EXPERTISE: A PHILOSOPHICAL INTRODUCTION

ALSO AVAILABLE FROM BLOOMSBURY

Critical Thinking, by Robert Arp and Jamie Carlin Watson
Epistemology: The Key Thinkers, edited by Stephen Hetherington
Problems in Epistemology and Metaphysics, edited by Steven B. Cowan
Problems in Value Theory, edited by Steven B. Cowan
The Myth of Luck, by Steven D. Hales

EXPERTISE: A PHILOSOPHICAL INTRODUCTION

Jamie Carlin Watson

BLOOMSBURY ACADEMIC
LONDON • NEW YORK • OXFORD • NEW DELHI • SYDNEY

BLOOMSBURY ACADEMIC
Bloomsbury Publishing Plc
50 Bedford Square, London, WC1B 3DP, UK
1385 Broadway, New York, NY 10018, USA

BLOOMSBURY, BLOOMSBURY ACADEMIC and the Diana logo
are trademarks of Bloomsbury Publishing Plc

First published in Great Britain 2021
Copyright © Jamie Carlin Watson, 2021

Jamie Carlin Watson has asserted his right under the Copyright,
Designs and Patents Act, 1988, to be identified as Author of this work.

For legal purposes the Acknowledgements on p. xxii–xxiii constitute
an extension of this copyright page.

Cover design Holly Bell

All rights reserved. No part of this publication may be reproduced or transmitted in any form or by any means, electronic or mechanical, including photocopying, recording, or any information storage or retrieval system, without prior permission in writing from the publishers.

Bloomsbury Publishing Plc does not have any control over, or responsibility for, any third-party websites referred to or in this book. All internet addresses given in this book were correct at the time of going to press. The author and publisher regret any inconvenience caused if addresses have changed or sites have ceased to exist, but can accept no responsibility for any such changes.

A catalogue record for this book is available from the British Library.

Library of Congress Cataloging-in-Publication Data
Names: Watson, Jamie Carlin, author.
Title: Expertise : a philosophical introduction / Jamie Carlin Watson.
Description: London ; New York : Bloomsbury Academic, 2020. |
Includes bibliographical references and index. |
Summary: "What does it mean to be an expert? What sort of authority do experts really have? And what role should they play in today's society? Addressing why ever larger segments of society are skeptical of what experts say, Expertise: A Philosophical Introduction reviews contemporary philosophical debates and introduces what an account of expertise needs to accomplish in order to be believed. Drawing on research from philosophers and sociologists, chapters explore widely held accounts of expertise and uncover their limitations, outlining a set of conceptual criteria a successful account of expertise should meet. By providing suggestions for how a philosophy of expertise can inform practical disciplines such as politics, religion, and applied ethics, this timely introduction to a topic of pressing importance reveals what philosophical thinking about expertise can contribute to growing concerns about experts in the 21st century"– Provided by publisher.
Identifiers: LCCN 2020019580 (print) | LCCN 2020019581 (ebook) | ISBN 9781350083844 (hb) | ISBN 9781350083851 (pb) | ISBN 9781350083868 (ePDF) | ISBN 9781350083837 (ebook)
Subjects: LCSH: Knowledge, Theory of. | Expertise.
Classification: LCC BD161 .W38 2020 (print) | LCC BD161 (ebook) | DDC 001.01–dc23
LC record available at https://lccn.loc.gov/2020019580
LC ebook record available at https://lccn.loc.gov/2020019581

ISBN:	HB:	978-1-3500-8384-4
	PB:	978-1-3500-8385-1
	ePDF:	978-1-3500-8386-8
	eBook:	978-1-3500-8383-7

Typeset by Integra Software Services Pvt. Ltd.

To find out more about our authors and books visit www.bloomsbury.com
and sign up for our newsletters.

For Aaron Thomas
Friend, musician, polymath

CONTENTS

List of Figures viii
Preface: The Big Questions about Expertise ix
Acknowledgments xxii

1 The Trouble with Experts 1

2 Philosophical Approaches to Expertise 29

3 Truth-Based Accounts of Expertise 49

4 Performance-Based Accounts of Expertise— Part 1 87

5 Performance-Based Accounts of Expertise— Part 2 109

6 Social Role Accounts of Expertise 137

7 The Cognitive Systems Account of Expertise 165

Notes 196
References and Further Reading 209
Index 240

LIST OF FIGURES

2.1 Taxonomy of Expertise in Plato's *Statesman* 30

2.2 Self-directors and Direction-takers 31

3.1 A Continuum of Competence in a Domain 54

3.2 A More Detailed Continuum of Competence in a Domain 55

3.3 True Beliefs Relative to Others on the Continuum 55

6.1 Harry Collins's Periodic Table of Expertises 157

7.1 The Cognitive Systems Account of Expertise 175

7.2 The Cognitive Systems Account of Expertise, Revised 176

PREFACE: THE BIG QUESTIONS ABOUT EXPERTISE

Socrates: *And when you call in an adviser, you should see whether [they] too [are] skillful [technikos] in the accomplishment of the end which you have in view?*
Nicias: *Most true.*
(Socrates in Plato's Laches 185d, Jowett trans., 1892)

Some concepts are so rooted in ordinary language that attempts to study them quickly become a series of quibbles over examples. *Expertise* is such a concept. We know what it means in general. We use it conversationally without any trouble. We know it has something to do with knowledge and something to do with skill. We tend to agree that experts—other things being equal—should be trusted as authorities in their domains. This is why we hire tax professionals when our finances get complicated, why we get a lawyer instead of representing ourselves, why we choose to work with certain grad school mentors over others, and why we seek out medical specialists about some of our symptoms. In other words, we know that some people stand, consistently, in a better position than we do with respect to some types of information or abilities.

It is easy to call such people experts. But is that what it means to be an expert? Is someone an expert just because they can do something better than we can, or do they also have to be great at it? Is it enough to be certified in a field or have a Ph.D. in an academic discipline to be an expert, or do you also have to work in that field a few years before you're an expert?

As soon as we start trying to pin down just what it means to be an expert and who fits that bill, things get murky. If your income tax documents are simple enough, an accountant might do no better than your Aunt Sally at filing them correctly. And not all tax professionals are the same. Someone who primarily does taxes for businesses may not know how to help individuals who would benefit from some types of tax protections. The same is true for medical conditions. If your symptoms are fairly common, your grandfather might do just as well at treating your symptoms as any physician (and your grandfather might not be opposed to adding a little bourbon to the remedy). If just anyone can do something, that something is not a good test of expertise.

Further, we know that some people are con artists, successfully posing as doctors, professors, and public officials. Frank Abagnale, from the (1980) book and (2002) film *Catch Me If You Can*, famously passed the Louisiana bar exam and became an attorney, despite the fact that he had never been to law school. He successfully impersonated a pilot and logged more than a million miles of flight time without a day of flight school. And for eleven months, he posed as a chief resident pediatrician in a hospital. Does this mean that Abagnale successfully *pretended* to be an expert, that he actually *became* an expert, or that the normal tasks of these experts (which, in this case, remember, included passing the Louisiana bar exam) were poor indicators of expertise? Abagnale's case is admittedly an extreme example, but that does not mean that imposters are rare. In 1984, evidence presented before the US House of Representatives showed that around ten thousand practicing doctors had fraudulent or outright bogus degrees (United States 1985: 3). And there is a growing number of people who impersonate doctors and pharmacists (especially online pharmacists [AARP 2018]) for years before getting caught (Mazza 2016; Mitchell 2017; Montague 2017).

When it comes to saying precisely what it means to be an expert, we're in the weeds before we've even started down a promising path. A central difficulty with studying expertise is that different scholars focus on different aspects of it. Some talk about what expertise *implies*, for example, why we should trust them, when, and how much. Others talk about *how we know* whether someone is an expert, such as their ability to smoothly and effortlessly do something or whether they have academic degrees or credentials. Some focus on *what it feels like* to perform as an expert, whether it is sustained, conscious judgment or unconscious "flow." Some are interested in *how society interacts* with experts, for example, whether society must acknowledge someone as an expert before they really are or whether someone appointed to an authoritative role like a judge or administrator is, by default, an expert. Still others are interested in *how people become* experts, whether it involves accumulating a lot of knowledge or many hours of a special kind of practice. As these discussions multiply, the task of saying precisely *what expertise is* gets more difficult.

The aim of this book is to introduce the major attempts, by philosophers, psychologists, and sociologists, to say what expertise is, to explore their strengths and weaknesses, and to develop a general account of expertise that accommodates those strengths while avoiding the weaknesses. When I say a "general" account of expertise, I mean an account that will explain what it means to be an expert, irrespective of the type of competence or field of study. A general account of expertise, as I approach it, is a social, applied, epistemological project. It offers criteria for being an expert, explains what constitutes the epistemic authority of expert testimony (how it puts normative demands on others to accept it), circumscribes the limits of expertise, and provides guidance for identifying and using expertise in practice. It draws together similarities of disparate types of expertise into a unified account of what makes them all instances of the same concept.

A general account is different from what I will call "operational" accounts. Operational accounts highlight one or two features of certain types of expertise, so they can be studied and understood distinctly from other types of expertise. For example, if you want to understand what makes a concert pianist, you will need a very different set of experimental conditions than if you wanted to understand what makes an expert historian. Operational definitions are important, and in this book, I rely heavily on the empirical findings of others who start with operational definitions of expertise. I largely take these empirical findings for granted, as I am not an empirical researcher. But it is one thing to study a phenomenon in the world, and another to say that that phenomenon fully exemplifies what we mean by a word, especially a word with as rich a history as expertise. I take it that operational definitions cannot do all the work that philosophers need them to, but I think they have important insights to contribute to that project.

The benefits of developing a general theory of expertise come as much from the process of constructing one as from the final product. It involves asking questions that inevitably frame the debate in a particular way. These questions can reveal misconceptions (either on my part or on the parts of others), and they can reveal previously unrecognized implications. If these questions frame the debate well, they provide avenues for studying the concepts in more depth.

Though this is foremost a work of philosophy, I have tried not to presuppose any robust background in philosophy. Where I invoke philosophical debates, I try to explain them with little jargon. I hope the book proves useful to anyone working in or wishing to learn about expertise studies, including psychologists, sociologists, political scientists, and neuroscientists. The literature on expertise across these domains is voluminous. And because there is so much written in each domain, it is easy to lose sight of what is being said about expertise in the others. My hope is that this book brings together the major threads of these discussions to provide a constructive foundation for interdisciplinary discussions of expertise and, thereby, that it breeds more interdisciplinary study of expertise.

To get us started, here is a working definition of our target concept:

Expertise: A high degree of competence in a domain

I'm using "competence" very broadly, to include knowledge, skill, performance, or aptitude. I'm leaving "high degree" vague because what counts as sufficiently high differs depending on who is approaching the question.

Note that this definition does not include anything about who or what might have expertise. As we will see in Chapter 2, expertise can be distributed through society in various ways, not least of which is technologically. Technologies called "expert systems" package expertise for use by others. They give novices the competence of experts, and they give other experts competence they didn't previously have. This means that not everything that exemplifies expertise (i.e., the processes or products of experts) is itself an expert. I will argue, however, that all manifestations of expertise ultimately trace back to experts, the people who create, build, discover, accomplish, or understand a domain well enough to exemplify expertise themselves, and, in some cases, package it for others. Thus, my working definition of *expert* restricts the relevant competence to agents:

Expert: A person who has expertise

These definitions are not uncontroversial, and I have intentionally rendered them ambiguous. For example, each aspect of this definition of *expertise* raises more questions: Does "high degree" mean higher than everyone or just some people, or high relative to all the truths in a domain? What or who determines what counts as competence in any particular domain: Can some experts just know things, or must they also be able to apply them or use them to predict future events? What counts as a "domain"?

Different scholars answer these questions differently. For example, some stipulate that experts are people who perform in the top 1percent of their domain (Ericsson and Charness 1994), so "high degree" is *very* high. Others say experts are people competent enough in the language of a domain to meaningfully interact with others in that domain (Collins and Evans 2007). With respect to what competence consists in, some say *explicit knowledge*, some say *tacit knowledge*, some say *embodied knowledge*, some say *performance*, and there are several others. Some questions depend for their answers on the domain at issue. For example, the competence of a chess expert may involve the speed and effortlessness at which they can see and execute the next appropriate move, while for an expert novelist, the writing may be difficult, time-consuming, and clunky, even if the finished product reads effortlessly, vividly, and compellingly. So, again, my working definitions are intentionally vague. But they orient us to what I consider the "big questions" in expertise studies:

1. What is an expert?
2. How does someone become an expert?
3. What does it mean to say that an expert has "authority," and how much should we trust authorities?
4. How does anyone recognize an expert, and how do we choose which experts to listen to?
5. How do we decide what to believe or do when experts disagree?

These questions are not new. Plato tells us that when Socrates attempts to understand the nature of rhetoric with the famous orator and teacher of rhetoric Gorgias, Gorgias brags to Socrates that his expertise as a rhetorician allows him to successfully mimic medical expertise: "Many and many a time have I gone with my brother or other doctors to visit one of their patients, and found him unwilling either to take medicine or submit to the surgeon's knife or cautery; and when the doctor failed to persuade him I succeeded" (*Gorgias* 456b). And to prove that his skill at this kind of mimicry is not just a matter of convincing patients, who do not know medicine, Gorgias contends that if a rhetorician and a doctor "enter any city you please" and debate before a group of city leaders over which of them should be appointed as a doctor "you would find the physician nowhere, while the master of speech would be appointed" (456b-c). Gorgias happily admits that rhetoricians have no knowledge of medicine; they are masters only of persuasion (459ff). So, Socrates concludes Gorgias's argument for him by saying:

> Then the case is the same in all the other arts for the orator and his rhetoric: there is no need to know the truth of the actual matters, but one merely needs to have discovered some device of persuasion which will make one appear to those who do not know to know better than those who know. (459c)

Who, then, is the real expert? The one who knows "the truth of the actual matters" or the one who can perform well enough to convince others they are an expert? Or must a real expert be able to do both?

As is typical in Socratic dialogues, the two do not arrive at a satisfying conclusion about the nature of rhetoric. But along the way, they also show that the nature of expertise is just as opaque. Are all doctors experts? And is public or institutional approval sufficient for being a doctor (the way some states still allow people with no law degree or experience to be elected as judges by popular vote)? Or would Gorgias eventually be found out? What distinguishes an expert from a novice such that the rest of us can tell them apart? All these questions are related, but in this book, I'll focus on questions 1 and 2, and leave sustained discussion of the remaining questions to other work.

The Backdrop

My interest in expertise stems from a lifelong fascination with the questions of whom to trust and what makes someone trustworthy. Raised in a religious household, I was regularly encouraged to trust sacred texts, and to trust those who interpreted them and taught from them. In school, we are all taught to trust teachers and textbooks. At the doctor's office, we are expected to trust the advice of the person in the white coat. In some courts, we are legally obligated to accept the opinion of a judge. And even after a substantial graduate education and extensive reading on trust, authority, and expertise, deciding whom to trust is not easy. For example, I believe that scholars who study ancient texts should be trustworthy in their conclusions about those texts, but I also believe that their own religious and professional convictions can influence the way they interpret them—even if they are trying their dead-level best to interpret them neutrally. I have observed that after one doctor offers an opinion, another often contradicts it. And I trust science as one of the more reliable processes for forming responsible beliefs, and yet I have extensive evidence that empirical research is fraught with error, bias, and fraud. To be sure, some scientists have discovered amazing things (antibiotics and vaccines have changed the world for the better). But at what point is our trust warranted? Must we wait until all the research arrives at equilibrium on a single conclusion, as it has with using statins to treat heart disease, or can we extend a little trust along the way as scientists work out the details, as when they're trying to figure out the right age and risk factors for getting breast cancer screenings?

A key insight from this interdisciplinary look at the nature of expertise is that competence in a domain falls along a continuum. Few of us are the very bottom of competence with most of the domains we encounter, and few of us are at the very top. We tend to know a few people who are just a little further up that continuum than we are. And they know people who are a little further toward the top than they are. This situation allows us a much richer picture of epistemic relationships than we typically find discussed either in popular culture or in the academic study of expertise, that is, the picture of a stark contrast between the *know-nothing novice* and the *superior expert*. Getting and using expertise well, we will see, has a lot to do with recognizing where we and those around are on that continuum and with learning how to talk with one another about our strengths and weaknesses in a domain.

Plan of the Book

In Chapter 1, I examine some problems with describing expertise in a society like ours—that is, a society inescapably infused with expert systems, bots, spyware, viral marketing, and so on. We will see that some arise from conflating expertise with other concepts, like professionalism or credentials, and some arise from the way experts are presented to us, distortions in the information we get from and about experts. Some of these distortions are dysfunctions in us (e.g., standpoint bias and the Dunning-Kruger Effect) and some are distortions in how society packages information (e.g., filter bubbles and echo chambers). And, of course, all this is in addition to the problem that some experts—that is, some people who are rightly called experts—often behave badly, letting other interests interfere with their willingness to serve responsibly as an expert.

In Chapter 2, I introduce several philosophical approaches to giving an account of expertise. I distinguish *definitional* from *methodological* accounts, *reductive* from *non-reductive* accounts, and *fixed criteria* from *process* accounts. Which of these approaches one chooses influences what an account of expertise will look like. Being aware of this influence can help inform our assessment of various accounts. Perhaps we will learn that all fixed criteria accounts of expertise face a fatal flaw or that attempts to construct a non-reductive account are committed to some form of disjunctivism[1] that they also have to defend for their account to be plausible.

It may turn out that no general account of expertise is plausible. If this is right, then we are faced with the possibility that only operational studies of expertise are possible. But some scholars contend there is a third option available that is derived from philosopher Ludwig Wittgenstein's notion of "family resemblances." Also in Chapter 2, I explain this Wittgensteinian approach to expertise. If such an account is plausible, then those who offer a general account face a serious question as to why we should prefer their approach to the Wittgensteinian approach. I contend that this account of expertise is not yet developed enough to constitute a challenge to the general accounts I explore in the remainder of the book. But I explain how such an approach might benefit expertise studies if these concerns could be allayed.

I close Chapter 2 with a discussion of how expertise is often exhibited through tools, machines, and programs called "expert systems." I explore the implications of expert systems both on experts in society and on expertise studies. I conclude that while expertise can be embodied by a wide variety of technologies, that embodiment ultimately traces back to expert agents.

In Chapter 3, I introduce what I call *truth-based* accounts of expertise, that is, the view that having reliable access to truths in a domain is a necessary condition for expertise. I then explore some prominent objections to truth-based theories and close with a suggestion for how to better capture what defenders of truth-based accounts find important for expertise while avoiding the worst of the objections.

In Chapter 4, I introduce performance-based accounts, accounts that regard expertise as primarily and necessarily a matter of *doing something well*. I start with the "embodied expertise" account, developed by Hubert and Stuart Dreyfus, which, in contrast with truth-based views, claims that expertise is exclusively a matter of know-how that is acquired through practice. Because expertise is distributed throughout one's body, by the time someone becomes an expert, they have lost the ability to communicate how they do what they do with non-experts. While the Dreyfuses' notion of embodiment captures the experiences of some experts, it leaves out the experiences of many others. After reviewing common criticisms of the Dreyfuses' account, I conclude that, while it captures some important elements of expertise, such as the role of experience in acquiring expertise, it does not have the resources to explain much of the empirical research on how experience produces expertise.

From here I turn, in Chapter 5, to the most widely discussed performance-based account of expertise, the "deliberate practice" approach developed by K. Anders Ericsson and his colleagues. I review the experiments that motivated the deliberate practice account and explain its power as an explanatory tool. I then explain some limitations and criticisms of the account. While deliberate practice does an exceptional job of explaining the development of expertise in a narrow set of conditions, such as those necessary for mastering chess or musical instruments, it does not account for the evidence that genetics, especially with respect to cognitive development and body structure, has a non-negligible role in determining when deliberate practice works and to what degree. I close this chapter by introducing attempts to explain performance-based expertise in a much wider range of conditions, such as those necessary for developing mastery in weather forecasting or political decision-making. The insights from this last section are crucial for the general account I develop in Chapter 7.

In Chapter 6, I introduce what I call *social-role* accounts of expertise, which is, very roughly, the idea that expertise is defined by and acquired through social processes. I begin by explaining a common concern that social-role accounts of expertise lead necessarily to theories of expertise that are inherently subjective or relativistic, and I demonstrate several options for how social-role theorists might avoid this objection. I then explain philosopher Steven Turner's objective social-role account, focusing on his explanation of how epistemic communities can legitimize expertise through a type of objective public assessment, even if, in practice, such assessment is a wholly social process. I then explore some problems for Turner's account and turn to the influential social-role account developed by sociologist Harry Collins and colleagues. Collins accepts much of Ericsson's deliberate practice approach, thus guarding it from charges of relativism. But he argues that there is an ineliminable social dynamic to developing and maintaining expertise that he calls "linguistic socialization." I close by highlighting some prominent criticisms of Collins's account while highlighting its most successful elements.

In Chapter 7, I take my conclusions from Chapters 3 through 6 and suggest that they point to a more robust account of expertise than currently exists in the literature. Starting with psychologist Daniel Kahneman's distinction between System 1 and System 2 thinking to describe different processes involved in decision-making, I argue that expertise is competence that is developed by training one of these two cognitive pathways. The competence that results from training System 1 thinking allows for fluid, superior performance in domains that are well-structured and have widely agreed-upon and easily accessible outcomes, and so I call this System 1 Expertise. The competence that results from training System 2 thinking allows for careful, reflective decision-making in domains that are loosely structured and for which determining the acceptable outcome is part of the judgment-forming process, and I call this System 2 Expertise.

I close the book with some brief reflections on how my conclusions in Chapter 7 can inform discussions of the remaining big questions about expertise—what sort of authority do experts have, how do we recognize experts, and how should we respond when experts disagree? Though these latter questions are often given priority in public discussions, they presuppose answers to the first two: What is expertise, and how is it acquired? If we have no consistent way of talking about expertise—if everyone uses the term slightly differently or inconsistently—we have little hope of figuring out whom to trust or how much. This book aims to serve as a foundation for standardizing talk about expertise so both researchers and the public can make clear their assumptions about expertise and avoid the simple mistakes of conflating expertise with concepts that do not serve it well.

A Note on Terminology and Presentation

For the sake of simplicity and consistency, I will use the word "domain" to refer generally to anything that typically goes by the names *subject matter*, *field of study*, *scope of practice*, *sport*, *area of specialization*, or *province*. It will become clear early in the book that domains are fuzzy, and determining who is an expert in what domain can be a conceptual mare's nest. Even those who work in expertise studies struggle to use the notion of a domain consistently. For example, well-known psychologist Daniel Kahneman (who, with his colleague Amos Tversky, launched the heuristics and biases literature), says in a *Time Magazine* interview that "there are domains in which expertise is not possible. Stock picking is a good example. And in long-term political strategic forecasting, it's been shown that experts are just not better than a dice-throwing monkey" (Luscombe 2011). This seems to take seriously the difficulties in developing expertise and identifying the sort of domains in which someone can be an expert. And yet, in another place, Kahneman calls psychologist Paul Rozin "an expert on disgust" (Kahneman 2011: 302). Is "disgust" a domain of expertise? If stock picking is not predictable enough to allow for the development of expertise, how might disgust be? It would seem that what people find disgusting is at least as arbitrary as which stocks will perform well in any particular quarter. I do think there is a way to make sense of both of Kahneman's claims, but it highlights the vast differences among domains, such that what counts as expertise in one domain—for example, predictive accuracy in the case of stock picking—can be very different from what counts as expertise in other domains—perhaps it is fluid understanding of a certain experimental literature in the case of disgust.

I will use the word "novice" synonymously with "non-expert" or "layperson," referring to anyone who is not an expert in the domain in question, or who is new enough to a domain not to be a competent knower or practitioner in the domain. Some reserve "non-expert" or "layperson" for people who have no experience in a domain whatsoever (e.g., most patients to their doctors) and "novice" for people just getting started in a domain (e.g., pupils to teachers and understudies to actors).[2] In general, I don't have a problem with this, I just find that it can be confusing. For example, aspects of many domains—even specialized domains, like cosmological physics—spill over into popular understanding, for example the Big Bang theory (not the TV show) and Darwinian evolution. Are people with a high school understanding of these domains laypersons or novices? If novices, what then do we call the college senior who is majoring in evolutionary biology? I am hesitant to call them an expert in any sense, but the college senior is more competent than the high school student. Trying to carve such boundaries seems unnecessary, as it does little explanatory work. Further, some people are experts in one domain but not in another. Are they then non-experts in the other or simply novices? I don't think the distinction in cases like these amounts to much, so I will use "novice" generally to refer to the continuum of competencies that fall below expertise. For some purposes, it is handy to distinguish the competence of someone who can merely do something from someone who can do it exceptionally. Aristotle suggests such a distinction between those who transmit an art and the artists themselves (*On Sophistical Refutations* 183b–184a). When it helps elucidate a point about expertise, I'll introduce one or more distinctions like this and explain their significance in that context.

When I introduce words from other languages, I first give their transliteration (how they sound in English) in italics and follow with the original language in parentheses: e.g., *techne* (τέχνη),; *sophia* (σοφία). After this initial introduction, I use only the italicized transliteration—*techne*, *sophia*.

Further, as someone writing in a domain that has traditionally favored men's voices over women's and that has, through its conservative commitment to a certain scholarly aesthetic, preferred masculine pronouns and masculine characters in its examples, I am sensitive to how these practices have alienated or indirectly devalued the voices and roles of women and other historically marginalized groups. In an attempt to be a small part of a trend toward correcting that, I have worked to use gender-neutral pronouns for my general examples, non-Western names in my specific examples, and I have changed masculine pronouns in quotations to gender neutral pronouns, using brackets [] to indicate that these changes are mine. If readers find the number of brackets distracting, I can only reply that this is evidence of the extent of the problem.

Finally, although this is a philosophical *introduction*, it is written with upper-level students and scholars in mind. I give as much background to technical discussions as space will allow, but I do engage with arguments and draw conclusions. This is less common in introductory works than it used to be, as there is now a much stronger distinction between *textbooks*, which presume to present both sides of an argument, leaving the conclusion to the reader, and *monographs*, which present a single line of argument throughout. While I think both types of book are valuable, I have benefited the most in my professional life from texts that incorporate a good deal of both, such as Bernard Williams's *Morality: An Introduction to Ethics* (1972) and David Coady's *What to Believe Now: Applying Epistemology to Contemporary Issues* (2012). It is in the spirit of these "introductions" that I have written this book.

Further, while it is a philosophical introduction, it is aimed at scholars working in any domain that engages in expertise studies. Because of this, I try not to presume too much background or technical terminology in any domain. This may cause some consternation. For example, psychologists may find my presentation of some of their history a bit elementary, and philosophers may find some of my background explanations of arguments overly simplistic. For that, I ask for your patience as you move into meatier sections of the text. Such is often necessary when space is limited. To mitigate the concern, I have included copious endnotes and references to guide readers to additional sources for these discussions.

And finally, each chapter builds on the previous, but I have made an effort to point explicitly to particular sections of past chapters when I reference them (e.g., "See 3.4"). So, if you are primarily interested in, say, social-role accounts of expertise, you should be able to read Chapter 6 independently of the rest, turning back to specific sections to fill any gaps.

ACKNOWLEDGMENTS

My first and most important acknowledgment goes to my partner, wife, and colleague, Dr. Laura Guidry-Grimes, to whom I am deeply grateful for enduring tireless conversations on most of the topics in this book, for giving me ample feedback, counterexamples, and suggestions, and for being gracious enough to help me organize my life so that I could write it all down. Sine qua non.

Second, I extend warmest thanks to Christian Quast and Markus Seidel for generously welcoming this largely unknown philosopher into the 2015 conference, "The Philosophy of Expertise: What Is Expertise?" in Münster, Germany. That experience—which included wonderful discussions with Harry Collins, Alvin Goldman, Barbara Montero, and Oliver Scholz—solidified my burgeoning interest in expertise studies.

Thank you, also, to Jesús Vega Encabo for organizing the 2019 Workshop on Epistemic Authority, Trust, and Autonomy at the Universidad Autónoma de Madrid, Spain. This book benefited from delightful conversations with Jesús Encabo, Elizabeth Fricker, Jon Leefmann, Sophia Dandelet, Winnie Ma, Jesús Navarro, Alejandro Vesga, and Aderonke Ogundiwin.

Others to whom I am grateful include Michael Bishop, who nudged me to take seriously empirical work on rationality and intuitions long before my "first philosophy" heart was ready. I did come around (mostly). Thanks to C. Thi Nguyen for insightful conversations about expertise, trust, and echo chambers, and his infectious enthusiasm for everything he works on. Thanks to Nathan Nobis and the editors of *1000-Word Philosophy* for helping to aim my entry on expertise at the right issues for the right audience. This greatly helped shape the structure of Chapter 1. Thanks to the editors and anonymous reviewers at the journals *Social Epistemology* and *Topoi* for their generous feedback on work that figures into parts of this book. And thanks to Colleen Coalter and Becky Holland at Bloomsbury for advocating for this project and guiding it through to publication.

Special thanks to my department chair, D. Micah Hester, who, despite the fact that I teach at a medical school and serve as a consulting hospital ethicist and plain language writer, generously allows me to pursue more traditional philosophical interests.

It is also fitting to acknowledge that a book like this wouldn't have been possible without extensive input from experts in a variety of domains. Others to whom I am grateful for suggestions, insights, critical feedback, and helpful conversation include (in alphabetical order):

Loïc Boulanger, M.D., breast surgery oncology
Logan Dwyer, J.D., law
Laura Guidry-Grimes, Ph.D., clinical ethics, disability ethics, psychiatric ethics
D. Micah Hester, Ph.D., American philosophy and bioethics
Scott Malm, Ph.D., toxicology
Adam Neal, Ph.D., religion
Jamie Michael Pearl, Ph.D.(c), ancient philosophy
Angela Scott, M.D., Ph.D., medical humanities and developmental pediatrics
Joshua Byron Smith, Ph.D., medieval and renaissance studies
Molly Wilder, J.D., Ph.D.(c), law and philosophy
Elizabeth Victor, Ph.D., philosophy

And last, but by no means least, I could not have put this book together without the diligent, careful work and feedback from my graduate assistant Rebecca Mullen. Many thanks, and I wish you much success.

All errors and omissions are, of course, my own. But I hope that, despite the book's imperfections, readers will find something insightful or useful for moving the debates over expertise forward. Onward and upward!

1 THE TROUBLE WITH EXPERTS

"And this I say, lest any [person] should beguile you with enticing words."

(*Colossians* 2:4, King James Version, 1611)

In this chapter, I review some contemporary difficulties with what it means to be an expert. I explore two common uses of expertise that impede efforts to develop a meaningful account of it (1.2–1.3). I then explore five cognitive and social mechanisms that have a distorting effect on whom we trust, that is, that make it easy to mis-identify experts (1.4–1.5). Whether individually or in combination, I call these distorting effects the *confounding of expertise*. I conclude that without a sense of what makes an expert an expert, it is difficult to combat these distorting effects and to develop strategies for trusting those who are trustworthy.

1.1 The Current State of Trust in Experts

- Your doctor tells you there's about an 80 percent chance you have cancer.
- Reverend Gloria Copeland tells you there is no flu epidemic.
- Political analyst Thomas Friedman tells you there will soon be another economic collapse like that of 2008.
- A builder tells you she can build a basement in your new house that won't leak.

Should you trust any of these claims? And if so, should you simply embrace them, adding them to your collection of beliefs, or should you hold them tentatively, taking them as an opportunity to look for more evidence?

These examples are not instances of simple *testimony*—one person's telling another person something with the aim of being believed on the basis of that telling.[1] The speakers do not merely have information to report, like a news source or textbook. They presume to understand something you are in no position to understand. They purport to be, in an important sense, the *author* of their claims; they offer those claims as a judgment formed after assessing evidence and applying it to a set of complex circumstances to answer a question they think is relevant to your interests (Austin 1946). If they are, in fact, authorities, in this sense, they are not only aware of that evidence; they understand how that evidence came about, how to use it, and perhaps most importantly, how it can go wrong. And they understand all this—again, if they really do—in virtue of an ongoing, intentional relationship with that evidence; they do not possess it by accident or by memorization. The presumption is that, if they really are speaking with authority, they are doing so because they are *experts*.

When experts speak from their expertise, they are claiming a certain authority in their domain. But trust in claims to authority has a spotty history. Political claims to authority have been met with revolution or war. Religious claims to authority have incited ... well, revolution and war. People advocating for new techniques or technologies are often regarded with suspicion. For example, in the mid-1800s, Hungarian physician Ignaz Semmelweis discovered that using a chlorine hand wash significantly reduced the spread of diseases like childbed fever. While this practice and Semmelweis's explanation of its success were well-received in the UK, Austrian and German physicians largely dismissed them both as naïve, even attacking them as "theology" rather than science. Mary Shelley's 1919 *Frankenstein*, written to lampoon uninformed distrust in innovation, also stands as a reminder of just how widespread cultural skepticism of new technologies can be and how it can shape which technologies are developed. Even today, highly educated people, people who create and innovate, are often called "elitist," "out of touch," or "impractical." And those who promote special interest groups, charities, or government agencies, regardless of their credentials or experience, are often dismissed for having ulterior motives.

A few types of people, however, seem to overcome this suspicion. It is usually—Semmelweis notwithstanding—those whose claims to authority can be demonstrated to others through various types of empirical success. For example, it is often easy to tell when clothes, tools, jewelry, carts, barrels, and candles are well-made. We trust people who have made good products to continue to make good products. And even when quality is not immediately obvious, online review platforms help distribute information about tools that break, clothes that wear out quickly or fit poorly, and jewelry that falls apart. Athletes are another example of experts who easily overcome suspicion. Few people who see Hannah Teter snowboard or Alina Zagitova ice skate question their expertise in their sports.

But there are many different types of expertise, and not all types are demonstrable in the same way. Economists and political analysts, for example, are notoriously bad forecasters.[2] Does this mean they are not experts or that their expertise is not in forecasting? Studies of psychotherapy outcomes suggest that trained psychiatrists and psychologists are no better than minimally trained counselors with no advanced degrees (Dawes 1994: 50–63).[3] Does this mean that psychiatrists are not experts or that a degree in psychiatry is not needed to be an expert counselor? Sommeliers are still widely regarded as "wine experts" despite extensive evidence that they perform no better than chance.[4] Have we set the wrong expectations for sommeliers, or do we now have good grounds to dismiss their testimony as, at best, guessing? And many people who were once regarded as experts have been outstripped by simple prediction algorithms.[5] Have these people lost their expertise? Did they have it in the first place?

Even in the physical sciences, which, arguably, have one of the best track records of successful discoveries, it is not easy to explain who counts as an expert and what expertise in a domain implies. On one hand, advancements in science and technology have—demonstrably and uncontroversially—helped humans (though not always other animals) live longer and better lives. If anyone fits the description of an expert, it would seem a scientist does. On the other hand, innovation is not the same as expertise. Few scientists ever make a "break-through" discovery. And many who do usually do so by accident. Wherein lies the expertise of someone who stumbles onto a single great idea, or who relies on decades of research from others before filling in the last piece that leads to discovery?

Further, whether scientists are experts because of their successes depends largely on how we define "success." Most scientific claims throughout history have proved faulty. Each time this happened, they were replaced with more useful theories, which also subsequently proved faulty, which were then replaced with other useful theories, and so on. Novelist Terry Pratchett made this point starkly in his satire of journalism *The Truth* (2000), when his imminently pragmatic character Lord Vetinari mused on the vicissitudes of science:

> "A thousand years ago we thought the world was a bowl," he said. "Five hundred years ago we knew it was a globe. Today we know it is flat and round and carried through space on the back of a turtle."[6] He turned and gave the High Priest another smile. "Don't you wonder what shape it will turn out to be tomorrow?" (33)

If we measure scientists' success in terms of usefulness, science does, indeed, seem successful. But if expertise is a matter of how much experts *know* in their domain, it is less clear which scientists, if any, are experts.

Further still, science has helped produce some of the most gruesome horrors in human history, from mustard gas, to the atomic bomb, to experiments conducted at the expense of human suffering and lives. Even if we allow that scientists are experts, there are serious questions about the sort of authority science engenders and the sort of trust that kind of authority requires from the rest of us.

Therefore, before we tackle the difficult work of identifying experts and sorting them from non-experts, we need to have a better sense of what it means to be an expert. Taking the concept of expertise seriously requires getting a sense of what role the concept plays in our language, learning which conceptions of expertise are plausible, looking for uncontroversial examples of experts in the world and seeing if our concept captures what they are, and then testing the strengths and limitations of this concept. This is not a simple project. It requires wading through both the pessimism and the optimism to see what holds up.

I'll start with two ways of talking about expertise that steer us away from a plausible conception of it. Then I'll review some psychological and social mechanisms that I think contribute to misunderstandings of expertise.

1.2 Are Experts Professionals?

Economist Roger Koppl defines an expert as "anyone who gets paid to give an opinion" (2018: 38). Koppl highlights some of the current discussions about expertise, but he is concerned that most current definitions favor treating experts as having a high level of knowledge or skill in their domains and that this biases meaningful discussion. He says such conceptions presuppose that experts are *reliable*, which, as he aims to demonstrate in his book, *Expert Failure*, is largely untrue. Further, he thinks his definition expresses what experts *are* in contrast to other current definitions that idealize expertise and attempt to say what experts *should* be. His descriptive definition of expert, he argues, also encourages a moralizing expertise that often comes with normative accounts. This raises concerns about whether experts can comment on morally charged topics like climate change or genetic theories of race without impugning their own expertise. As a corrective, he says his definition "leaves it an open question whether experts are reliable or unreliable" (38).

Koppl's definition renders *expert* roughly equivalent to "professional," someone who is hired to fill a special, paid role, in this case, giving an opinion, whether in private or public life. This has the benefit of taking some of the pressure off deciding what counts as a domain of expertise—it is defined by the type of opinion needed—and it takes some pressure off the notion that credentials are evidence of expertise—they are not. For Koppl, judges who are elected by popular vote are experts even if they have no law degree, no previous experience with the law, and no knowledge of the law whatsoever (which is still possible in some states). Further, Koppl claims that his definition lets us ignore all questions about who is trustworthy, whom we should trust, and how we distinguish "real" experts from fakes. It allows us to focus solely on successes and failures. If someone hired to give an opinion gives us a bad one, then we can respond to that failure rather than worrying whether the person was an expert in the first place. This definition also makes it easy for Koppl to argue that experts fail. If people hired to give an opinion are experts, and those people fail to give good advice, then experts fail.

To be sure, many professions, like medieval guilds, have instituted gatekeeping mechanisms for ensuring at least some degree of competence in their domains: education requirements, experience requirements, certifications, references, and so on. But Koppl does not require this for his definition. If you hire your eighteen-year-old nephew to advise your business manager on how to do the business's taxes, your nephew is now an expert on business tax. This example shows that not all professionals are experts and not all experts are professionals, and it is a mistake to conflate them.

Koppl's central argument for his definition is that, if we define people according to their competence, then we are committed to the notion that everyone is an expert. This is because everyone has privileged knowledge of their corner of the world, which gives them authority on that knowledge, and, thereby, makes them an expert on that perspective. But, if everyone is an expert, then no one is an expert (2019).

A moment's reflection shows that this argument is faulty. If we put ten doctors in a room, each of whom has expertise in a different subspecialty—cardiology, orthopedics, neurology, and so on—would we say, "Well, look, everyone in here is an expert, so no one is an expert"? Clearly not. What if everyone in the room were an expert in the same domain? Would that mean there were no experts in the room? That's not obvious, either. If everyone in the world took the time to study the piano, and everyone in the world became as good as any master pianist (set aside the empirical implausibility of this), it would not be meaningful to say that no one can play the piano very well. If this is right, then the claim, "if everyone is an expert, then no one is," is false.

In addition to losing this central motive for his definition, Koppl's use of the term *expertise* is muddy. He agrees with most accounts of expertise that "experts have knowledge not possessed by others" (23) and that "different people know different things, and no one can acquire a reasonable command of the many different fields of knowledge required to make good decisions in all the various domains of ordinary life" (23). But then he says, "There is perfect moral, epistemic, and cognitive parity between experts and nonexperts" (37). His basis for saying this seems to be the assumption that non-experts need no special help in assessing the claims of experts, that is, he thinks it resolves what philosophers have called the "recognition problem" for expertise. Yet, imagine our ten doctors again. Would we say that the cardiologist's advice is no better than the neurologist's even if the question is about heart disease? In the process of making *expertise* more manageable, he's eliminated any substantive difference between experts and non-experts.

Perhaps the biggest problem with Koppl's definition is that it doesn't actually eliminate the question of who is highly competent in a domain, it just pushes that question onto the person who hires them. Even if Koppl isn't concerned about who actually knows something in a domain, the person who hires them certainly should be. Even though experts often give the wrong opinions, when they give the right opinion, experts (real experts, that is) give them for the right reasons. It is no accident that a doctor can distinguish one type of cancer from another, whereas a novice cannot. It is no surprise that an expert musician makes fewer mistakes over time on a complicated piece of music than a novice who happens to know how to play that piece. In conflating professionalism with competence, Koppl draws an unwarrantedly skeptical conclusion about experts generally.

To be sure, Koppl may not want to use the term "expert" for those highly competent in a domain, but that seems like an arbitrary choice. Would he prefer to the term "specialized competence"? If so, then that's what this book is about. Mainly because that is what people care about when they have talked about expertise since ancient Greece.

Koppl's misuse of *expert* highlights the confusion that's possible when we are only concerned with one aspect of a concept. For Koppl, this is how to mitigate error in the use of science in finance and public policy. Yet, Koppl could use the term "professional" instead of "expert" and get more from his argument, and he would also avoid denuding the very different concept of expertise of its historical, intuitive, and colloquial underpinnings.

1.3 Is Expertise Dying?

Tom Nichols, a professor of national security affairs, believes expert skepticism is growing in unprecedented ways. He argues that the problem has grown from mere widespread ignorance among citizens—which he admits has always been a problem—to "positive hostility" toward those we traditionally think of as experts and toward what those experts regard as "established knowledge." This positive hostility, Nichols argues, is leading to a social catastrophe he calls the "death of expertise" (2017: 20).

What does Nichols mean by "expert"? "Experts are people who know considerably more on a subject than the rest of us, and are those to whom we turn when we need advice, education, or solutions in a particular area of human knowledge" (29). This definition suggests that someone is only an expert if they know more than others, but Nichols does allow that experts can rely on one another, too. And as Nichols describes experts, it becomes clear that he doesn't think expertise is solely about relative knowledge; "true expertise," he says, "is a combination of education, talent, experience, and peer affirmation" (30). Importantly for his central thesis, Nichols does treat expertise as an objective phenomenon. Even if no one accepted the authority of experts, there could still be experts in the world.[7]

Does Nichols really think that expertise is dying, that is, becoming less prominent in the world? Not exactly. Nichols argues that people are increasingly suspicious either of the idea that there are experts in the traditional sense of scientists, doctors, or engineers or of the idea that experts stand in a better position than the rest of us (Nichols 2017: 20–1). Nichols thinks this strong, public resistance to traditional experts is the result of five factors:

1 **The commodification of higher education**
    Nichols argues, first, that colleges are now overflowing with students who are often unprepared to be there, led by people with second-rate degrees who are incentivized to give *A*s and *B*s regardless of the quality of a student's work, and who spend their time teaching the basic reading and writing skills those students should have had before walking into class. The result? Everyone has a decent GPA. Everyone gets a degree. According to Nichols, this result instills a feeling of authority and exceptionality in even the most underprepared and underaccomplished student. It turns out, they surmise, becoming well educated is not all that hard. Who needs experts when we are all experts now?

2 **Changes in the structure of information**
    Second, he argues that technology has made information easy to package and disseminate quickly, and this has led, in turn, to a distilled and unnuanced view of sophisticated domains. As we benefit from "on demand" service in entertainment and shopping, now news, politics, and science are available instantly. And we expect roughly the same things from these that we do from sources of entertainment: "We want it broken down, presented in a way that is pleasing to our eye … and we want it to say what we want it to say" (111). But, of course, packaging information this way has a doubly vicious effect. By necessity of structure and time, it glosses over details that matter, so that (1) it makes us feel like we know more about a topic than we do, and (2) it does so in ways that make us worse off than if we didn't know anything about the topic at all. The result, again, is that we are losing the sense that we need experts.

3 **The complicity of journalists with clickbait culture**
   Third, while the emergence of the twenty-four-hour news cycle contributes to number 2 on Nichols's list, it, along with other journalistic strategies, also plays a distinct role in fostering hostility toward expertise. To compete with other forms of media, news outlets now target audiences and cater to their entertainment interests as much as they cater to (and sometimes despite) their interest in information. Nichols traces this trend to 1996, when Fox News "made the news faster, slicker, and, with the addition of news readers who were actual beauty queens, prettier" (153). What's worse, the new formats catered to niche political content, setting up Fox and CNN as rival political sources in addition to rival news sources. Overlay this with the advent of news satire, through programs like *The Daily Show*, which Americans in 2014 said they trusted as much as CNN, and you have a recipe for the death of expertise: clickbait politics spun by celebrities and dressed up with multi-million-dollar aesthetics tells us all the information we need to know about complicated political issues. We don't need experts to connect the dots for us.

4 **The increasingly low quality of scientific research**
   Fourth, it turns out that experts may not be the trustworthy bastions of information that they are supposed to be. A 2015 study attempted to replicate 100 psychological studies only to find that the effects reported in half could not be reproduced. Cancer researchers found something similar in 2016: "Fully half of all results rest on shaky ground, and might not be replicable in other labs" (185). And hundreds of scientific publications are retracted every year for either methodological or ethical failures. The number of retractions doubled between 2003 and 2009, and growth didn't level off until 2012, still leaving nearly 1,000 in 2014 (Brainard and You 2018). This increase is partly because the number of published papers doubled during that time (around 2.5 million in 2015, according to one report [Ware and Mabe 2015]), so the retraction rate reflected the growth rate. And the leveling off does suggest better oversight on the part of journal editors, but it's still the case that about 4 out of every 10,000 articles published are retracted.[8] If scientists are uncertain about their own work, the public has little reason to trust their expert judgment.

5 **The bad behavior of traditional experts**
And finally, even if their quality were better, there is still the question of experts' character. Politicians and religious leaders may clash over political agendas and self-serving policies, but scientists are supposed to be immune from that. Nonetheless, increasing access to scientific controversies shows more clearly than ever that science is a human endeavor. Sixty percent of the retractions mentioned in number 4 were due to fraud (Brainard and You 2018). In a 2005 study, 14 percent of scientists admitted to seeing other scientists falsify data (Martinson et al.). If experts cannot be trusted to have integrity with their own work, then they cannot be trusted to help novices with the issues that matter to them.

These five factors strike me as worth taking seriously, though it is worth noting that Nichols restricts his claims to factors that primarily affect the United States. Different problems may threaten expertise in other socio-political contexts, and therefore, may call for different responses.[9] Nevertheless, Nichols's list should motivate us to consider the ways information is distorted by context and medium wherever we are, and to work out new strategies for understanding and using scientific results.

But the critical question is: Are these five factors bringing about the death of expertise? Not according to Nichols's definition of expertise. There aren't fewer scientists, doctors, or engineers. And it isn't obvious that more scientists, doctors, or engineers are out of work due to a lack of public trust. In fact, the changes in the structure of information and the algorithms on which people rely for news and other information is actually evidence that we rely on many more experts than just traditional experts. We are beholden to everyone who is responsible for getting information to our smart phones, from our internet or cell provider to the programmers who work to ensure our devices are not hacked.

If Nichols is right, expertise is not dying, rather, the people we are publicly claiming to trust as experts are changing. Rather than trusting doctors directly, we are relying on websites like WebMD and Mayo Clinic. Rather than listening to boring CNN prattle, we get the same news stories packaged in a more interesting way by Trevor Noah. This is not completely irrational. Individual doctors can be biased, but medical websites can, if done well, transmit collected wisdom. And given how little citizens can do to change the political landscape of large swaths of the country, better to be pessimistic and a little entertained than pessimistic and distraught. Why would Nichols be upset that people are trusting different experts as long as the real experts are behind the curtain keeping things moving in the right direction?

It seems the real question he is addressing is why people would trust a website where no authors (and therefore, no author credentials) are listed rather than doctors, or a comedian rather than people who have specialized training in medicine and journalism. What sort of attitude would lead people to believe they can know whom to trust without investing in the domain themselves? I think this is a great question. People are expressing (at least publicly) less trust in traditional experts and expressing trust in other putative experts without knowing whether they are trustworthy. But the point I want to highlight is that Nichols is conflating the objective conception of expertise with trust in a specific set of experts. He is saying the shift away from trusting traditional experts is the death of expertise. Maybe this is bad, and maybe it isn't. Perhaps traditional experts should be traded in for a different set. But keeping our concept clearly in focus will help us identify and address the right problems.

Should we be worried that trust in experts is on the brink of demise? I think the answer, broadly speaking, is no because I don't think Nichols has identified the right problem. We are not facing the death of expertise or even the death of trust in experts. We are seeing a shift in the experts that some people trust and the way they trust them, and that calls out for an explanation.

1.4 A Different Hypothesis: Expertise Is Often Confounded

Why do I think this is only a shift? For two reasons. First, everyone, no matter how skeptical of *some* kinds of experts they are, still trusts *some* other people *as* experts. And second, empirical evidence suggests that the level of trust in traditional experts has not changed much.

It is nearly impossible to live in a technological society without trusting some people as experts. If you search the internet for a video on how to change the headlight on your car, then you are trusting someone you think is in a better position than you. If you look, specifically, for a video created by a mechanic or parts manufacturer (i.e., someone who specializes in that type of work), then you're trusting that person as an expert. All of us trust some news sources and not others if we think they have a reliable track record of presenting information accurately. We trust some talking heads about nutrition and health and not others, sometimes based only on their credentials. We trust accountants, electricians, IT professionals, and pilots based on their experience, education, certificates, degrees, ratings on consumer review sites, or rankings by independent accreditors. Sometimes we trust them just because they are wearing a certain uniform.[10] We trust some religious leaders and not others, not necessarily because of their competence as theological or biblical scholars (though sometimes we do), but because of the role they play in our religious organizations. When in doubt, we even set up our own experts. Philosopher Josh Reeves points out:

> Evangelicals, who tend to be most distrustful of human authorities, are also more likely to form groups around charismatic figures (e.g., the megachurch phenomenon). In the area of theology and science, even the most strident critics of scientific experts set up their own alternative institutions, publish their own research, cite their own scientific credentials, etc. In practice, critics of scientific expertise themselves function as experts; they just work outside the mainstream institutions of science. (Reeves 2018)

Setting up our own experts is not a new phenomenon, either. Corporations regularly create or fund scientific projects to produce data consistent with their financial interests, as when companies tried to manufacture doubt about the effects of smoking (Oreskes and Conway 2010), conduct biased studies on pesticide safety (Mie, Rudén, Grandjean 2018), and market overly high doses of pharmaceuticals like opioids just to be able to market anti-addiction drugs later on (Lopez 2019; Winter and Fieldstadt 2019).[11] Some universities even have programs designed to produce experts who defend specific economic or theological views.[12] But in each of these cases, the goal (and arguably, the result) is not to undermine *expertise*, but to redirect trust (intentionally or unintentionally) to different experts or different types of expert or to make us think certain people are experts (whether they are or not). All but the most reclusive anti-experts still trust attorneys to protect them from liability and hospital doctors when they have a broken limb or cancer.[13] So, while Nichols may be right that his factors are pointing to a social problem worth solving, it is not clear it is the problem he claims.

Further, it turns out that trust in scientific experts, while not as high as many of us would like, has "remained stable for decades." Pew Research Center reports that public trust in science has remained at around 40 percent since 1973 (Funk and Kennedy 2019). This study also shows that slightly more Americans—about half—accept the almost unanimous scientific opinion that genetically modified foods are not worse for health than non-GMO foods (Funk, Kennedy, and Hefferson 2018).

Of course, expertise is not "Expertise" (capital E), a monolithic enterprise whose representatives should engender uniform confidence. Different sciences and disciplines have different success rates. But interestingly, the novice public seems to understand that, as well. For example, a 2013 study found that trust in financial institutions rose sharply with the economy in the 1980s and 1990s but then fell sharply again from 2007 to 2010 in the wake of the housing market's collapse, while their trust in the sciences, broadly speaking, remained relatively stable (Smith and Son 2013). The 2019 Pew study showed that despite overall stable confidence in science, confidence in medicine "declined in the early 1990s and has ticked downward again in more recent years, from 41% in 2010 to 36% in 2016 and 37% in NORC's most recent survey." And a 2018 study of 3,367 experts and novices found a similar degree of confidence in science overall but distinct differences in confidence in climatologists (Beebe et al. 2019).

To be sure, we may not think such dips in public confidence are warranted in every case. But the reasons respondents give for their skepticism is telling. When asked whether disagreements in climate science suggest that *the methods of climate science are unreliable*, significantly more undergraduate students and novice college graduates thought the answer was yes. The same was true for whether disagreement among scientists suggests that *more than one theory is correct*. When asked whether disagreement among scientists suggests that there is *no correct theory*, novice college graduates were much more likely to say yes than *climate scientists or undergraduates*, somewhat allaying the sense that all undergraduates are relativists. And when asked whether disagreements in a domain are healthy for that domain, the majority of all respondents agreed that the answer is yes. But when asked whether *political ideology or financial incentives were the most likely reason for disagreement*, undergraduates and novice graduates were much more likely than experts to say yes. The authors of the study conclude that "while non-experts express less confidence in climate scientists than other scientists, they express very high levels of confidence in both" (Beebe et al. 2019: 47).[14]

These studies suggest that (a) trust in science has been stable for decades, (b) trust in particular sciences is mitigated by social influences, and (c) nevertheless, trust in science as a whole is not especially low. Thus, whatever else Nichols's list suggests, it is not obviously a wholesale rejection of expertise.

Instead, the problem that Nichols is trying to address is, to my mind, better described by the less radical notion that certain cognitive and social structures shift public trust toward different sets of putative experts. There is a gulf between exercising expertise in a domain and the public's perception of expertise in that domain. That gulf is much like the uncertainty in a controlled experiment in science: Between the bit of nature an experiment is trying to uncover and the results of the experiment, variables can distort, or "confound," the results. Let's call this less radical phenomenon "the confounding of trust in experts." Trust is confounded when we are led to trust people as experts who aren't experts and to refrain from trusting experts when we should, when we are motivated to trust experts to the wrong degree, and when we are led to persist in the illusion that we are as knowledgeable as experts in a domain when we are not. Trust has been confounded in the past by propaganda campaigns[15] and changes in technology,[16] and we are discovering ever new ways this can happen.

1.5 How Is Expertise Confounded?

What variables confound trust in experts today? Over the past two decades, we have learned a number of ways that information can be distorted. Some of those ways are internal to us—how we interpret and use information—and some are external to us—how information is presented to us. Whether any one of these confounds trust in experts for any particular person is an empirical question. And, of course, different combinations of them can have different effects on the social reception of experts. But understanding how each can individually shape our perspective on information, and thereby, on experts, can help us better calibrate our own trust as we develop strategies for identifying genuine experts.

1.5.1 Tribal Epistemology

One possible confounding variable is that people get stuck in a "tribal epistemology," a phenomenon named by *Vox* writer David Roberts (Roberts 2017). Tribal epistemology is a way of understanding the world that is based, not on standard rules of evidence or experience, but on the way our epistemic communities interpret others' claims and on the value those communities put on certain beliefs. Roberts explains tribal epistemology as a way of processing information:

> Information is evaluated based not on conformity to common standards of evidence or correspondence to a common understanding of the world, but on whether it supports the tribe's values and goals and is vouchsafed by tribal leaders. "Good for our side" and "true" begin to blur into one. (Roberts 2017)

In epistemological terms, we might call tribal epistemology a "theory of justification" (Watson, n.d.). Theories of justification tell us the conditions under which we should believe something, or those under which it is permissible to believe or not believe something. In considering whether to accept a new claim, such as "Humans are contributing to climate change" or "There is a military-level crisis at the U.S.–Mexico border," traditional epistemologies tell us that these are justified for us only if we have sufficient reasons to believe[17] that they are true and lack reasons sufficient for undermining them: What evidence is there that global temperatures are rising? What evidence is there that human behavior is correlated with this rise in temperature? Tribal epistemology, on the other hand, requires that we ask whether a claim is consistent with other claims held by people with whom we most closely identify, those we trust in virtue of their beliefs and values, that is, by our epistemic communities. Is this a claim pundit Rush Limbaugh would endorse? Is this a claim economist Paul Krugman would endorse?

If this is how people process information, it is easy to see how it could confound trust. Whereas some people trust traditional experts—doctors, scientists, engineers, tax accountants—others divide up the set. Perhaps they trust engineers and tax accountants but not doctors or scientists, preferring instead to trust, say, practitioners of alternative medicine, political commentators from certain news outlets, or politicians from certain political parties. The problem is that an epistemic community's beliefs are not obviously tied to any objective measure of epistemic value, such as truth-seeking or coherence or one's total evidence. A community, like an individual, can hold beliefs for any number of faulty reasons. Thus, the degree to which someone trusts their "tribe's" epistemology over standard evidential sources negatively affects their ability to adequately identify and weigh the claims of experts.

It is worth noting, though, that there is nothing about tribal epistemology renders it impossible to overcome. Roberts titled his article "The *Rise* of Tribal Epistemology," but people have been making decisions on the basis of group values and interests for centuries. Many Catholics filter information through the lens of ecclesiastical process, Protestants filter information through various interpretations of the Bible, and both conservatives and liberals vet information through their preferred economists and political ideologues. Nevertheless, many of these people regularly engage in constructive collaborations with experts and policymakers with whom they disagree. So, while tribal epistemology may explain some shifts in who people trust as experts, it surely does not explain them all.

1.5.2 Standpoint Epistemology

It is important to point out that tribal epistemology is distinct from "standpoint epistemology," a view that arose in feminist epistemology[18] and feminist philosophy of science[19] and that has important implications for reasoning about any social issue. Whereas tribal epistemology is an account of what we should do with information, standpoint epistemology is a theory about the role of social and historical factors in shaping what information means to us in the first place. Philosopher Tracy Bowell explains that, according to standpoint epistemology:

> The social situation of an epistemic agent—her gender, class, race, ethnicity, sexuality and physical capacities—plays a role in forming what we know and limiting what we are able to know. They can affect what we are capable of knowing and what we are permitted to know. (Bowell n.d.)

Traditional approaches to epistemology are grounded in concerns about what individuals are justified in believing given their evidence. To the extent that people are, broadly speaking, rational, they should be able to observe the world around them and then to draw fairly reliable inferences from their experiences and understanding. The problem is that much of what we observe in the world around us—what we pay attention to, what we regard as important to our beliefs—can be altered by features of our own identities, especially the identity formed in light of how others treat us based on our sex, race, class, abilities, etc.

To get a sense of the implications of standpoint epistemology, Bowell asks us to consider an example from philosopher Terri Elliot (1994):

"Person A approaches a building and enters it unproblematically. As she approaches she sees something perfectly familiar which, if asked, she might call 'The Entrance'. Person X approaches the same building and sees a great stack of stairs and the glaring lack of a ramp for her wheelchair." (424)

The experience of person A is of the entrance to a building. Whereas the experience of person X is of a barrier to entrance and (at best) an inconvenience. Person X's social location—qua person with a disability—means that the building presents differently to her from how it does to someone without a disability. (n.d.)

Would Person A understand the "entrance" in a way that implies someone *should* put a ramp on this building (understand it such that it constitutes a normative implication)? Presumably, since the entrance presents no problem to Person A, they would not give it much thought at all beyond what is needed for their particular epistemic needs: *I want to go in this building. Building entrances are the way to do that. This is the entrance to this building.* Person A wouldn't, without help, understand the entrance as an obstacle without understanding the perspective of someone like Person X. The key insight from standpoint epistemology is that Person A *could* understand the entrance that way if they were willing to engage epistemically with people who understand it differently. Thus, tribal epistemology is not related to or motivated by standpoint epistemology.

Standpoint epistemology makes an important contribution to how we know in social groups. It does not directly challenge whether individuals can reason well about the information they have, rather it challenges the assumption that individuals, by themselves, can have all the information they need to make good decisions about what to believe without engaging with others from multiple standpoints.

Could standpoint epistemology's key insight—that we process information differently depending on our social and historical backgrounds—contribute to the confounding of trust? I think, like tribal epistemology, the answer is yes, to some degree. Given our social and historical limitations, there will be information we cannot "see" as well as we should, and some that we cannot see at all. This matters because those beliefs affect—directly or indirectly—the welfare of others. Our beliefs about abortion, disability, race, and sexual minorities, for example, affect how we vote, how we write private and public policies, how we talk to and about other people in our daily lives, and thus, how we form beliefs about social problems and their solutions.

Nevertheless, we retain this limited view when forming beliefs only when we refuse to seek out or engage with the perspectives of those with a vested interest in those beliefs. If we vote on, say, whether third trimester abortions should be legalized before we understand relevant medical, social, historical, and economic factors that account for why people have abortions, that is, before we admit that the perspectives of those most affected by a policy are valid, then we are presuming that any one individual perspective on a topic is sufficient for forming a judgment on that topic. But if, instead, we are humble enough to admit that we are dependent on others for an accurate perspective on the world (and take advantage of the vast amount of information easily available to us), we can start to see the world through multiple perspectives and choose more nuanced and more strongly justified beliefs. This is not always easy. As Alessandra Tanesini puts it, those whose perspective is socially dominant—the "privileged"—"are often ignorant of the facts about their privilege because they have an incentive not to know the truth about themselves" (2020: 340). But it is not impossible. And the groundswell of cultural commentaries on race, gender, sexuality, and disability attest to humans' ability to address this epistemic obstacle.

Standpoint epistemology seems to explain a set of beliefs, namely, those where the believer's privilege is at stake, as in the case of public support for tariffs, decisions about abortion policy, and opinions about publicly funded health care. But it does not adequately account for the motive not to seek out multiple perspectives in social areas where privilege is not (at least not obviously) at stake, such as public policy on guns, animal welfare, homeopathy, or conspiracy theories. If this is right, then standpoint epistemology does not fully explain shifts in who some people trust as experts. For a fuller explanation, we must look for additional mental or social processes that affect how people process information.

1.5.3 The Dunning-Kruger Effect

A third possible confounding variable in who people trust is the counterintuitive cognitive phenomenon called the *Dunning-Kruger Effect*: the less one knows in a domain, the more likely they will believe they are knowledgeable in that domain. In 1999, social psychologists Justin Kruger and David Dunning published the results of four experiments that showed people who score in the bottom 25 percent on tests of humor, grammar, and logic significantly overestimated their abilities in these areas relative to other participants. And all those who scored in the bottom 50 percent overestimated their abilities to some degree.

What's behind these results? Kruger and Dunning conclude that the knowledge and abilities one needs to work competently in a domain are also needed to recognize that one is not competent in that domain. Thus, the Dunning-Kruger Effect is the claim that people who are incompetent have little insight into their incompetence (Dunning 2011).

To get a sense of how bad the problem is, even before the "Effect" was coined by Kruger and Dunning, a 1977 study found that 90 percent of faculty at the University of Nebraska rated themselves above average for teaching ability (Cross 1977). And a 1992 study of software engineers at two high-tech companies showed that 32 percent at one and 42 percent at the other rated their skills as being in the top 5 percent of their companies (Zenger 1992). Since their four original studies, Dunning and others have replicated their findings in a variety of domains. In a 2016 *Politico* piece, Dunning writes:

> We have found this pattern in logical reasoning, grammar, emotional intelligence, financial literacy, numeracy, firearm care and safety, debate skill, and college coursework. Others have found a similar lack of insight among poor chess players, unskilled medical lab technicians, medical students unsuccessfully completing an obstetrics/gynecology rotation, and people failing a test on performing CPR. (Dunning 2016)

From here, it is easy to see how the Dunning-Kruger Effect can confound trust in experts. The point is not simply that people don't know enough to be competent. It's that the information they have distorts their beliefs about their competence. As Dunning explains, "the key to the Dunning-Kruger Effect is not that unknowledgeable voters are uninformed; it is that they are often misinformed—their heads filled with false data, facts and theories that can lead to misguided conclusions held with tenacious confidence and extreme partisanship" (2016). The result is that trust is diverted away from trustworthy sources by the very mechanism they use to assess what's trustworthy: their own minds.

Again, though, this is likely not the only factor at play in the confounding of expertise. Not everyone whose trust has been confounded is in the bottom 25 percent of competence in a domain. And the degree and topics on which someone is overconfident vary widely. Few people (I assume, fingers crossed) would volunteer in an emergency to try to land a passenger jet if they had no experience at all flying planes, or to perform heart surgery without any prior training. The domains in which people tend to be overconfident are those from which they are insulated from the practical consequences of their beliefs. Most people will never know whether a public policy aimed at addressing, say, climate change or drug abuse has any effect on those problems. So, either way they vote, they're safe. Thus, in addition to ignorance, the degree to which a belief is risky can also affect confidence.

1.5.4 Filter Bubbles[20]

As noted earlier, Nichols says that the way we receive information changes the way we think about and use information, and a clear example of this is what journalist and cultural critic Eli Pariser (2011) calls a "filter bubble."[21] The speed and volume of information on the internet has produced a marketplace for the free exchange of ideas that could not have been imagined by the classic defenders of free speech like John Milton and John Stuart Mill. Perhaps ironically, some of the by-products of this technological free exchange of ideas now threaten our ability to pursue true beliefs.

Though the internet promises almost unlimited access to ideas, humans cannot sort and comprehend vast amounts of information. Algorithmic filtering tools are needed to make these sources useful and fast. They offer a way to ease the effects of information overload by tailoring the vast amounts of information on an issue to that which best fits the data that companies already have about us.

To be sure, filtering of one sort or another has always occurred. There has always been too much news to report. News outlets decide which stories are hot, interesting, or worth reporting and reject the rest. They must also frame stories in a historico-political context, which presupposes a particular interest in geography and history on the part of their audiences. This is why Americans see very little news about Chile or Argentina but see volumes about Venezuela and China. News outlets also have limited time to cover the topics they choose, so they must also decide how much of a story to explain. For example, one 2015 item was that US President Obama proposed reducing tariffs *to increase American jobs*. Basic economics tells us that lower tariffs typically means outsourcing domestic labor, so it isn't clear from this headline how lower tariffs are supposed to *increase* domestic jobs. Economists know this, but the general public does not. And while some critics highlighted the worry, neither the New York Times nor *Huffington Post* explained the economic relationship between tariffs and domestic jobs for their readers (Baker and Davis 2015; Johnson 2015). The novice public was left to deal with the uncertainty some other way.

Internet filtering tools offer even greater scope and precision than traditional journalistic judgments, which raises questions about how the algorithms should be designed. Classically, liberal democracies have rejected the idea that a state-sponsored mechanism can effectively or justly filter, so citizens are obliged to look for alternatives. Importantly, the same concerns that apply to government control of the news can apply to private individuals (such as those at large-scale media outlets).[22] While news outlets generally make decisions like other businesses, on the basis of their customers' needs and interests, there is nothing to keep them from having a political agenda. And, indeed, as Nichols pointed out, we now have news outlets, like Fox News, that are explicitly associated with a certain interpretation of political issues. What better corrective, then, than to design advertising mechanisms aimed, not just at broad demographics, but to our individual interests? And this is precisely what happened.

Algorithms developed by Amazon, Google, and Facebook paved the way for data gathering through free services like Gmail—where users, in trade for an account, volunteer personal information through *click signals*—the data we produce when we search, scroll, click, read, open email ads, and buy on the internet. This data includes the topics we search for, the length of time we look at them, which ones we *like* on Facebook, which ones we share, the types of devices we use to look at them, where we are when we look at them on our devices, etc. In his 2011 book, Pariser explains:

> By getting people to log in, Google got its hands on an enormous pile of data—the hundreds of millions of e-mails Gmail users send and receive each day. And it could cross-reference each user's email and behavior on the site with the links he or she clicked in the Google search engine. (2011: 33)

Click signals are recorded and mined for patterns that allow producers to cater to users' narrow interests. This is why the shoes you were shopping for on Zappos now appear in an ad on your Facebook page. It also explains why one person's Google search looks different from another's,[23] and why two people with many of the same Facebook "friends" see very different posts in their newsfeeds—they *like* different posts, and subsequent posts are filtered according to those preferences.

The data gathered on internet users is now staggering, and companies like Acxiom store and sell this information to companies. Acxiom has information about "96 percent of American households and half a billion people worldwide," including "the names of their family members, their current and past addresses, how often they pay their credit card bills[,] whether they own a dog or cat (and what breed it is), whether they are right-handed or left-handed, what kinds of medication they use (based on pharmacy records) ... the list of data points is about 1,500 items long" (Pariser 2011: 43). This information is for sale to anyone willing to pay, and it is available to the federal government on demand.[24] All this raises significant moral concerns about privacy. But what about epistemic concerns? How does this data gathering affect our ability to pursue what's epistemically valuable?

A result of filtering for individual interests is what Pariser calls the "filter bubble." Filter bubbles occur when the information you volunteered to websites along with your click signals form an isolation bubble of information that almost perfectly suits you, and that, in turn, excludes other viewpoints that are relevant to which beliefs you form. "We're never bored. We're never annoyed. Our media is a perfect reflection of our interests and desires" (2011: 12). If you regularly visit conservative websites and *like* conservative posts, the information you see from non-conservatives (say, liberals and libertarians) will diminish or disappear over time. Given that the world looks conservative (or liberal or libertarian) to you, it will be difficult to take an opposing point of view seriously. Those must be minority views, you conclude, by sheer dint of their scarcity on social media.

So far, though, these are not *new* concerns about epistemic responsibility. People have always been free to stick their heads in the sand. The problem arises when we combine the invisibility of filter bubbles with an understanding of how human behavior can be manipulated by others. We are faced with the question of whether filtering algorithms shape content so much that companies and governments can engage in an invisible structuring of our world such that we see primarily what *someone else* wants us to.

Using your personal information to invisibly influence future preferences and purchasing behavior is called *persuasion profiling*.[25] Pariser explains, "In the wrong hands, persuasion profiling gives companies the ability to circumvent your rational decision making, tap into your psychology, and draw out your compulsions. Understand someone's identity, and you're better equipped to influence what he or she does" (Pariser 2011: 123).[26] Just as advertising agencies have always created markets by convincing us we need things we've never thought of, corporations and internet barons can now use our personal information to manipulate and change even deeper interests. If this is right, then it can also affect whom we perceive to be experts, and thereby confound our ability to trust people who are trustworthy.

Filter bubbles can confound trust, but it is heartening to note that they can also be burst. Pariser offers a number of suggestions for popping filter bubbles, from using virtual private networks (VPNs) for browser searching to actively seeking out diverse perspectives on a topic. Philosopher C. Thi Nguyen (2018a) notes that "we can pop an epistemic bubble simply by exposing its members to the information and arguments they've missed." That may be easier said than done. Motivating people to care enough to consider more information than they already have is no mean feat. But, it is not substantially different from resolving disagreements over evidence in other contexts.

Given the ubiquity of these personalized digital worlds, our lives are now largely shaped by what philosopher James Williams calls the "attention economy" (2018), as advertisers and politicians vie for the scarce resource of our attention. But though they are everywhere, they are not comprehensive. And this fragility means they contribute to, but do not fully account for, shifts in whom we trust as experts.

1.5.5 Echo Chambers

A fifth likely confounder of trust in experts is what political scientist Kathleen Hall Jamieson and communication researcher Joseph N. Cappella call an "echo chamber" (2010). An echo chamber is an evidence set that both feeds and is a function of your interests and values as a knower—the evidence you find echoes back to you what you already believe is right. Echo chambers are like filter bubbles in the sense that they isolate you from relevant alternative or contrary evidence that would enhance the accuracy of your beliefs. But they differ in that echo chambers are a function of the way you (rather than others) select the sources you find trustworthy. Further, an echo chamber is a social structure that explicitly manipulates your trust.

Consider an innocuous sort of filter bubble of our own making:

> Suppose I believe that the Paleo diet is the greatest diet of all time. I assemble a Facebook group called "Great Health Facts!" and fill it only with the people who already believe that Paleo is the best diet. The fact that everybody in the group agrees with me about Paleo shouldn't increase my confidence level one bit. They're not mere copies—they actually might have reached their conclusions independently—but their agreement can be entirely explained by my method of selection. (Nguyen 2018a: 5)

Note that the fact that we don't know how people we select came to believe Paleo is the best diet is important. If all the members were just my students who I convinced to accept Paleo, then I would know their beliefs are not extra reasons for me to accept Paleo. But the fact that they have their own, independent reasons suggests that they are all "reasonable people," just like me, and this seems to confirm my belief—though it shouldn't—that the Paleo diet is best.

This case is worrisome but not inescapable. A little knowledge of statistics would tell me that increasing my confidence in Paleo on these grounds would be fallacious, an instance of what's called "self-selection bias." What's more, I probably have regular contact with healthy people whom I trust but who are not fans of Paleo, whether friends or co-workers, any one of whom might, given the opportunity, erode my confidence.

But imagine I got into Paleo because some people I trust deeply told me that Paleo is the only empirically based diet, and that all other diets miss fundamental nutritional elements. Further, imagine the literature they give me to read confirms this suspicion and gives ample arguments that other diet programs are simply for-profit ploys. This literature convinces me that any putative scientific claims offered in support of non-Paleo diets is contrived and fabricated.

Now, my evidence-gathering system is structured so that I will dismiss out of hand any putative evidence against Paleo or for another diet. In essence, I've set up the following conditions:

1   I rely on specially chosen experts (Paleo gurus) to check and reinforce my reasoning and beliefs.

2   I evaluate others' experts (evidence for any other diet) through my reasoning and beliefs, which have been structured by my experts.

3   I leave no option to check for failures in either my own or my experts' reasoning and beliefs.[27]

By allowing (intentionally or unintentionally) select experts to shape my belief-forming mechanisms, I have conditioned those mechanisms to regard any non-Paleo or anti-Paleo evidence as unreliable. I don't even need to start the Facebook group to maintain my beliefs, and I don't have to worry about running into naysayers at the office; I have reason to believe all the evidence they could have is faulty. No one could convince me otherwise.

Now imagine a less innocuous case. Let's say you want to start a Facebook group with only people who hold the "right" views of politics. Many people will claim they aren't Paleo fans, but no one will admit they have the wrong political beliefs. So, how do you select people for this group? Presumably, based on what you believe about politics. You don't think you have wrong beliefs, either, but the only gauge you have of the rightness of others' beliefs are your own beliefs on the matter.

To be sure, if you are humble enough, and if at least some of your reasoning abilities in the area of politics are functioning properly, then you have a shot at calibrating your beliefs in a way that orients you to trust trustworthy sources. You will hear the random contrary bit of evidence and incorporate it into your overall belief system, nudging down your confidence here and there. But if your reasoning abilities about politics are off-track from the start (perhaps you were raised with a certain tribal epistemology or are not well-positioned to consider different epistemic standpoints), then anyone you choose to trust will have beliefs selected based on your starting assumptions. Why would you choose to trust people who say things that don't make sense to you? Without intending it, you have become trapped in an echo chamber.

Echo chambers are especially vicious when what is echoed is the unreliability of any source that disagrees with you. When political commentators on one side of a political topic constantly discredit those from any other perspectives as biased or partisan or corrupt, then the echo chamber is sealed from the inside. And from here, the concern for expertise is clear. Echo chambers can confound our trust by directing it to untrustworthy sources while continually reinforcing the belief that those sources are trustworthy.

Philosopher Jennifer Lackey (2018b) thinks that echo chambers are not actually a problem for expertise because echo chambers are content neutral. If we're locked in the right chamber (the one where all the best information and methods of assessing evidence is reinforced), then all the better. She says, for example, that she has no problem being in an echo chamber that dismisses climate change deniers because requiring her to hear them out is asking her to place value on something besides truth.[28] The problem is not the *structure* of an echo chamber, according to Lackey, but the *content*, when the echoes reinforce "an utter disregard for truth." She argues that "to identify the problem as involving an echo chamber—rather than lies and ignorance—is to put the epistemic cart before the horse. This matters because lies spread far faster, and more widely, than the truth does online" (Lackey 2018b).

Unfortunately, Lackey's criticism begs the question. The climate change denier is just as convinced as Lackey that his beliefs are true and that his evidence-seeking process is reliable.[29] What's worse, his echo chamber—assuming he is in one—reinforces this way of thinking about evidence and truth. The climate change denier might be as committed to finding truth as Lackey but simply ill-equipped to do so given the structure of how he receives information. Lackey seems to view those who help build certain kinds of echo chambers the way Nichols does, as encouraging the death of expertise. But people in echo chambers still trust people they think are experts and for the same reasons that others do: because they believe they're telling the truth. Their trust is simply confounded.

1.6 Summing Up

Understanding how information can be distorted can help us be more sympathetic to skeptics about expertise. It can also suggest ways of mitigating those effects when experts purport to speak authoritatively in a domain. For example, recognizing the influence of a "tribe" on a demographic's beliefs can help us package information in a way that coheres with that group's basic assumptions about the world. And recognizing the importance of intellectual humility can help us hear evidence that challenges our "standpoint" in a productive way. But even more important at this stage in the conversation is getting clear on what we mean by expertise. Without a firm grasp of the phenomenon, we can too easily conflate expertise with other concepts or get distracted by trying to identify it before we know what it is we are looking for. The central project of this book is to explore the groundwork that others have laid in attempting to describe expertise, and it is to that groundwork that we now turn.

2 PHILOSOPHICAL APPROACHES TO EXPERTISE

"No art is ever closed within itself."
(Cicero, *De finibus bonorum et malorum*, Book V, § 6, trans. William Carew Hazlitt, 1877)

In this chapter, I review an ancient taxonomy of expertise to help orient us to the project of developing a general account of expertise (2.1). I then highlight three distinctions that shape general accounts of expertise (2.2). It is possible, however, that no general account will prove satisfactory. With that possibility in mind, I review a Wittgensteinian "family resemblance" approach that could, with some further development, help save expertise studies from relativism (2.3). But because I do think a general account remains in the offing, and because I find current versions of the Wittgensteinian account unsatisfactory, I set it aside for the purposes of this book. I close the chapter with a discussion of how technology shapes expertise (2.4). While I think a wide range of technologies can exhibit expertise, I argue that responsibility for their creation, use, and evaluation falls ultimately on human[1] experts, and so I restrict the remaining discussion in this book to expertise as it is acquired and exhibited by agents.

2.1 The Oldest Taxonomy of Expertise

What is arguably the oldest taxonomy of expertise carves expertise much the way contemporary lexicographers do, into *practical* or *performance-based* expertise, on one hand—the ability to do something well in a domain—and *theoretical* or *cognitive* expertise, on the other—having true beliefs or knowledge in a domain. In Plato's dialogue *Statesman*, an unnamed visitor to Athens asks a young student named Socrates (though not the Socrates we know and love) to help him describe the ideal political leader. They begin by distinguishing two types of knowledge, *practical* and *theoretical*:

> **Visitor:** Well then: isn't it the case that arithmetic and some other sorts of expertise (*technai*) that are akin to it don't involve any practical actions, but simply provide knowledge?
>
> **Young Socrates:** That's so.
>
> **Visitor:** Whereas for their part the sorts of expertise (*techtonikein*) involved in carpentry and manufacture as a whole have their knowledge as it were naturally bound up with practical actions, and use it to complete those material objects they cause to come into being from not having been before?
>
> **Young Socrates:** What of that?
>
> **Visitor:** Well, divide all cases of knowledge (*epistemas*) in this way, calling the one sort practical knowledge (*praktikein*), the other purely theoretical[2] (*gnostikein*). (258d–e, trans. Rowe)

They then distinguish those who *direct* others to do practical things (the master builder, for example) from those who *actually do* them (the carpenter). The person who performs the skillful labor has practical expertise. But the person who directs "has a share in the theoretical sort of knowledge" (260a), so they talk of directive knowledge as a species of theoretical knowledge. Of course, not everyone who has theoretical expertise directs others, so they add *theoretical judging* expertise next to theoretical directing expertise (260b). So far, then, we have something that looks like Figure 2.1.

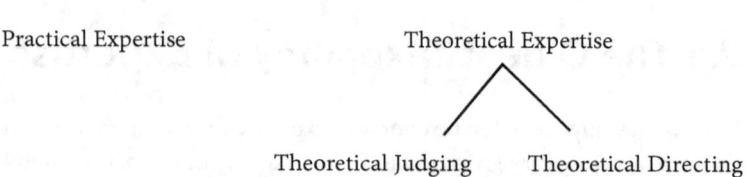

FIGURE 2.1 Taxonomy of Expertise in Plato's *Statesman*.

They further divide Theoretical Directive into *self-directing* expertise, those who work for themselves, for example, those who direct how their own goods are made and sold, from those we might call *direction-taking* expertise, who take direction from others before giving directions themselves—the middle-managers of the ancient world: "The retailer, I think, takes over someone else's products, which have previously been sold, and sells them on, for a second time. ... [T]he class of heralds takes over directions that have been thought up by someone else, and itself issues them for a second time to another group" (260d). This suggests a distinction between those who produce items with expert skill and those who understand how to use those items. There are innumerable examples of this, as when one person writes a computer program and then teaches someone else to use it. The person who uses it may or may not be able to write programs like that. There are also ambassadors who do not make political decisions but know how to convey them in attractive and relevant ways. There are musicians who do not write songs but simply play the songs of others. This suggests a second branch in our taxonomy along the lines of Figure 2.2.

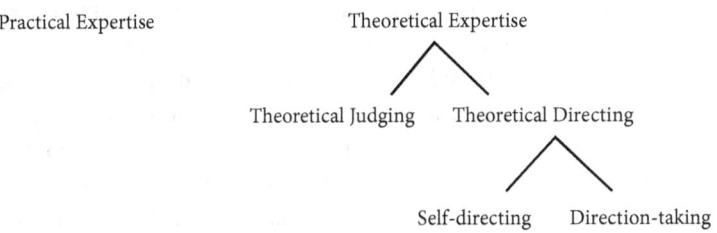

FIGURE 2.2 Self-directors and Direction-takers.

The Visitor and Young Socrates pursue the ideal political leader by further dividing the self-directing theoretical experts into directors over animate and inanimate objects, directors over animate objects into directors over individual rearing and herd-rearing creatures, directors over herd-rearing creatures into directors over aquatic and dry-land creatures, and so on (walking vs. flying, horned vs. non-horned). The discussion culminates in directors over what Diogenes of Sinope, by plucking a chicken, lampooned as "Plato's human": the featherless biped.[3]

This taxonomy is noteworthy for several reasons. First, early in this conversation, it becomes apparent that the interlocutors view expertise as something objective in the world, not simply a matter of title or reputation. In considering the person who has the knowledge to advise a king, they admit this person need not be a king:

> **Visitor:** And isn't it the case that the person who possesses this, whether he happens to be a ruler or a private citizen, in all circumstances, in virtue of his possession of the expertise itself, will correctly be addressed as an expert in kingship?
> **Young Socrates:** That's fair. (259b)

The idea that expertise is not constituted solely by social recognition or public appointment is consistent with most of the views we will encounter over the next four chapters. As we will see in Chapter 6, even though some theorists argue that expertise is a largely social phenomenon, few actually defend the claim that it is solely a social phenomenon. Rather, the idea that expertise is solely a matter of reputation or social approval is most commonly posed as a foil to demonstrate the strength of other views rather than as a view that anyone actually holds.

Second, we see that those whose skill is in performing specialized tasks (whether practical expertise or direction-taking expertise) are regarded as experts in their own right. While we might be tempted to place practical expertise underneath theoretical directing expertise, this does not reflect either the social or the conceptual relationships among experts we find in the text or in the world. For example, while a carpenter may work for a master builder, it is not part of her expertise qua carpenter that she does so.

And third, practical expertise is almost immediately left behind, being mentioned later in the dialogue only to highlight other aspects of expertise. This suggests that, at least on the face of it, it is reasonable to focus study on one type of expertise, giving account of it independently of others. The accounts in Chapter 3 tend to focus on one type of expertise while acknowledging that other types exist outside their scope of interest. For example, some philosophers who offer accounts of expertise approach the topic through epistemology—the study of knowledge—which, because of its central interest in true beliefs, shapes their interest in expertise as certain kind of epistemic state, namely, having a substantial fund of propositional knowledge in a domain. That is, they focus on what Plato's characters call theoretical expertise: knowledge *that* rather than knowledge *how*. There are exceptions among philosophers, such as Hubert and Stuart Dreyfus (see Chapter 4) and Zoltan Majdik and William Keith (later in this chapter), but many epistemologists explicitly restrict themselves to the cognitive dimensions of expertise, and this is consistent with ancient discussions of expertise.

2.2 Developing a General Account of Expertise

Plato's taxonomy is a useful starting point for two reasons. First, it confirms some of our twenty-first-century intuitions about expertise, centrally, that expertise is largely about knowledge or proficiency in a domain. Second, it frees us to explore expertise using a variety of evidence. Unlike so many ancient philosophical discussions, this one is not driven by *a priori* assumptions about nature, but by real-life examples of experts—herdspeople, salespeople, political rulers, and so on. While the Visitor and Young Socrates were using conceptual tools, their discussion was informed by their contemporary understanding of these social roles. Because of how expertise is acquired and employed in society, the study of expertise is, necessarily, a social project. This suggests that drawing some initial conceptual distinctions can be helpful for getting started but that we do not have to hang onto them if further evidence from philosophy, psychology, sociology, or neurology renders them impractical.

With that in mind, there are three conceptual distinctions that currently help shape expertise studies: the distinction between definitional and methodological accounts of expertise, between reductive and non-reductive accounts, and between fixed criteria and process accounts. Philosophers Oliver Scholz (2009; 2018) and Christian Quast (2018a, b) help illuminate some of these.

2.2.1 Definitional vs. Methodological Accounts

A classic philosophical way to approach a concept is by trying to *define* it according to necessary and sufficient conditions. On this approach, we might say someone is an expert *if and only if* they meet conditions *x*, *y*, and *z*. Classic examples of this definitional approach include the idea that something is knowledge if and only if it is justified true belief, and the idea that something is a body if and only if it is extended in both space and time. Truth-based accounts of expertise as discussed in the next chapter tend to be definitional in this sense.

On the other hand, one might think that definitional accounts have proved, over the many philosophical attempts to develop them, too restrictive and inconsistent with the way concepts work in the real world. Instead, one might attempt a less-restrictive, *methodological* account. Oliver Scholz (2018) explains:

> A few concepts may be blessed with precise definitions of the "if and only if" variety, e.g., "triangle" or "circle" in the terminology of geometry …. [And] some concepts (e.g., "Scandinavian country," "member of the Vienna Circle") can be introduced by enumerating their extension [what they pick out in the world]. Many concepts can be taught by giving examples and hoping that the learner catches on. Some concepts ("red") are best explained ostensively. And some concepts may be so fundamental (e.g., "good") that they cannot be defined in an illuminating way. Anyway, most concepts seem to be "cluster concepts"; the meaning of such a concept is "given by a cluster of properties" (Putnam 1975: 52) or a set of (possibly context-dependent) criteria. (31)

Whether we believe a concept is strictly definable or a loosely definable cluster concept will influence how we approach developing an account of it and what adequacy criteria are necessary for determining whether the account successfully expresses the concept.

Scholz, for example, rejects strict definitional accounts of expertise in favor of what he calls a "symptoms" account, that is, an account that explains expertise in terms of features of expertise as it appears in the world. Scholz follows philosopher Nelson Goodman in defining "symptom" as "neither a necessary nor sufficient condition but rather a feature that we think may, in conjunction with others, make more probable the presence of a given disease or other notable state" (Goodman 1984: 135). Scholz offers some categories of symptoms by which expertise might be identified (32):

1 Individual cognitive abilities, achievements, and goods
2 Social relations
3 Modes and degrees
4 Effects and concomitants

He then offers some methodological strategies for distinguishing experts from novices: *weighted checklists* that weigh items in the symptom lists against details and expectations of the domain, and *ideal expert* criteria, with which one constructs models of expertise for various social uses (33).

Whether a definitional or methodological account is more promising will depend largely on what sort of concept expertise turns out to be and what we need from an account of it.

2.2.2 Reductive vs. Non-reductive Accounts

Philosopher Christian Quast (2018a, b) argues that most contemporary accounts of expertise are insufficient because they are *reductive*, that is, they attempt to reduce expertise to more fundamental concepts, and thereby, miss important, non-reducible features of expertise.

In general, a reductive account of a concept fully explains that concept in terms of more basic concepts. For example, some have argued that "knowledge" is fully explicable in terms of "justified true belief." In other words, there is nothing about knowledge that cannot be explained in terms of these more fundamental concepts (but see the ongoing debate over "Gettier Problems"). So, while the view that knowledge is justified true belief is definitional, as we saw in the last section, it is also reductive. Other concepts are not fully reducible. For example, philosophers and mathematicians Bertrand Russell and Alfred North Whitehead tried to reduce all the rules of mathematics to the rules of logic, but they, by their own admission, failed. And since no more successful attempt has come along, the consensus is that mathematics is something over and above logic, and, as such, is irreducible to it.[4]

Reductive accounts of *expertise*, then, attempt to explain expertise in terms of more basic concepts, for example, "an extensive fund of usable knowledge" or "superior performance."[5] Non-reductive accounts contend that there is something about expertise over and above any particular instance of these more basic concepts. For Quast, this is the mutual interdependence of the concepts that comprise expertise. Expertise is not reducible to competence, outcomes, or social functions because there are examples of a person having each of those who is, intuitively, not an expert. Therefore, according to Quast, an expert must demonstrate all three because, in being an expert, they take on a deontic (duty-based) obligation to use their competence adequately when called upon: "Someone is an expert only if she is undefeatedly[6] disposed to fulfill a contextually salient service function adequately at the moment of assessment" (16).

We might ask whether this account succeeds in being non-reductive. It doesn't reduce expertise to a single criterion, but perhaps it reduces it to a set of them (competence, outcome, and function). Just as knowledge is not any particular instance of justification, truth, or belief, but only instances of the combination *justified true belief*.[7] Or perhaps Quast's point is that the relationship among them cannot be specified independently of the context in which they are exemplified, and therefore, expertise is not reducible to any *a priori* specifiable relationship among them. This might mean that expertise is analogous to the view in ethics called *particularism*, according to which a moral claim can only be evaluated as true or false in a particular set of circumstances (see Dancy 2001). There are no generally specifiable reasons that explain whether a moral claim is true, and any sufficient reasons for whether a moral claim is true include the details of a particular circumstance to which the claim refers. If expertise is like moral particularism, then Quast is right that expertise cannot be reduced to any set of conditions that does not include the details of a particular circumstance in which we are evaluating putative expertise.

The reductive/non-reductive distinction may prove fruitful for expertise studies in the future. For now, non-reductivism about expertise is still in a young stage of development, so the remainder of this book is concerned with reductive accounts.

2.2.3 Fixed Criteria vs. Process Accounts

Fixed criteria accounts set a minimum threshold for who can count as an expert and then define experts as anyone who meets or surpasses that threshold. For example, we might call Scholz's symptoms account a fixed criteria account because anyone who exhibits certain symptoms to a certain degree is likely to be an expert. Other fixed criteria accounts include Goldman's (2001), Fricker's (2006), Coady's (2012), and Watson's (2018).

Process accounts, in contrast, explain expertise in terms of the environments and methods necessary for acquiring expertise. On a process account, whether someone achieves expert-level competence depends primarily on the standards of a domain rather than on a set of strictly specifiable conditions. For example, Barbara Montero (2018) defends a process account which views experts as "*individuals who have engaged in around ten or more years of deliberate practice* [to be defined in Chapter 5], *which means close to daily, extended practice with the specific aim of improving, and are still intent on improving*" (64, italics hers). Process accounts allow for a continuum of competence from novice to superior performer, and they can help explain varying degrees of competence among experts.[8] Other process accounts include Dreyfus and Dreyfus (1986), Collins and Evans (2007), and Ericsson and Pool (2016). Whether this distinction is useful and which type of account is more promising will depend on the sorts of questions we ask of an account of expertise. Laying my cards on the table, I think fixed criteria and process accounts are not mutually exclusive, and I think there are benefits to incorporating aspects of each into a general account, as I will argue in Chapter 7.

2.3 Whither Wittgenstein? (Is a General Theory of Expertise Misguided?)

What if the central assumption behind this chapter is wrong? What if no objective general account of expertise is plausible? In her (2016) discussion, Barbara Montero acknowledges this possibility but sets it aside:

> I shall proceed with the assumption—one prevalent in the current scientific and philosophical literature on expertise—that there are significant commonalities across the various domains of expertise, and thus in formulating a theory of expertise, I'll shoot for a theory of everything, while being well aware that such a theory might not be feasible. (16)

But what if we find out it is not feasible? Are we stuck with a sort of relativism about expertise? Or should we content ourselves with operational accounts, which study only what expertise means in limited contexts, such as expert chess playing or expert weather forecasting, recognizing that what we mean by "expert" will likely vary according to who is operationalizing the definition, perhaps allowing even for expertise in naturopathy or astrology?

Not necessarily. There is another option that may allow us to make sense of expertise without sending us down either of these paths. Rather than a unified concept, some argue that expertise is pluralistic, that is, instantiated by a cluster of concepts, some of which may be mutually exclusive but that are, nonetheless, objective. This approach draws inspiration from philosopher Ludwig Wittgenstein, and philosophers Zoltan P. Majdik and William M. Keith (2011) call it the Wittgensteinian approach to expertise.

Majdik and Keith begin by noting the limitations of accounts of expertise that conceive of it solely in terms of truth, knowledge, or performance:

> Conceptualizing expertise as bodies of knowledge elides ways in which expertise can be a [sic] practice oriented primarily not toward different forms of knowledge, but toward the resolution of a problem. From this perspective, the defining characteristic of "expert" and "expertise" is not bound (simply) to the possession of knowledge, or processes of knowledge acquisition or production, or connections to knowledge networks, but instead flows from problems that require resolutions. Problems (and solutions) are relative to situations and vocabularies of description, and subject to be validated and justified as legitimate in the eyes of relevant others. (2011: 276)

Rather than attempting another kind of general account, Majdik and Keith note that expertise is often identified and employed in the service of solving certain problems. The nature of the problem needing to be solved seems to determine the type of expertise needed to solve it. But since problems vary widely, expertise may, as well. In fact, it may be just as difficult to pin down a general definition of expertise as it is to pin down a general definition of "game" or "number," as Wittgenstein points out:

> Consider for example the proceedings that we call "games". I mean board-games, card-games, ball-games, Olympic games, and so on. What is common to them all?—Don't say: "There must be something common, or they would not be called 'games'"—but look and see whether there is anything in common to all.—For if you look at them you will not see something that is common to all, but similarities, relationships, and a whole series of them at that. ... Look at the parts played by skill and luck; and at the difference between skill in chess and skill in tennis. ([1958] 2000, §66: 182)

Some games are fun, some are not, some are played alone, some with others, some are competitive, some are cooperative, and so on. Thus,

Wittgenstein says we identify games by their "family resemblances" rather than according to some strict definition. What unifies these family resemblances so that we always know what is meant by "game" when we hear it? As it turns out, in English, context does most of the work we need when it comes to practical, daily usage. Consider the word "love." No one would be confused or concerned if someone said "I love ice cream" and then turned to their child and said "I love you," even though "love" means something importantly different in the two sentences. And while tracing the various attitudes associated with the English word *love* to various Greek terms (*philia* [φιλία], *eros* [ἔρος], etc.) has scholarly (and enjoyment) value, it is not necessary for understanding and using "love."

Unfortunately, the same does not seem to be true for expertise. Unlike "love" and "game," there is widespread disagreement over what it means to be an expert, who counts as an expert, how we identify experts, and how we should react to them once we have identified them. So, how might the Wittgensteinian approach work with expertise?

Majdik and Keith propose to treat "expertise" as a heuristic—a type of practice that can repeatably solve problems over time. This takes the focus off the particular knowledge, beliefs, or skill of an individual practitioner (e.g., is their expertise based on a substantial fund of true beliefs in their domain?) and locates it between the putative expert's judgment and the success in solving a problem over time (2011: 278–81). To demonstrate, they contrast three fictional oncologists.

Imagine three oncologists who all have a patient die while in their care. The first oncologist made all her decisions about treatment in accord with "accepted treatments and principles" in oncology. The second oncologist rejected standard treatments and principles and, instead, relied on her own judgment to make treatment decisions. The third made decisions based on non-standard treatments and principles (279, 283). Even though a patient died in all three cases, Majdik and Keith say we would regard the first oncologist as an expert but not the second because standard treatments and principles repeatedly get better results than shooting from the hip. What about the third oncologist?

To answer that, they argue we have to be able to extend the problem space into the future. If the third oncologist's judgment was a function of their understanding of how such judgments affect populations of patients over time, then that has the markers of expertise. They ask us to imagine that the third oncologist "uses non-traditional treatments that over time help as many people or more patients than the first oncologist's traditional treatments" (283). In such a case, they think we would also regard that oncologist as an expert. The benefits of these non-standard practices for solving the problem are repeatable. Even though no one could give a substantial reason why the third oncologist has such good results, "the expertise is embedded in the situation and in the possibility of justification, even if no one asks for justification" and that "allows for the resultant practice to be, in principle, intelligible to others" (283).

They argue that this "practice-oriented" approach is not intended to replace what many find valuable in more traditional accounts of expertise, but to supplement them in order to leave "room for enactments of expertise that vary significantly" (278). So, in some cases expertise will be determined by "certification, in others it requires knowledge, in others training, in others it is grounded in personal values, and so forth" (285). But the key to staving off relativism is that expertise gains legitimacy by demonstrating that it can solve problems in the eyes of "a public that encounters the same or similar problem as the expert does" (284).

As a point of clarification, as I understand their view, rather than adding to current accounts, their approach is intended as a meta-account that can accommodate other accounts by unifying them under a methodological principle, namely, apparent success in solving problems over time. As they note, "Expertise emerges as a fluid concept that *can only be judged against the particulars of a situation, problem, or exigency that necessitate the enactment of an expertise*" (281, italics theirs). But it is worth pointing out that, even as a meta-account, it cannot accommodate all definitional accounts of expertise. For example, their "meta" move does not seem to "add to" the veritistic account that we will look at in the next chapter, but rather to supersede it. Veritism claims that having reliable access to true beliefs in a domain is a necessary condition for having expertise. The Wittgensteinian approach rejects that in order to expand the concept to include various standard uses of the term "expertise" that do not reduce to truth conditions. In contending that only some instances of expertise depend on reliable access to truth, the Wittgensteinian approach displaces veritism. This is not necessarily a problem for the view, but in order to make this move, Majdik and Keith owe us more in the way of explaining why some instances of "expertise" (as it is used colloquially) actually count as *expertise*. To see why, consider two problems for this approach.

First, the ability to reliably solve problems is not co-extensive with expertise. An eight-year-old child can reliably solve addition and subtraction problems, but this does not mean they are an expert in arithmetic. Further, while some domains are problem-based (such as politics and engineering), others are not. Violinists don't seem to solve problems. Nor do trick pogo-stick jumpers or expert mixologists.

Second, even if we allow "problem" to be defined so widely that it includes, say, figuring how to land a particularly difficult pogo-stick jump, setting up "problem solving" as a standard for expertise renders expertise hopelessly subjective. Consider the rather robust anti-vaccine movement. For many, vaccines solve an important social problem with very low risk. For others, vaccines do more harm than good—they are not an appropriate solution to public health dangers that include, for example, autism. How should we decide whose perspective on this problem legitimates the relevant expertise? As pluralists about expertise, it would seem that Majdik and Keith would have to concede that there is expertise on both sides—two different communities find a problem "solved" in mutually exclusive ways. But this is a type of relativism that Majdik and Keith explicitly claim they want to avoid.

While I don't think Majdik and Keith's Wittgensteinian approach is sufficient as it stands, I think a successful account in the Wittgensteinian spirit might be developed. If someone does pursue this avenue—and perhaps Christian Quast's non-reductive, pragmatic approach (2018b) is a good starting point for a project like this—its strengths and limitations would need to be balanced against other plausible accounts in the domain.

2.4 Expertise Producers, Expertise Users, and Expert Systems

Up to now, I have only discussed expertise in terms of experts, people who have the relevant competence in a domain. But it is important to recognize the ways technology shapes expertise, displaces some experts, and creates others. Consider Plato's distinction between self-directing expertise and direction-taking expertise. As self-directors construct efficient systems of production and sophisticated tools for producing products that previously only artisans could produce, new opportunities for expertise emerge.

Consider that there was a time when going to an auto mechanic meant going to a specialized expert. Much like a physician, an expert auto mechanic could look, listen, and experiment with your car to diagnose abnormalities, explain those abnormalities in light of your use of the vehicle, and prescribe a solution that meets your needs as a driver—that is, the aim was not to press options that cost a lot of money or merely fit some preconceived notion about what a car needs, but to offer options and advice that are, to some extent, tailored to your needs. Although never a professional auto mechanic, my father is one of these (now) rare experts, owing to decades of immersion in hobby restoration and engagement with other experts like himself. If you present him with an array of twenty or thirty multi-colored unattached wires and a set of electrical problems, he can trace the function of each wire and fix the problems within a matter of hours. If you present him with a structural defect in, say, the frame or one of the axles, he can design (and usually build) a part that will address the defect.

This is not, however, the sort of competence you typically encounter in auto mechanic shops now. Instead, diagnostics are conducted by electronic scanners that connect to your car's on-board computer. Maintenance recommendations are based, not on the user's need and current state of the vehicle, but on standardized factory recommendations and the mechanic's company policies. In one respect, this is understandable. Contemporary cars are significantly more complex than the ones my father is used to working on. The mechanics of internal combustion and electric current have been superseded by electronic fuel injection, electronic power steering, and electronic temperature control. This means that the expertise needed to diagnose problems requires advanced training in computer technology in addition to the mechanics of internal combustion engines, CV (constant velocity) joints, coolant systems, and brake lines—training that few people have. Nevertheless, advances in technology have allowed that pool of experts to remain relatively small while allowing the number of automotive technicians to expand exponentially and indefinitely. Further, those diagnostic tools can, for some problems, outstrip expert judgments in reliability. When a few experts develop technologies that embody their expertise and then teach novices how to use them, their expertise is transmitted widely without any direct effort from them. Today, if you were to ask why you need a new fuel regulator, the most common answer will be: Because the scanner found a problem with it.

What does this imply for today's auto mechanic? They are clearly not experts in the sense my father is. But are they not experts in any sense? They still have to know how to use the diagnostic tools, understand what they imply in the specialized language of automotive parts and services, and then apply that understanding to addressing the problem. Given how many parts of contemporary cars are controlled by computers, my father cannot do any of this. Today's mechanic is almost surely an expert. But there is also a difference between the sort of mechanic my father is and the sort of mechanic one typically encounters in the service center of an auto dealership.

This example has affinities with a distinction that Aristotle draws in *On Sophistical Refutations*. Aristotle says that some teachers don't teach their expertise; they teach only the findings from their domain of expertise:

> For some of the [paid teachers of contentious argument] gave their pupils to learn by heart speeches which were either rhetorical or consisted of questions and answers, in which both sides though that the rival arguments were for the most part included. Hence the teaching they gave to their pupils was rapid but unsystematic; for they conceived that they could train their pupils by imparting to them not an art but the results of an art, just as if one should claim to be about to communicate knowledge for the prevention of pain in the feet and then were not to teach the cobbler's art and the means of providing suitable foot-gear, but were to offer a selection of various kinds of shoes. (183b–184a, trans. E.S. Forster)

Here we see two examples of experts who pass on the conclusions of their domain to students who merely repeat those conclusions to others.[9] The student of the orator, who simply recites speeches written by others that express the generally agreed upon views of the domain, and the cobbler, who teaches someone which shoes help with which foot pain but doesn't explain why. To be sure, there may be some expertise in the *presentation* of arguments or the *selling* of apparel, but set that aside.

These examples show that certain technologies allow us to "package" expertise in ways that other experts and novices can use to perform better than they otherwise would (and better, in some cases, than experts would on their own). Some of those procedures are so simple that a novice can do them. As philosopher Stephen Turner puts it, expert knowledge is "hidden" in routines, processes, and "objects: drugs, weapons, and so forth are used by people who do not have the knowledge to make them" (2014: 6). He cites novelist Herman Wouk's *The Cain Mutiny*, in which a character says, "The Navy is a master plan designed by geniuses for execution by idiots. If you're not an idiot, but find yourself in the navy, you can only operate well by pretending to be one. All the shortcuts and economies and common-sense changes that your native intelligence suggests to you are mistakes. Learn to quash them" (1951: 93).

This category of ability is broad and does not capture nuances in abilities. It could include the person who knows only how to take pictures on their new Nikon D500 (but none of its fancy features), someone who knows how to play a handful of songs on a guitar (but doesn't understand music generally), and someone who has learned how to maintain an office copy machine (change the toner cartridge, trouble-shoot jams, and operate the settings). In each case, the user of the technology read or heard some basic instructions they have learned to follow, but their competence ends where the instructions do.

The distinction between localized and specialized expertise is helpful, but it's not all that we need. The person who merely receives the results of an art is not analogous to today's mechanic. What we find is that some packages of expertise are too complicated for Wouk's naval officers. In some cases, experts don't merely pass down the results of an art; rather, they teach a different art. Contrast the ability to use Microsoft Word well with the ability to use Microsoft Excel well. For someone who already has basic computer skills, it is fairly easy to be a competent user of Word; it is very difficult for the same person to be a competent user of Excel. The complex skills required to use Excel well strikes us as a type of expertise compared with the skills needed to use Word. But note that neither the competent user of Word nor the competent user of Excel need understand the programming used to create those programs. That is a whole other domain of specialization.

A more striking example is found in the domain of toxicology. Toxicologists can specialize in a number of different scientific domains, like biochemistry or epidemiology. But even if a toxicologist is highly trained in biochemistry, for example on the core principles of adverse reactions between chemicals and the human body, their professional roles might require them to work in a much wider range of activities for which they may not have been trained, such as epidemiology. Because of this, other experts have developed tools that a highly trained scientist in biochemistry or epidemiology can use outside their area of specialization, such as the EPA's Human Health Risk Assessment process (Human Health Risk Assessment, n.d.). A toxicologist's expertise is sufficient for using the tool even if it is not sufficient for addressing the problems that the tool addresses. In other words, the expertise of human health risk assessment has been packaged in a way that other types of experts can use to expertly solve problems outside their personal scope of expertise.[10]

This suggests that there are three types of people who engage with expertise: those competent to create and package new technologies (*expertise producers*), specialists who are competent to use technologies (*expert expertise users*), and non-specialists who are competent enough to use technologies (*novice expertise users*).

The practice of packaging expertise for non-specialists and other specialists to use started as an engineering project called "knowledge engineering." The goal was to try to produce strong artificial intelligence (AI) machines, but it was immediately seen to have implications for expertise research. Knowledge engineers would take a set of general rules that experts use to complete a task (the "knowledge base") and turn them into formal rules that could be computed digitally. They would then write a separate program (the "inferential engine") to address particular problems by searching the knowledge base and then drawing judgments that mimic those of experts.[11] Early examples are computer chess programs. The moves and rules available to the computer are exactly the same as those available to the chess grandmaster. The trick was to program a machine to apply those rules more quickly than a human; and the results were an astounding success. Advancements in technology and computer learning have rendered this process exponentially more complex. The program AlphaZero, for example, taught itself to play chess and then built its skill level by playing innumerable games against itself.[12] The domain that designs and studies packaged expertise is now called "expert systems."

An expert system is a technology that allows someone to perform the job of an expert with a success rate that is the same or greater than experts'. There are two broad types of expert systems: (1) systems that attempt to mimic *the way experts form judgments* (in some cases, with their cognitive limitations like limited short-term memory intact) and (2) systems that attempt to mimic *the successful outcomes of expert judgment*, irrespective of how experts actually achieve that success.[13] To see how these differ, contrast two examples.

First, imagine you are faced with the question: *How likely is it that the person sitting at my desk will default on a loan?* If you work for a bank and are considering whether to offer this person a loan, this is a question that matters a great deal for your institution's financial stability. Someone who fancies themselves an expert judge of such things may try to collect and weigh myriad bits of evidence, anything from the person's type of employment, income, and employment history, to their clothing, speech, social manners, and history of paying off loans. Of course, we now know many of these things are irrelevant to whether someone will default on a loan. We have a pretty good sense of which bits are good evidence and which are bad. But, how did we figure those out? And, now that we know them, do we need *experts* to evaluate them in every case where someone wants a loan?

What's interesting is that even the expert who understands the good evidence and tries to focus on it, and rightly believes that information about how the person looks (e.g., the person's dress and social manner) is irrelevant is still highly influenced by irrelevant factors (often because of cognitive biases or heuristics). An expert system, on the other hand, is not distracted by these. In our example, an algorithm has been developed that calculates a credit score using only the good bits of evidence, and we need not worry that the algorithm will be biased against the applicant's Miley Cyrus T-shirt. This expert system mimics the way human experts think, yet it outstrips human experts in predicting who is likely to default. The credit score, in effect, eliminates the role of human experts in making this decision—credit scores are so much better than human experts that we don't want humans trying it anymore.

Other expert systems mimic the success of expertise *without* reflecting the process of expert judgment. Consider how researchers might figure out the criteria for a happy marriage. They might pore through self-help guides and testimonials and come up with a tangle of advice that includes some combination of, say, love languages, financial stability, work–life balance, and the ability to negotiate household responsibilities. Alternatively, one might just find happy marriages and start looking for similarities across these marriages. One project did just that and discovered what is now called the "F minus F" rule. This rule says that couples who fight more than they have sex tend to be unhappy, and couples who have sex more than they fight tend to be happy.[14] If this is right, we can gloss over the details of *why* a couple might have sex more than they fight (perhaps for some couples it *is* a matter of financial stability or love languages) and focus on the results of the formula. This expert system mimics the outcome an expert should be able to give us (what makes a happy marriage) without employing how experts reason about such things.[15]

Why is all this important for an introduction to expertise? First, it highlights two important distinctions that help focus our discussion. The first is between experts who design, create, and produce new knowledge and technologies (what I am calling *expertise producers*) and those who use that knowledge and those technologies (*expertise users*). The second is between expertise users who need specialized expertise to be able to use expert systems and those who do not. Just as an Excel user must have some specialized skills, so do radiography technicians, dental hygienists, respiratory therapists, and, touching back to our opening case, contemporary auto mechanics; they are all expertise users, but they are also experts themselves (*expert expertise users*). On the other hand, almost anyone can learn to use Microsoft Word competently or decide whether to loan someone money just by knowing whether their credit score is within a certain range; these are expertise users who do not need expertise to use the products of expertise (*novice expertise users*). My focus in this book will be on the expertise of the first two types of people (the expertise producer and the expert expertise user) and not on the novice expertise user or the expert system itself.

A second important point for this book is that, in areas where expert systems outperform their human counterparts, we should be intellectually humble enough to admit it and turn our human efforts to more efficient uses. Packaged expertise improves the quality of knowledge and performance across numerous domains, from the 100-meter dash (the shoes, the clothes, the track material) to the book you're reading. And to the extent that expert systems (like Google's seemingly magical search algorithm) enhance human activity, we should be careful to avoid attributing that additional advantage to human competence where it has been unseated from former competence.[16]

A third point is that, even in those areas where expert systems outperform humans, the system is not "authoritative" in the way that experts are.[17] The system works like a tool. Hammers are not authoritative (except, perhaps, metaphorically, as when wielded by an assailant), but carpenters are. Expert systems have expertise because they are designed to act like experts, but they are not, for all their successes, experts.[18] (Recall the distinction between expertise and expert in the preface.) In Chapters 3 through 7, we will see that how people become experts and how they exhibit expertise are very different from how machines—even highly complex computational machines—do so. But further, we should not forget that expert systems can be designed well or poorly, and they can be used well or poorly, and the responsibility for those uses lies with humans. We can imagine expert systems that exacerbate harms, for example, a more efficient farming technique that causes the animals more suffering, and ones that make people better off, such as a medical advancement that gives a doctor more time to focus on the personal and social implications of a surgery for a patient.

A final point, which is an extension of the previous, is that, while expert systems obviate the need for expertise producers under some conditions, they do not obviate the need for experts generally. Expertise producers are still needed to discover and design expert systems, and in many cases, specialized expertise users are needed to use and evaluate the expert systems. However accurate medical diagnosing becomes, its accuracy will depend on the myriad of human researchers collecting and organizing data that produce those diagnoses. And however simple medical diagnostic technologies become, we will still need experts to interpret their outputs in light of the needs, values, and preferences of particular patients. The emerging technologies of self-driving cars and personalized medicine are already raising concerns about implicit race- and sex-based bias. Only human experts can detect and remedy these problems. Some human experts will be replaced by expert systems, but the need for human expertise will not disappear.

While expert systems are fascinating and worthy of extensive study, I set them aside for the remainder of this book to focus on human experts, what it means to be an expert and how one acquires it. Whatever expert systems can do and whatever advantages they bestow, they owe their benefits to the experts who design them and use them. And it is those groups that have the strangely compelling ability to understand what they're talking about and use it to their and others' advantage. They are the ones with the cool confidence and careful reasoning that motivate us to take note and follow advice. In looking for what might account for such abilities, I start with truth-based accounts of expertise.

3 TRUTH-BASED ACCOUNTS OF EXPERTISE

Sages now trust to Fairy Scenes no more,
Nor venture farther, than they see the Shore:
They build on Sense, then reason from th' Effect,
On well establish'd Truths their Schemes erect;
By these some new Phaenomena *explain;*
And Light divine in ev'ry Process gain.
    (Samuel Bowden, *On the New Method of Treating Physic*, 1726: 8)

Over the next five chapters, I will introduce and evaluate four general accounts of expertise: truth-based accounts, performance-based accounts, social role accounts, and the cognitive systems account. In this chapter, I start with accounts that ground expertise in true belief, whether in *reliable belief* alone or in the richer notion of *knowledge* (3.1). I focus on the key feature of truth-based accounts, which I call the Reliable Access (RA) condition (3.2), and I review the central arguments for adopting this condition (3.3). I then explore what I take to be the most salient objections to truth-based accounts generally, and to RA specifically (3.4). At the end (3.5), I explore how proponents of a truth-based account might avoid these objections, but I argue that while aiming at truth remains a premier epistemic goal, achieving it is not a plausible criterion for expertise. Nevertheless, I argue there is an objective epistemic criterion, which I call "epistemic facility," that is consistent with the reasons that motivate truth-based accounts while avoiding the most serious objections.

3.1 Truth-Based Accounts of Expertise[1]

To say that experts know more than novices about their domain seems like a truism. Even experts who primarily *perform* their expertise—chess

---

Parts of this chapter are adapted from Watson (2018) and (2019).

grandmasters, Olympians, sharpshooters, etc.—tend to know more about their domain than regular chess players, amateur athletes, and recreational shooters. But is *knowledge* what makes an expert an expert? Do they have to know something about their domain, or does the knowledge come along with the ability to perform?

In some domains, it is easy to think knowledge is fundamental to if not exhaustive for expertise in that domain. Consider mathematics, which, according to Plato in *Statesman*, doesn't "involve any practical actions, but simply provide[s] knowledge" (258d, trans. Rowe). Consider also art history, philology, semiotics, and classics. What is expertise in these domains apart from knowing things? To be sure, one might argue that experts in these domains also have certain performative skills, such as defending a thesis, writing compellingly, researching thoroughly, and teaching well. But all of these performances seem dependent on and secondary to knowledge in these domains.

In other domains, it is hard to see, on the face of it, what role knowledge plays. Sure, a teenager learning to play basketball must know the rules of the game. But the rules don't tell her how to hold her arms to shoot, how to move her feet, how to handle the ball. And these aren't things she learns from a textbook. She starts by playing with the ball, and then someone shows her a few moves, and then she practices those moves until she is better and better. It is not obvious to her how she gets better, that is, how practice improves her performance. In shooting dozens of free-throws, she isn't gaining knowledge *that* her muscles are doing so-and-so to remember how to move or knowledge *that* the myelin sheathing around the fibers in her nerve cells is changing shape or *that* her brain is neutrally plastic in some way that helps her retain this ability over time.

In still other domains, knowledge and practice are bound up tightly together. Consider the expert surgeon or the video game designer. Both knowledge and skill are necessary but individually insufficient for having expertise in these domains. And in both, new knowledge emerges through practice, which, in turn, improves performance.

These examples do not contradict truth-based accounts. They simply emphasize that knowledge plays different roles in different types of expertise. And those who defend truth-based accounts acknowledge this. They simply focus their accounts on what they often call *cognitive expertise*.[2] To the degree that working in a domain involves collecting, manipulating, producing, and distributing information, expertise in that domain—

according to truth-based accounts—ensures that that information is likely to be accurate, is more likely to be something we know about the world.

To the extent that specialized expertise is a matter of tracking truths, it could range from knowledge of single truths (David Coady [2012] claims to be an expert on what he had for breakfast) to a robust understanding of the propositions in a domain (Myles Burnyeat [1987: 20] says that expertise with a single claim is nonsense[3]), including how they came to be part of that domain, how they are related to each other, how they can be employed to answer standard questions in that domain, and how they can be employed to answer new questions in that domain.

Whether experts actually do apply their competence in practice or display is secondary, on this view, to having the *ability* to apply it. On truth-based accounts, an expert may acquire expertise that they never subsequently use or demonstrate to anyone. Nevertheless, they have expertise in that domain.

Elizabeth Fricker (2006) defends an account according to which being an expert makes any judgment likely to be *knowledge*:

> S is an expert about P relative to H at t just if at t, S is epistemically well enough placed with respect to P so that were she to have, or make a judgment to form a conscious belief regarding whether P, her belief would almost certainly be knowledge; and she is better epistemically placed than H to determine whether P. (2006: 233, italics hers)

David Coady (2012) argues that expertise consists of having *more true beliefs* in a domain than most everyone else. Similarly, Scott Brewer (1998) says:

> For A to be an epistemic authority for B on some subject matter, B must judge that A has some sufficient knowledge, intelligence, or wisdom which makes it reasonable to believe either that what A says on that subject is more likely to be true than the results reached by B through B's independent investigations, or is no less likely to be true than the results that would be reached by B through B's independent investigations. (1588)

Other veritistic accounts include those of Jean H.M. Wagemans (2011) and Jimmy Alfonso Licon (2012). Wagemans argues that "for a person to be rightly called an expert, the person should not only know something simpliciter, but [they] should also be able to give an account of what [they] know[]" (330). Licon says experts must, at minimum, meet three conditions, a reliability condition, a scarcity condition, and a heuristic condition:

The reliability condition	S is an expert in X just in case S is a reliable source of outputs relating to X.
The scarcity condition	Within their community, experts with regard to X should tend to be in the minority.
The heuristic condition	S enjoys expertise with regard to X just in case S knows, more so than those who are not experts, how to apply what knows she about X to novel situations. (2011: 452)

One of the most widely discussed truth-based accounts of expertise is Alvin Goldman's *veritism* (2001, 2018). Goldman calls his view veritism (from the Latin *veritas* for "truth") because it is essentially "truth-linked" ([2001] 2002: 145), that is, reliably formed true beliefs are necessary for expertise on his view. Goldman's most recent formulation of veritism is a reductive account that is constituted by a specific set of *capacities*, which he labels CAP:

[CAP] S is an expert in domain D if and only if S has the capacity to help others (especially laypersons) solve a variety of problems in D or execute an assortment of tasks in D which the latter would not be able to solve or execute on their own. S can provide such help by imparting to the layperson (or other client) his/her distinctive knowledge or skills. (2018: 4)

According to CAP, an essential goal of expertise is to improve the epistemic placement of others by conveying knowledge or skills. Narrowing his focus to "informational or cognitive domains," Goldman then sets out to say what it would mean for someone to be in a position to improve epistemic placement in cognitive domains. Goldman has formulated several versions of the "truth-linked" condition for CAP over the years, but his most recent is labeled [TL2]:

[TL2] S is an expert about domain D if and only if
(A) S has more true beliefs (or high credences) in propositions concerning D than most people do, and fewer false beliefs; and

(B) the absolute number of true beliefs S has about propositions in D is very substantial. (2018: 5)[4]

While (A) and (B) are presented as jointly sufficient for expertise, Goldman ([2001] 2002) also says that experts must be able to "deploy or exploit this fund of information to form beliefs in true answers to new questions that may be posed in the domain" (145), and I take it that most proponents of veritism would accept this as a third necessary condition.[5]

[TL2, revised]: **S is an expert about domain D if and only if**
(A) S has more true beliefs (or high credences) in propositions concerning D than most people do, and fewer false beliefs; and
(B) the absolute number of true beliefs S has about propositions in D is very substantial (2018: 5); and
(C) S has the ability to use this fund of information to form beliefs in true answers to new questions that may be posed in that domain.[6]

This account is noteworthy for Goldman because it represents a reversal of a concession he makes in a piece from 2009. There, in light of criticism of truth as a necessary condition for expertise,[7] Goldman broadened his criteria allowing "other epistemic values or desiderata, beyond truth and false belief, to enter the picture, in particular such notions as justification and rationality" (275). But when entertaining that possibility again in (2018: 5), he reverts to his original (2001) commitment to truth as a necessary condition, arguing that truth better accounts for why we consult experts in the first place and, unlike justification-based or evidence-based accounts of expertise, truth-based accounts avoid epistemic relativism.

Interestingly, Goldman (2018) says that he takes these issues to be secondary to the social epistemological questions of *how to identify experts* and the *epistemic norms that govern expert testimony*, and he says he is not attempting "to fix any precise *margins* or *thresholds*" for expertise (6, italics his). But whether Goldman holds veritism firmly or weakly, it is an influential view that is worth exploring.

3.2 The Reliable Access Condition for Truth-Based Accounts

Whether a truth-based account focuses on mere reliably true belief (Goldman; Licon) or on the richer concept of knowledge (Fricker;

Wagemans), all truth-based accounts have as a necessary condition that experts have *reliable access to true propositions*. Call this the reliable access (RA) condition on expertise:

> Reliable Access Condition (RA): S has reliable access to a domain, D, such that, any belief P in D she holds (or is placed well enough to hold) is more likely to be true than the beliefs of those in some reference class.

Even in cases where novices have an abundance of true beliefs in a domain, novices' access to those truths is typically unreliable, random, and often accidental, while experts tend to form true beliefs intentionally and strategically, through extensive training. Reliability helps explain why we turn to experts when we need information or advice and not to hobbyists. Expert testimony places novices in a better position to obtain what they need from a domain than they might otherwise be.

The introduction of a "reference class" is also important. Most accounts of expertise allow that competence in a domain falls along a continuum. At one end of the continuum, people have almost no competence in that domain—think of people who cannot play the harmonica or who cannot explain what cancer is. At the other end of that continuum are highly competent people, that is, experts—think of famous harmonica player John Hopper from the band Blues Traveler or a board-certified oncologist. To be sure, there may be no set upper end of that continuum. Competence may grow indefinitely. Nevertheless, at some point, a person has moved far enough along the continuum to be considered an expert (Figure 3.1):

Novice   Expert

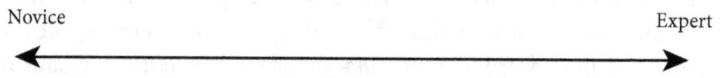

FIGURE 3.1 A Continuum of Competence in a Domain.

Interestingly, there is a lot going on in the space between the novice and the highly competent expert. There is the hobbyist in a domain, the person just out of college in that domain, the person just out of graduate school in that domain, the person who specializes in one domain but has extensive knowledge in another just in virtue of the kind of domain it is. Consider the domain of oncology (cancer medicine). To be a cancer doctor, you have to have extensive knowledge of other domains of medicine: cardiology, pulmonology, hematology, nephrology, hepatology, and so on. So, while one might specialize in oncology, they nevertheless have general expertise in other domains of medicine.

To help keep that in mind, let us add two more categories of competence, recognizing that these have no hard boundaries but that they do track objective gains in ability as someone studies or practices in a domain (Figure 3.2):

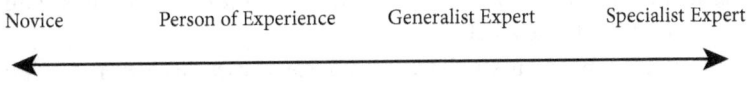

FIGURE 3.2 A more Detailed Continuum of Competence in a Domain.

Returning to the issue of a reference class, according to truth-based accounts, placement on the continuum is determined by how many true beliefs someone has in a domain. But how many relative to what? What place someone gets on the continuum depends on whether they have *more truths than X*, where X is some reference class. Philosophers are divided over what the relevant reference class is. Most say that it refers at least to everyone below the expert on the continuum, that is, an expert is someone who has more true beliefs in a domain than anyone else (Figure 3.3).

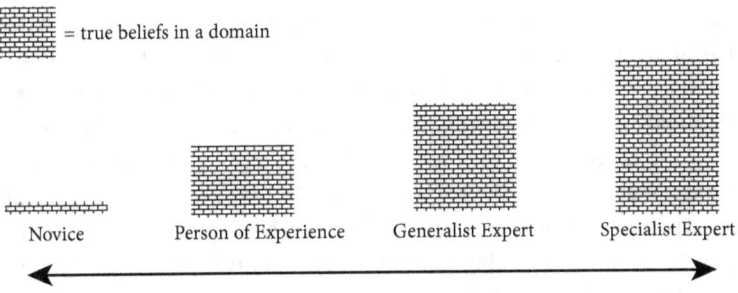

FIGURE 3.3 True Beliefs Relative to Others on the Continuum.

Goldman adds to this that an expert has more true beliefs *and fewer false* in a domain. Scholz argues that this is problematic: "The following situation may easily arise: *A non-expert may have more true beliefs and fewer false beliefs about D than the expert*. Or, at least, it might happen that *a non-expert may have fewer false beliefs about D than the expert*" (2009: 193, italics his). Scholz's point is that, since this account is merely about the collection of beliefs and not how they were acquired, it could happen purely by accident that a novice has more true beliefs and fewer false than an expert. Consider someone who reads about a domain constantly.

What they read is true, and they don't form any other beliefs about it or try to draw inferences that may turn out to be false. Yet someone who has worked in a domain for many years (someone we would intuitively call an expert) and who does draw inferences has surely formed a number of false beliefs about the domain over time. In this case, the hobbyist would have more true beliefs relative to false than the trained specialist and would therefore be an expert (and fall higher on the expertise continuum than the trained specialist).

David Coady concurs with Scholz and offers a case that is even simpler: "If one could be an expert on a subject just by having significantly fewer false beliefs about it than most people, one could acquire expertise in a subject by the simple expedient of taking little or no interest in it" (2012: 29). How could "taking little interest in a domain" make it so that a novice has fewer false beliefs than an expert? Precisely because experts have a significantly larger base rate of beliefs in that domain: "They inevitably acquire more beliefs about those subjects and so run a greater risk of believing falsehoods about them than laypeople do" (2012: 29). Novices just don't have many beliefs, so the number of false beliefs they have about that domain will be similarly limited.

One might object that whether Scholz's and Coady's critiques are damaging depends on what they mean by the "and." If they mean the novice has "more true beliefs relative to false beliefs," then this could be true for the reason that Coady gives. As long as the novice doesn't take much interest in a domain, they may end up with fewer false beliefs relative to true beliefs than the expert. But if they mean both more true beliefs and fewer false beliefs, then it is unlikely that a novice could have more true beliefs than an expert (unless we come up with some contrived example where a novice points to a stack of textbooks in the expert's domain and says, "I believe everything in those books").

However, this objection would miss the mark. The key to *defining* expertise according to this reference class is that someone has more true beliefs and fewer false beliefs in a domain. So, if it is even possible that someone who has not studied in a domain could meet that criterion, they would count as an expert whether we intuitively think of them that way or not. There is no requirement on truth-based accounts that experts must have acquired their true beliefs a certain way or through a certain type of study or experience.

However, Goldman's condition (B) is supposed to allay this worry. He requires that "some non-comparative threshold of veritistic attainment must be reached" in order for someone to be an expert (2001: 91), though he admits that such a threshold is vague. As long as someone meets an objective threshold of true beliefs in a domain, then whether they have studied or trained or not, they are rightly regarded as an expert. Coady thinks we can avoid this problem altogether by just leaving out the *fewer false beliefs* requirement. On his view, "Being an expert is simply a matter of having a significantly greater store of accurate information about it than most people (or most people in one's community)" (2012: 28).

A different sort of objection to including less competent people in the reference class is not tied to the RA condition. We can imagine a world where everyone except a handful of highly trained specialists in a domain is wiped out. Are the remaining specialists no longer experts just because they are not more competent in their domain "than most people"? They still have their specialized knowledge and skills, they can still speak authoritatively about their domain to each other, and if all of their knowledge and skill is comparable, then they are still epistemic peers. Further, they could still turn to one another for a review of their own work and collaboration (they turn to them precisely because they have that knowledge and skill), things they could not do with people who lacked their level of knowledge and skill. If expertise is to be grounded in an objective competence in a domain, and these people lose none of that competence in the case where everyone else has disappeared, then it seems arbitrary to withhold the term "expert" from them.

3.3 The Case for Truth-Based Accounts

Why hold a truth-based account? There are two primary reasons and one ancillary for adopting RA as a necessary condition for expertise. First, RA easily explains the epistemic authority of expertise by grounding it in a central epistemic aim, either knowledge or a necessary condition for knowledge (viz., truth). Second, RA shows how expertise could be an objective phenomenon in the world,[8] staving off concerns that expertise is merely assigned arbitrarily according to cultural preference or is merely a socially constructed tool of political or organizational power. In other words, grounding expertise objectively helps stave off concerns with epistemic relativism. And third, RA explains why people seek out experts in the first place, namely, to be put in an epistemically better place than they would otherwise be. I call this an ancillary reason because it is not about the concept of expertise but rather how expertise is regarded by others.

With respect to the first reason, philosopher Moti Mizrahi explains: "The fact that one is an expert ... is supposed to make one's assertion that p significantly more likely to be true. Any argument from authority makes this implicit assumption" (2013: 60). Similarly, Licon (2012) appeals to epistemic authority as constitutive of RA:

> The addition to our account of expertise is based on the following intuition: an expert with regard to X should be able to, at least to a greater degree than his non-expert peers, improvise solutions to novel problems related to X. Surely, experts should be better equipped, than their non-expert peers, to handle novel problems relating to their field of expertise. Put differently, an expert in X should have methods and heuristics to able to apply to novel situations that arise related to her area of expertise. Put differently: an expert with respect to X should have greater knowledge-that and knowledge-how than most of her peers, ceteris paribus. (451)

Licon takes the idea that experts are better equipped than novices to discharge their epistemic activities in a domain as a way of expressing RA. Note that this move is not an *inference* for Licon (i.e., they can solve problems, therefore, they are reliable); rather, he uses the comparative success of experts over novices as *a way of saying* experts can solve problems better than most of their peers.

The desire to ground expertise in a central epistemic aim is, on the face of it, a strong reason for adopting RA: If someone is likely to be *right*, objectively, about propositions in a domain, they are epistemically better placed in that domain than we are. All things being equal, we have a reason to defer to people who are well-placed in a domain, especially if they are better placed than we are. Their claims in that domain are prima facie authoritative for us.

The second reason for adopting RA is that it avoids concerns about epistemic relativism with respect to expertise. If expertise is grounded in nothing more than social agreement, the idea that experts are authoritative is as credible as the idea that politicians care about citizens. The epistemic aims of truth and knowledge are not merely desirable, and therefore, normative; they are also, presumably, objective features of the world. Identifying expertise with an objective standard provides a means of assessing claims to expertise, debunking charlatans, and adjudicating among competing claims to expertise independently of purely social decision procedures like voting and favoritism, which are inherently relativistic.

A third reason someone might adopt RA is that it is consistent with why people seek out experts in the first place. Goldman (2018) says that an advantage of veritism is that:

> it makes smooth and straightforward sense of the familiar, longstanding activity of consulting experts when we have questions to which we do not know the answers ourselves .... The standard goal of people seeking informational experts is precisely to learn the true answers to their questions. (6)

An uncharitable interpretation of this argument is that because people seek experts for true beliefs in a domain, we should formulate our account of expertise such that experts are more likely to have true beliefs in a domain. But it would be strange to formulate a concept in a certain way just because people think it should work that way. A more charitable interpretation is that experts have a track-record of serving the social function of providing truths and that veritism explains how they do this. For example, expert professors have answers to questions in their domain that those outside their domain (viz., students) do not. Pilots have answers to questions in their domain that passengers and flight attendants do not. Surgeons have answers that hematologists do not, and vice versa.

Quast (2018a: 18) also argues that we should not leave this social role of expertise out of accounts of it and suggests that "the conceptual function (point, role) of expertise is to substantially improve the social deployment of available agential resources apt for an accurate attainment of cliently relevant ends." And Licon (2012: 453) says that "we value justification instrumentally because it is a reliable guide to discerning truth-tracking propositional attitudes from those that are not." If the function of expertise is to make people better off, epistemically speaking, then RA explains how it performs this function.

3.4 Objections to Truth-Based Accounts

Truth-based accounts face a number of important criticisms. In some cases, these criticisms simply highlight areas of weakness that can be shored up with some conceptual work. In other cases, the criticisms are more serious. Here, I will highlight five objections that figure prominently in the literature.

3.4.1 RA Is Not Sufficient for Expertise

As we noted above, simply having more true beliefs or knowledge than some relevant class of others is not sufficient for expertise. The expert must also be able to apply those true beliefs effectively. As philosopher Julia Driver (2006) humorously puts it:

> Satan could well be an example of a being with superior moral knowledge, but it would be unwise to defer to Satan's judgment on what to do. I might be confident in his ability to know, but not confident in his accurate transmission of that knowledge. (630)

We might, of course, still allow that Satan is an *expert* on moral knowledge but simply not *trustworthy* in that domain, which is a different issue.[9] David Coady makes this move:

> Suppose Jones has acquired significantly more accurate information about a subject than most people, but that, as a result of some cognitive impairment, Jones is no longer able to accurately answer new questions that arise about the subject. Is Jones an expert? It seems to me that Jones is an expert, at least until such a time that the subject in question has changed (or lay knowledge of it has expanded) to the point that Jones's store of accurate information on the subject is no longer significantly greater than most people's. (2012: 29–30)

The problem with this argument, however, is that it turns Jones into little more than a print copy of an encyclopedia: a repository of information that is incapable of employing that information over and above regurgitation. In actual practice, expertise is dynamic—a continuous engagement with old and new information in the act of answering questions (tacit or explicit) and solving problems. And different domains require different abilities on the part of their experts. Some domains require "problem-solving, pattern recognition, situational discrimination, experience … testifying to a lay public … agreeing with other experts … ability to make reliable forecasts … ability to identify other experts in the same domain" and teaching abilities (Scholz 2018: 32). If this is right, then characterizing expertise—even cognitive expertise—solely in terms of RA proves too restrictive.

Goldman (2001/2002: 146) seems to acknowledge this problem and adds to his account the additional condition: "and a set of skills or methods for apt and successful deployment of this knowledge to new questions in the domain." And recall that Goldman's CAP makes the ability to improve others' epistemic placement necessary for expertise (2018: 3–4). Would Satan's character allow him to perform this function even if we grant that he has the knowledge to do so?

Perhaps a better way to pose this question is to follow Oliver Scholz (2009) in asking, "Is the resulting explication still purely veritistic? It seems that [unlike Coady] Goldman has tacitly introduced an additional epistemic desideratum" (2009: 193). If this is right, then RA is not sufficient for cognitive expertise.

I don't think this is a serious problem for veritistic accounts. Even if RA is not sufficient, it may still be a necessary condition for expertise. Some people call this "impure veritism" (see Shaffer 2013). And in each of Goldman's formulations, he explicitly allows for such contingencies, pointing out that he is not trying to have the final word on expertise, but simply trying to push the debate forward. Thus, if RA can be included as no more than a necessary condition on expertise, so be it. Perhaps it can be a key necessary condition for expertise without being fully sufficient. Unfortunately, this is not the only challenge for RA.

3.4.2 RA Rules out Past Experts

A second reason to reject RA stems from the revolutionary nature of scientific progress. Perhaps unsurprisingly, there are a number of people to whom it seems perfectly appropriate to ascribe expertise but for whom we believe RA is not met. For example, it seems justifiable to regard Nicolaus Copernicus and Isaac Newton as experts in physics even though, given our current understanding of physics, we think most of their beliefs were false. In addition to his credible belief in heliocentrism, Copernicus held the putatively false beliefs that "wandering stars" (planets) are carried through the heavens affixed to concentric crystalline spheres and that these spheres turn against a background of fixed stars (cf. Cohen 1985: 24–5). And though Newton's theory of motion was the most successful account of motion for over two hundred years, we are now led to reject his beliefs that the laws of motion remain invariant in all reference frames (an idea he picked up from another putative expert, Galileo) (cf. Newton 1952: 19), that there is an ontological distinction between space and time (Newton 1952: 8–9), that space is structured according to Euclidean geometry, and that alchemy held serious promise for the understanding of matter.[10] If it is right to regard Copernicus and Newton as experts when we believe RA is not met for most of their beliefs in their domains, RA is not necessary for expertise.[11]

Consider, further, the case of Ignaz Semmelweis.[12] In 1847, Semmelweis discovered that people who wash their hands in a solution of chlorinated lime before delivering babies are less likely to transmit puerperal fever to the mothers. By instituting a policy of handwashing in this solution, Semmelweis cut mortality rates from the disease in his maternity wards by more than 90 percent. One might contest whether Semmelweis was an expert in his domain. His experiments were, by today's standards, naïve and clumsy. His discovery was accidental—he had no reason to believe chlorinated lime would do the trick. But his success in reducing hospital disease with antiseptics won him an honored place in the history of medicine (though, sadly, not within his lifetime).

Unfortunately, Semmelweis's explanation of why the lime solution worked is simplistic and, by contemporary standards, false. Semmelweis discovered that many who worked in the maternity wards also worked in the morgue, and he hypothesized that they brought "putrid matter" from dead bodies to the delivery tables when examining pregnant patients (Hempel 1966: 6). Today, experts in disease transmission believe puerperal fever is caused by infectious organisms, most commonly, Beta haemolytic streptococcus, Lancefield Group A (Hallett 2005). Streptococcus bacteria are easily transmitted to the genital tract of pregnant women, particularly when examination conditions are not sterile, and its transmission has nothing to do with dead bodies. The lime solution happened to work because it killed the bacteria, not because it cleaned off "cadaveric particles" (Hempel 1966: 8).

By all accounts, Semmelweis was a competent physician. But did his false beliefs render him inexpert? In hospitals today, doctors routinely engage in trial-and-error to figure out what's wrong with patients and which treatments might help. Analogously, we must ask: Does the possibility that contemporary scientific claims are similarly susceptible to vast revision render contemporary researchers inexpert? If the answer to these questions is no, we have a reason to give up RA.

We might try to solve this problem by defining expertise relative to the current state of science. We might, for example, say that Newton was an expert in his own time even though he would not be one today. But veritism will not allow this qualification; it requires reliable access to true propositions in a domain. But if the current state of physics is correct, Newton did *not* have reliably true beliefs in physics in his own time because he did not have *true* beliefs in physics. The force of this argument comes from the fact that the current state of physics—and any domain, for that matter—is just as likely to undergo the same eclipse as classical physical theories. If physicists two hundred years from now turn out to be right, and this implies that physicists today are wrong, then current physicists are not experts according to RA, either.

But even if this were so, it is surely the case that physicists today can and should be trusted over non-physicists to confer justification on propositions in physics. If the epistemic authority of trained physicists is not in question and if we have good reason to believe there are experts today, then the problem must be with RA.[13]

One might reply that this objection applies only to an unsophisticated sort of veritism. Veritism, someone might argue, is consistent with the idea that historical figures were experts in their own time because they had more true beliefs than *most people at that time*. This is where Goldman's condition "fewer false beliefs" might give his account an advantage over Coady's. Coady's account cannot explain how past physicists could be experts, but perhaps Goldman's could. Surely Newton had, on balance, more true beliefs about physics and fewer false than others in his time, just because he had spent time learning about the domain.

But on closer examination, adding the qualification "than most people at that time" cannot save RA. If past physicists' basic assumptions about the natural world are false now, they were false then. Even if the beliefs they derived from these assumptions proved practically useful—and more useful than their contemporaries'—they were derived from spurious premises—which is unlikely to yield true beliefs except by accident. So, even if Copernicus and Newton were experts only relative to their contemporary epistemic communities, it is not because they had a substantial fund of true beliefs relative to those contemporaries.

Goldman (2018) presents a new response to this concern, arguing that just because we cannot discern whether someone is an expert "until decades, or even centuries, after [they are] dead—because we may not be able to tell how many of the propositions believed are true or false," that does not mean "there are no facts of the matter. Facts may simply be elusive," "such is life" (2018: 5). The idea here is that even if we cannot identify an expert because we do not *know whether* they have a substantial fund of knowledge, this does not mean that expertise is not truth-linked. Those who have a substantial fund of knowledge in a domain are experts whether we know it or not.

Unfortunately, this revised argument leaves veritism no better off than the previous. Now, centuries hence, we can conclude (presumably definitively) that Copernicus and Newton were *not* experts according to veritism. Their fundamental assumptions about space, time, etc., were not borne out by future research. We can tell. And they were wrong. Yet, if we were able to go back in time, we would not denounce them as untrustworthy, as we do those who promote pseudo-science. We would enthusiastically encourage their contemporaries to trust them as experts. We would, unabashedly, defend Galileo against Bellarmine.

3.4.3 Current Experts Do Not (Sufficiently) Meet RA

A third objection to RA is that people we are currently justified in regarding as experts do not meet RA. There are two ways to make this argument. One is to argue that we cannot, in principle, know whether they meet RA, so whether they do is beyond our ken, and the concept of expertise is functionally irrelevant to any practical application of the term. That is, there is no way to substantiate the attribution of expertise to anyone, even ourselves. A second is to argue that experts' actual track record shows that they do not meet RA. If, in fact, experts do not have more true beliefs than some relevant set of others, then RA is not an adequate condition on expertise.

The first strategy involves appealing to an old problem in epistemology, called the "problem of the criterion."[14] Though this problem applies to knowledge claims generally, it constitutes a particularly difficult problem for RA. The concern, roughly, is that any criterion by which we attempt to justify beliefs about the world is also subject to some criterion that also needs justification. If the criterion is subject to itself, its justification is circular. If it is subject to some other criterion, *that* criterion is subject to some criterion, and the problem rematerializes. The skeptical conclusion is that all justifications are either circular or they regress ad infinitum, rendering all beliefs, ultimately, unsupported.[15]

The most widely accepted way to avoid the problem of the criterion is to reject internalism about justification in favor of some version of externalism: If a subject's beliefs are formed according to a procedure or process that yields more true beliefs than false in an environment for which that procedure or process is fitting, that subject's true beliefs are rightly regarded as justified, regardless of whether the subject knows whether the procedure or process is reliable. Under such conditions, a subject's belief system is appropriately connected to the world. Of course, this does not alleviate the problem of the criterion *for the subject*. If a subject is asked whether any of her beliefs were formed according to such a procedure or process or whether she employed such a procedure or process in a fitting environment or which beliefs formed according to such a procedure or process are true, she would be, justifiably, unable to provide a non-skeptical answer.

Whatever concerns the problem of the criterion poses for epistemology generally, they are exacerbated for veritistic accounts of expertise because expertise seems to have an inherently social dimension. Truth-based accounts of expertise are supposed to *explain how* someone's testimony constitutes a source of authority for a proposition. But the *attribution* of expertise is substantiated by comparing and contrasting the competence of a putative expert with a domain's historical trajectory and its current claims and methodologies as understood by others working in that domain. Does this process reflect a reliable connection with truth? Could an expert's competence be explained *apart* from a reliable connection with truth? I think we have to answer yes to this latter question. As John Hardwig (1985) puts it, "If one defines 'expert' in terms of the *truth* of [their] views …, it is often impossible in principle to say who is an expert—even if one is an expert oneself!—since it is often impossible to say whose view is coincident with the truth" (340, n.2, italics his).

If this is right, RA is simply one way of explaining why an attribution of expertise would be successful if it were successful. It makes it in-principle impossible to determine whether anyone is actually an expert. This raises the question of why we should accept RA over alternatives that can help us identify experts. The response, if veritism is right, is that there is no such alternative; RA is the only sort of criterion that could stave off relativism. We will assess this claim in 3.4.5.

One might try to save veritism by replacing RA with a different theory of knowledge or truth that better captures the way experts are developed and identified. But this would give away too much. Whatever account we give of "knowledge" or "truth" that is not reliably connected with the world will, if not supplemented with alternative, objective epistemic criteria, reopen the door to relativism. As philosopher Stephen Turner (2014) explains:

> A theory of knowledge is not ... going to help much. ... At best, we can work with a functional notion of knowledge: A routine can do things for us that a justified true belief can do; tacit knowledge can do what explicit knowledge can do; an instrument can do what a trained body can do; a person merely following a routine can do what a person who is knowledgeable about the process itself can do. Objects created by design can also serve as functional substitutes for knowledge. (7)

Whatever we call "knowledge" or "truth" in these expertise attributions, they amount to no more than "something cognitive in origin that enables someone to do something they could not otherwise do" (Turner 2014: 10). This leaves veritists in a lurch.

To be clear, I am not a skeptic about expertise. But I do think philosopher Hilary Kornblith is too cavalier when he writes that "one would have to be a radical skeptic about mathematics, logic, probability, and decision theory to think that convergence of opinion is not, at this point in the history of those fields, evidence of truth" (2010: 40–1). The history of science and law has shown many times that convergence of opinion is evidence only of propositions' usefulness for answering questions that are constrained by a paradigm of assumptions—convergence is a *reason* to believe a proposition is true, but it is unclear whether it reveals reliable connection with truth (see Martini 2015: 4–7). So, comparative success cannot be construed as an indicator of RA.

The second strategy for arguing that experts do not meet RA is empirical. Philosopher Moti Mizrahi (2013, 2018) offers two arguments that, if sound, show that experts do not meet RA, and therefore, that arguments from expert opinion are weak.[16] Mizrahi's first argument goes like this:

[**Mizrahi – 1**]
1. Arguments from expert opinion are weak arguments unless the fact that expert E says that p makes it significantly more likely that p is true.

2. [As empirical evidence on expertise shows] the fact that E says that p does not make it significantly more likely that p is true.
3. Therefore, arguments from expert opinion are weak arguments.

(2013: 58–9)

RA commits us to premise 1, so I will take that as a given for the sake of the argument. In favor of premise 2, Mizrahi highlights a series of studies from a number of different domains that show experts performing no better than or worse than novices. He offers eight pieces of empirical evidence in support of premise 2, which I paraphrase and supplement with citations here:

1. Over a twenty-year study, psychologist Philip Tetlock (2005) found that expert forecasters in economics, public policy, and journalism predicted political events more accurately than "dart-throwing chimpanzees," by which he means, no better than chance.

2. About two-thirds of findings published in top medical journals are rejected after a few years.[17]

3. Most studies published in economics journals are rejected after a few years.

4. There is a one-twelfth chance that a physician's diagnosis will be wrong such that it endangers patients.[18]

5. Tax returns prepared by professionals contain more errors than those prepared by non-professionals (Paskin 2008).

6. Clinical psychologists are no better at providing therapy than novices (Dawes 1994; Ericsson and Lehmann 1996).

7. Attending physicians are no more accurate in predicting patients' preferences for end-of-life care than interns, despite spending more time with the patients (Wilson et al. 1997).

8. There is research showing that experts' decisions are no more accurate than novices' decisions and are much less accurate than decision aids (e.g., decision procedures, and what Bishop and Trout [2005] call "statistical prediction rules" [SPRs]; Camerer and Johnson 1991).

From this evidence, Mizrahi (2013: 58) concludes: "As research on expertise shows, expert opinions are only slightly more accurate than chance and much less accurate than decision procedures." Thus, "arguments from expert opinion, i.e., inferences from 'Expert E says that p' to 'p,' where the truth value of p is unknown, are weak arguments."

There are some important qualifications for Mizrahi's argument. By "arguments from expert opinion" he means arguments that appeal *solely* to the fact that an expert is an expert. For example, the following argument counts as an argument from expert opinion:

> *Expert:* It is better to invest in real-estate than in bonds.
> *Non-expert:* Why?
> *Expert:* Because Expert E say [sic] so, that's why! (60)

A second important qualification is that arguments from expert opinion are not those that are "simply reporting what the majority of experts about subject matter S accept or what is considered to be common knowledge in a specific domain of knowledge by virtue of being privy to this knowledge" (61). In fact, Mizrahi seems to be okay with two uses of expertise: (1) experts who construct decision procedures (expert systems) that perform better than human experts (2013: 66), and (2) agreement among experts. As he notes, "Once we take into account considerations of evidence for p and whether or not p is common knowledge in a field, then an argument from expert opinion is no longer just an appeal to expert opinion. Rather, it is an appeal to expertise, evidence, and agreement among experts" (2013: 71). And arguments based on evidence can be strong. In fact, Mizrahi's argument depends on their being strong. In his (2014) reply to an objection from Markus Seidel, Mizrahi writes, "I do not accept p because p is asserted by E or because E judges that p is the case. Rather, I accept p because p is a result that was arrived at by experimentation" (8).

So, what sort of expert opinion is Mizrahi aiming at? Presumably, his argument is supposed to undermine any appeals to expert testimony that p under conditions of uncertainty, "where the truth value of p is unknown" (58). What he means by "unknown" is unclear. Reading him charitably, it doesn't mean that a student who asks a question in a math or science class isn't justified in accepting the professor's answer. Even though the student doesn't know the answer, the answer is, presumably, widely known among experts in the domain. But what about a nurse who is trusting a doctor with respect to medicine dosing for a complex patient? Empirical data is based upon an aggregation of data across many patients, canceling out unique differences and combinations of illnesses. Thus, which specific medicines or dosage will benefit a particular patient is unknown to both the nurse and the doctor. Does Mizrahi mean that, in those circumstances, the nurse would do no better by asking the patient, as opposed to the doctor, which medicines would benefit her? Without further qualification from Mizrahi, it is difficult to say. For now, we will just say that he means some general sense of "decisions under uncertainty."

Mizrahi (2018) presents a second line of argument that arguments from expert opinion are weak, this time based on research on cognitive biases and heuristics. Since the late 1960s, research in the domains of cognitive psychology, economics, and behavioral economics has produced extensive examples of the ways our minds deceive us. This research is commonly referred to as the *heuristics and biases literature*.[19]

Cognitive *heuristics* are subconscious rules of thumb or shortcuts we use to reason more quickly and, in some cases, more efficiently than if we were to spend time consciously reasoning about a belief or decision. The heuristics in question are not general rules of thumb we consciously choose. They are, rather, shortcuts that our brains use automatically and unconsciously, for example, remembering painful events more readily than pleasurable ones (hedonic asymmetry) and drawing comparisons based on similarities (the availability heuristic).

In simple contexts, where risks are explicit and options are few and clear, these cognitive heuristics serve us fairly well. In evolutionary terms, they may lead us to simple overcautiousness when the harm is considerable, such avoiding anything that looks like the berries that made us sick that one time. What we lose in the pleasure of learning the flavor of a new fruit we gain in safety.[20] Unfortunately, as contexts become more complex, risks become difficult to assess, and options are many and imprecise, heuristics often lead us astray. While refusing to eat berries that look similar to poisonous ones may keep us safe, treating someone like a criminal because they dress like someone we have known to be a criminal can lead to unjust prejudice and, thereby, to discrimination.

Cognitive *biases* are subconscious dispositions to treat information a certain way. For example, if I am biased toward pessimism, I am likely to regard even very good events as mediocre. Similarly, if I love someone, I am likely to interpret their immoral behavior more charitably than a stranger's. In evolutionary terms, biases may have helped us form protective communities, leading us to care more about people we know and regard strangers suspiciously, to pay more attention to our own anecdotal situations as opposed to including evidence that also applies to everyone (base rate neglect), and to unreflectively follow the beliefs and behaviors of our communities, or worse yet, to rationalize our commitment to their ideologies (bandwagon effect). But, as with heuristics, in highly complex societies where social relations are not constrained by biology, geography, or highly scarce resources, biases almost always lead us to irrational conclusions. And while some biases can be made explicit, such as our preferences for certain types of political positions and certain religious views, others are implicit. Implicit biases can lead people to treat women or minorities or older people or foreigners differently than others, albeit completely unintentionally and even in contrast to explicit desires not to be biased along these lines.

With this in mind, Mizrahi asks whether experts are any less susceptible to the errors associated with heuristics and biases than novices. He argues that the answer is no:

[Mizrahi – 2]
1. An expert's judgment that p is (defeasible) evidence for p only if experts are not susceptible to the sort of cognitive biases that novices are susceptible to.
2. It is not the case that experts are not susceptible to the sort of cognitive biases that novices are susceptible to.

Therefore,

3. It is not the case that an expert's judgment that p is (defeasible) evidence for p.

As with [Mizrahi – 1], Mizrahi points us to the empirical literature for evidence in support of the idea that experts are no better than novices when it comes to cognitive biases:

1 Expert police drivers are just as susceptible to illusions of superiority as everyone else (Waylen et al. 2004: 323).

2 Judges are just as susceptible as legal novices to anchoring, hindsight bias, framing, and other biases when analyzing legal cases (Guthrie, Rachlinski, and Wistrich 2001, 2007, 2011).

3 Medical decisions made by patients, medical students, and physicians are equally subject to framing bias (McNeil et al. 1982).

4 Philosophers are not less subject to ordering biases in philosophical dilemmas (Schwitzgebel and Cushman 2012).

5 Software engineers are no less subject to confirmation bias than novices (Leventhal et al. 1994).

Mizrahi does the same with erroneous heuristics, offering seventeen additional bits of evidence (which I won't reproduce here). He further says that he found no studies that "report that expert judgments are immune to cognitive biases or that expertise provides protection against cognitive biases" (9), though he admits that some studies show that experts are *less* affected by confirmation bias than novices.

What do Mizrahi's arguments imply for veritism? Without clarifying what he means by cases where "*p* is unknown," the conclusion is pretty grim. They imply that patients, nurses, and medical students are never epistemically justified in taking orders from doctors about complex patients (patients for whom there is little empirical evidence) with respect to the type of medicine to give complex patients, medicine dosage, treatment decisions, or long-term care planning just because they are doctors. It means that construction workers are never justified in taking advice from architectural engineers on new projects just because they are architectural engineers. It means that empirical researchers are never justified in trusting the statistician they have hired to organize and interpret their data just because they are a statistician. And it means that companies are not justified in trusting their company accountants just because they are accountants—they could do no worse by choosing a random employee to compile the tax returns for their company. To be sure, we might have to rely on these experts as a matter of administrative authority and practical efficiency (someone has to do it; it might as well be the accountants). But if they are not really better at their jobs than novices, we have a real problem on our hands.

There are at least four responses to Mizrahi in the literature (Seidel 2014; Walton 2014; Hinton 2015; and Botting 2018). Douglas Walton's (2014) criticisms are aimed at the structure of [Mizrahi – 1], but he largely agrees with Mizrahi's conclusions, arguing that we always need more than mere expert testimony to be justified in a belief. Markus Seidel takes the empirical claims of [Mizrahi – 1] largely for granted but offers five arguments against the conceptual aspects (e.g., the definition of expert and relative differences in the strengths of different types of expertise). Mizrahi (2016) finds none of these compelling and contends that the conceptual aspects are not problematic, so if anyone would object, they should do so on empirical grounds. Martin Hinton (2015) argues that Mizrahi and Seidel are talking past one another because they are using the terms "expert" and "opinion" differently, and since (Hinton argues) neither gives a sufficient account of either, this leaves their arguments inconclusive. David Botting (2018) seems to suggest that, reliability aside, if an expert demonstrates trustworthiness as a witness, they meet the standard conditions for trust in testimony, and, therefore, arguments from trustworthy expert opinion are not weak.

Mizrahi's arguments and the critiques so far are interesting and worth exploring. There is much more room for discussion. For now, I will just sketch three of my own concerns to try to nudge the discussion forward. One concern with [Mizrahi – 1] is that, once we look closely at the evidence he offers, it is not clear that it does the work he claims it does. We can set aside piece of evidence 8 because we can agree with Mizrahi that if expert systems outperform experts, then we should choose expert systems. Yet, we saw in Chapter 2 that expert systems are not cause for alarm over the general reliability of experts since experts are still needed to create and evaluate these systems. This also addresses concerns about piece of evidence 5, because a number of expert systems are being developed in accounting to address this problem (and many others) (see Marr 2017).

Pieces 2 and 3 point out rates of research retractions. But research retractions are irrelevant to expert accuracy. Scientific articles are retracted for a number of reasons—primarily, errors in research methods, fraud, ethical mistakes, and unreproducible results. A retraction suggests nothing about experts' ability to predict or work in their domains. Empirical research is different from research in social science or humanities domains that are largely argument-based. In the latter, retractions typically raise concerns about limiting freedom of speech and nefarious political ideologies, either on the part of the author or publishing organization. But in empirical research, each study is subject to confirmation or disconfirmation by future studies; they are, as it were, individual data points on a trend line. Rather than cause for alarm, research retractions in empirical domains are a sign of a healthy program of peer oversight.

Piece 4 is misleading because the empirical research on physician performance is mixed—it doesn't present a univocal picture of expert failure. A number of factors seem responsible for physician performance: whether the problem is well structured (Patel and Groen 1991), whether the problem is within the scope of the physician's domain of specialization (Patel and Groen 1991), whether the experiments are conducted in natural or artificial (lab-based) environments (Klein 1998; Montero 2016), and the expert's domain of specialization (surgeons and radiologists, for example, improve significantly over time) (Maruthappu et al. 2015; Grinsven et al. 2014; Ericsson and Pool 2016: 139–41).

Piece 7 is also misleading because the studies cited compare licensed physicians to interns (medical residents), not novices. Medical residents are MDs with clinical experience. They count as specialized experts, even if only weakly on our continuum of expertise. If licensed physicians perform no better than residents, this is not evidence that they perform no better than novices or no better than chance. It could simply be that the tasks evaluated are what are called *low performance ceiling* tasks (Camerer and Johnson 1991: 202ff)—tasks that require specialized training, but training that is fairly easy to learn. The competence needed for low performance ceiling tasks does not allow much enhancement of performance even with ongoing specialized training. The game checkers is an example of a task with a relatively low performance ceiling. Whereas with chess, one can practice for a lifetime and only get marginally better, chess seems to have an upper level of performance that is widely achievable. This raises the possibility that the decision tasks the residents and attendings were asked to perform could be the sort of skill that residents have already learned and that do not admit of much improvement over time. But, again, this does not tell us anything about physicians' performance as decision-makers.

With respect to piece 1, like 5 and 8, I think we can concede Tetlock's conclusion here, allowing that, where decision procedures outperform experts, we should prefer them to expert advice. Interestingly, though, while Mizrahi cites Tetlock's (2005) conclusions about financial and political forecasters as evidence for premise 2, he does not note that Tetlock spent the next few years studying how to enhance forecasting abilities, and in his 2015 book with John Gardner shows not only a number of cases where expert political forecasters outstrip chance, but what sorts of practices enhance predictive competence. Rather than supporting Mizrahi's skeptical conclusion, Tetlock's ongoing research testifies to the reliability of suitably trained experts.

This leaves piece 6 to stand alone in support of premise 2 of [Mizrahi – 1]. And since this is evidence from a single domain, it seems to lack the necessary generalizability to sufficiently support his conclusion.

My second concern with [Mizrahi – 1] is that there does seem to be a significant amount of empirical evidence showing that some types of expert decisions *do* outstrip chance. For example, empirical studies on surgeons show that they get better over time (Vickers et al. 2007; Vickers et al. 2008). Do novices improve at surgery over time? (Hint: We do not let non-surgeons practice surgery.) Would Mizrahi suggest that surgical decisions, even with improvement, are no better than chance? Is there a measure of how well novice surgeons perform? (No.) Further, in the same volume where Camerer and Johnson suggest that decision procedures outperform experts (Ericsson and Smith 1991), Patel and Groen (1991) explain three experiments comparing medical competence across a range of competence levels, from first-year college student to licensed physician. Their results show unequivocally that third-year medical students and physicians significantly outperform first- and second-year medical students on diagnostic tasks. They also performed better on recall tasks, where the results "indicate rather reliably that recall was nonmonotonically related [they are associated, but this association was discovered independently of level of expertise] to the length of the training period or the level of expertise" (111).[21] This is important because recall proved significant in predicting diagnostic accuracy. Further still, psychologist Gary Klein (1998) shows that expert firefighters and military commanders significantly outperform novices in domain-specific decisions. And psychologist Anders Ericsson and science writer Robert Pool highlight dozens of studies showing that the training strategy called *deliberate practice* improves decisional performance far beyond what was previously expected in many different areas of competence, including rock climbing, medical diagnosis, surgery, chess, flying a fighter plane, and novel-writing (2016).

If all this is right, then it would seem that Mizrahi's conclusion is hasty, based on incomplete and misleading studies. At most, Mizrahi has shown that, under some circumstances, some types of experts are not reliable decision-makers, and that, in some of those cases, decisions would be improved by a decision tool. Yet, again, no one doubts these conclusions. As social scientists Harald Mieg and Julia Evetts summarize the literature:

> We find consistently high accuracy of judgment by experts in domains such as weather forecasting, chess, or soil quality, and low judgment accuracy by court judges, clinical psychologists, or stockbrokers. The findings for physicians diverged. For example, radiologists show good decision performance, psychiatrists a poor one. (2018: 142)

The difficulty is that expert competence is a mixed bag, and we cannot draw blanket conclusions about the strength of appeals to expertise from a narrowly curated set of studies.

With respect to [Mizrahi – 2], premise 1 seems false. Even if, descriptively, experts are just as subject to cognitive biases as novices, there is evidence that experts use tools to mitigate biases. Consider confirmation bias, the tendency either to look only for evidence that confirms a belief or to weigh confirming evidence more heavily than disconfirming evidence. What's the solution? Typically, confirmation bias can be mitigated either by protecting yourself from learning which outcome the evidence supports, through experimental controls like double-blind experimental conditions, or by submitting your judgment about the evidence's relevance for your belief to peer review by other experts or to peer experts at professional conferences. These are by no means perfect, but they provide oversight over and above mechanisms novices typically have at their disposal. Unlike novices, experts are aware of these tools, and it is often part of their research protocols to use them.

Further, even in cases where experts predict only marginally better than novices, Camerer and Johnson note that experts "seem to have better self-insight about the accuracy of their predictions [called *calibration*]" (1991: 202). They explain that "most people are poorly calibrated, offering erroneous reports of the quality of their predictions. ... There is some evidence that experts are less overconfident than novices" (1991:202). And a number of studies show that the level of a person's expertise ameliorates bias (Keren 1987; Shanteau 1989; Smith and Kida 1991; Cohen 1993; and Bornstein, Emler, and Chapman 1999).

Mizrahi might respond to these criticisms by saying, nevertheless, in those cases where decision procedures outstrip expertise, we should be much less trusting of expert judgments and look for more opportunities to develop and use decision aids. I am sympathetic with this conclusion, and I think the development of expert systems will continue to render some types of expertise obsolete or undermine them altogether. I am not, however, as sanguine as Mizrahi that once expertise has been occluded by technology (e.g., the likelihood of defaulting on a loan) people who were formerly called experts, and whose skill level no longer meets the minimum competence for expertise in that domain retain the right to be called experts. In that case, the domain has outstripped human ability, and thus, there is no one with a high competence relative to the domain at the time. But this does not mean that expert systems have outstripped every type of expertise. That is an empirical question, and on that point, I am not sure that Mizrahi has made his case.

What does all this mean for truth-based accounts? If veritists intend to construct an internally consistent account of expertise, [Mizrahi – 1] and [2] would imply that there are very few experts in the world. No one is more reliable than anyone else in any domain, and thus, no one meets RA. Interestingly, Mizrahi does not draw this conclusion. He allows that there are experts; he simply concludes that they are not reliable, and therefore, appeals to their authority are weak. I have raised concerns for Mizrahi's conclusions that warrant further analysis. Nonetheless, Mizrahi's arguments present the right sort of challenge to veritists, especially to those who argue that expertise should help novices improve their epistemic placement. To stave off concerns like these, veritists would do well to look for empirical support that experts are able to do what veritists claim for them.

3.4.4 Even Cognitive Expertise Is Not All That Cognitive

Another concern for veritism is that it assumes cognitive expertise can be distinguished from performative expertise. Despite the long tradition, beginning with Plato, of distinguishing cognitive (theoretical) from performative (practical) expertise, some argue that veritism's basic assumption that one can define cognitive expertise in contrast to performance is implausible. Expertise in any domain you choose, they contend, ultimately comes down to what someone can do.[22] Philosopher Michael Polanyi expresses this view when he writes, "Science is operated by the skill of the scientist[,] and it is through the exercise of his skill that he shapes his scientific knowledge" (1962: 49). Anders Ericsson and Robert Pool (2016: 130–7) contend that the psychological research is clear that, for expertise, doing is more important than knowing: "The bottom line is what you are able to do, not what you know, although it is understood that you need to know certain things in order to be able to do your job" (131). While substantial knowledge often enhances expertise, it is, according to Ericsson and Pool, only a by-product of extensive practice rather than characteristic of the expertise produced.

Imagine getting advice from an expert chef. While her advice about which foods have the right acidity for which sauces or which part of an animal does not get chewy when braised is likely to be accurate, the understanding that accounts for that accuracy is developed as much through practice as through learning from other teachers. The same goes for construction forepersons and photographers. To be sure, veritists might resist the claim that these types of expertise are cognitive. But the point is that even if they are right that knowledge is necessary for some types of expertise, it is not knowledge qua knowledge that explains the authority of an expert, but knowledge acquired in the right way. If this is right, then even if we can make sense of truth-based accounts, they can only be developed through practice and performance, so that the more fundamental competence of expertise is performative.[23] At best, veritism could only be impure veritism.

Another more specific problem with the claim that cognitive expertise is truth-linked is that many types of cognitive expertise are explicitly aimed at goals other than truth. Research shows, for example, that most people's beliefs about space, motion, density, etc., reflect a commitment to what is called Naïve Physics (McCloskey, Caramazza, and Green 1980; Kaiser, Jonides, and Alexander 1986; Smith and Casati 1994), which is roughly the view of physics described by Aristotle, Galileo, and Kepler (see Cohen 1985). Experimentation has long debunked these naïve beliefs, but they nevertheless make it possible to get effectively through our day. Naïve physics is so much a part of how we view the world that AI developers have attempted to program naïve physics into computers so they can handle "common-sense" problems (Smith and Casati 1994; Bertamini, Spooner, and Hecht 2004). If this is the case, many expert performers—stock car racers, trapeze artists, pilots—likely have as many false beliefs about physics related to their performance as those who cannot perform at their level.

Further still, truth-based accounts leave out important types of cognitive expertise. Many types of cognitive expert judgment are evaluated as better or worse, or more or less fitting, rather than true or false. Consider physicians in palliative care medicine, a domain that manages symptoms and stress in seriously ill patients. Given the complexities of serious illness, there is rarely a single plan of care that could be regarded as "medically correct" for a patient. The expertise of palliative care medicine involves, among other things, working closely with patients and families to formulate a plan of care that achieves increasingly better results under conditions of ineliminable uncertainty—that is, when the course of an illness makes it impossible to form a judgment about what a "best" result might be. It is also extremely difficult to determine which treatments are causally related to positive outcomes. Different pain medications manage different patients' pain differently, and complex care involves a significant amount of trial and error (see Prasad and Cifu 2015). This sort of expert judgment is also common in teaching, contract law, and some types of consultation. If these are legitimate instances of expertise, and their epistemic or technical authority is such that novices have a reason to trust them in their respective domains, then having a substantial fund of knowledge or true beliefs cannot be a necessary condition for expertise.

Perhaps the problem is attempting to carve out distinct types of expertise in the first place. Rather than attempting to talk about cognitive expertise independently of performative expertise, or arguing that performance is more fundamental than knowledge, what if we accept that both cognitive and performative activities are essential to expertise but allow that their contribution to an explanation of expertise depends on the domain. In other words, we might ask what role understanding is playing in a particular instance of expertise. Consider the difference between stock-car racing and cooking. Is one domain more cognitive than the other? If we say yes, what implications might this have for our understanding of expertise? What about painting and dancing? Barbara Montero (2016) suggests that a more productive distinction than cognitive or performative for some domains is between large and small muscle groups:

> One reasonable suggestion would seem to be that we can draw the line between gymnastics and tennis on one hand and chess and poetry on the other in terms of how these activities differentially employ large muscle movements. That is, one might say that while both gymnastics and poetry involve hard mental work, gymnastics and golf also involve hard bodily work, as measured by the strength of large muscle contractions, where as chess and poetry ... are physically undemanding. (71)

She also suggests "success" conditions as a meaningful categorization tool: "In gymnastics, for example, the success of an action seems intimately connected to the bodily movements the gymnast makes, whereas in chess the grandmaster's exact bodily movements seem incidental" (71).

The point is that attempting to divide expertise into cognitive and performative before understanding the details of the domain seems as arbitrary as thinking of leadership expertise in terms of caring for land animals versus sea animals, or four-footed animals versus two-footed animals. It could be that truth-based accounts are not so conceptually problematic as wrongheaded. They may be the featherless bipeds of expertise studies.

3.4.5 RA Is Unnecessary for Expertise

Veritists' biggest concern with giving up RA seems to be the worry that it leaves us with epistemic relativism (Goldman 2018: 6). Since we cannot appeal to truth to arbitrate our search for answers, we must specify which normative epistemic system to appeal to in order to justify claims in a domain. But then, one putative expert could appeal to epistemic system A to justify the claim that p, and another could appeal to epistemic system B to justify not-p—leading to an unacceptable epistemic relativism. To avoid "potential trouble on this front" (6), Goldman argues, we would need an additional assumption, namely, that there is only one correct epistemic system. But this would simply push concerns about truth-linked accounts to the level of epistemic systems, leaving the problem unresolved.

With this problem unresolved, the concern continues, if we do not adopt a version of RA, we are giving up an *objective* account of expertise in favor of a merely *reputational* one (Goldman 2018: 3). A reputational account is the view that someone is an expert because they are widely regarded as an expert. The person functions as an expert regardless of whether they are sufficiently knowledgeable in the veritistic sense.

Of course, the fact that people come to be regarded as experts through social processes is not, in itself, problematic. A necessary condition for trusting someone as an expert is regarding them as an expert. And some people develop reputational expertise for the right reasons—they are regarded as experts because they *are* experts. Biologists, chemists, and engineers come to engender trust from their epistemic communities through certain social processes, just as religious figures, politicians, and health gurus. Call this *descriptive reputational relativism*: someone functions as an expert because a large portion of their epistemic community regards them as such. This view allows *being an expert* and *being regarded as an expert* to come apart.

However, if expertise lacks a strong connection with truth, being an expert may not be distinguishable from being regarded as one: someone functions as an expert *solely* because they are widely regarded as such. This is the species of epistemic relativism Goldman is concerned about; call it *normative reputational relativism*. On this view, an expert on, say, nutrition (as conferred by a community because they undertook years of education, scientific study, and professional experience) could have the same epistemic authority as an "expert" on nutrition (as conferred by a community unified by their skepticism about traditional science or medicine). Even more disturbing, normative reputational relativism is consistent with the claim that both have the same epistemic authority in the same epistemic community. Normative reputational relativism leads to incoherence in attempts both to characterize expertise and to apply it.

I contend, however, that rejecting RA does not leave us at the mercy of normative reputational relativism. Expertise can be inherently *social* without being *merely* reputational. Consider Stephen Turner's (2014) account of the epistemic authority of scientists in a democratic society:

> The cognitive authority of scientists in relation to the public is, so to speak, corporate. Scientists possess their authority when they speak as representatives of science. And the public judgments of science are of science as a corporate phenomenon, of scientists speaking as scientists. (23)

Turner's point is that, when scientists speak publicly, on behalf of their shared commitment to a certain epistemic process, their collective voice carries presumptive epistemic authority. This presumption is legitimated partially by successful advancements in science and engineering that are perceived by that community as beneficial and partially by the commitment of the scientific community to certain kinds of epistemic safety practices, such as peer review and research oversight, which, when it works well, provides something like a mechanism for continuous calibration, a check on one another's competence. So, while not grounded in truth per se, the epistemic authority of scientists is legitimated by a process of gathering and assessing evidence in an epistemically responsible way, and this way is at least partly independent of public opinion, and, therefore, does not reduce to mere reputation. We will explore Turner's view further in section 6.3.

And Turner's view is not the only alternative to veritism. I contend that what justifies our trust in experts is evidence that they have a certain type and degree of competence in a domain, where the sufficiency of that type and degree are determined by the state of skill and information in that domain at whatever time we face the question of whether to trust a putative expert (see Watson 2019). I call this the *domain-at-a-time* condition. For example, in some cases, the standards of a domain-at-a-time will determine that having a certain amount of information combined with the ability to use processes aimed at truth (such as experimentation and statistical analyses) are sufficient for expertise. In other cases, the standards of a domain-at-a-time will determine that being able to perform at a certain skill level with whatever mental agility this requires, such as ballet or chess, is sufficient for expertise. In still others, those standards will determine that the ability to explain and use best practices shown to improve someone's circumstances, such as palliative care medicine or financial advising, are sufficient for expertise (for more on the domain-at-a-time condition, see Watson 2019).[24]

Whether any of this evidence gives us reliably true beliefs is beyond our ken. We cannot say that scientists today discover truth with any more surety than Copernicus could in 1530. But we have good reason to trust physicists now irrespective of that fact, even if new research 500 years hence suggests they are wrong. Therefore, it is both implausible and unnecessary to believe that expertise is linked, essentially, with truth. It can be linked with other objective criteria, and those criteria are sufficient for explaining the authority of experts.

To be sure, this sort of objectivity may not give us everything we want from expertise. For example, Goldman says that "the standard goal of people seeking informational experts is precisely to learn the *true* answers to their questions" (6, italics his). Since my condition does not include having a fund of true beliefs as a necessary condition, my account fails to capture this desired use of experts. To that concern, I can only return his earlier reply: "Such is life." Scientists have been attempting that feat for centuries. Whether they have achieved something close is an open question in philosophy of science. That does not, however, mean there are not good reasons to trust experts whose beliefs are, nonetheless, well-supported according to the current state of their domains. Rather than pursuing a veritistic view of expertise, I contend that an account that starts from the current objective standards set in domains more adequately explains expertise.

3.5 What's Left for Theories of Cognitive Expertise?

Given that many domains of expertise do require intense mental rigor, a rich background of information, and understanding of the complex relationship among bits of information in a domain, it seems there is still something to say about this account of expertise. We would still benefit from an account of the cognitive competence of experts even if no instance of expertise is wholly or even largely cognitive. But if such an account is not truth-linked, what might it look like?

I don't think we can just replace knowledge or truth with justification. That would avoid objections to veritism but raise other important concerns: What adequate theory of justification is not truth-linked in some important respect? How do we account for primarily cognitive types of expertise that aren't propositional or that aren't aimed at forming beliefs? I think an account of expertise has to be settled prior to the justification question, that is, before we know what experts might do with their expertise. Whether expert competence is aimed at justifying belief or building trust or being helpful or performing an experiment depends on the domain and the context in which it is employed. And this suggests that the responsible ability to process information is central to the cognitive competence of experts.

Following Catherin Elgin (2012, 2016, 2017, 2018) and Oliver Scholz (2018), I take *understanding* to be critical for the cognitive competence of experts, whatever experts aim to do with that understanding.[25] Scholz agrees, saying that understanding "typically refers to more complex and more involved phenomena [than knowledge]. ... [U]nderstanding is directed towards complex relations, structures and patterns. In other words, it is *more holistic* than knowing" (2018: 35, italics his). Elgin offers a rich account of understanding that I won't elucidate here except to note that she argues that understanding is tethered to the world in a way that establishes objectivity without truth through a concept she calls "exemplification" (2012). The terms and models of a theory exemplify relevant features of the world to the extent that they are representative of them, that is, those features that a theory picks out constitute a reliable example or representative sample of the part of the world the theory describes. There is much to tease out here, and Elgin is transparent that our commonsense notion of understanding is "hideously murky" (2012). But I think a thoroughly worked out account of understanding is critical for a defensible account of the cognitive competence of experts. Alas, that is a topic for other books.

For now, I will stipulate that such an account is in the offing and say that experts understand propositions in their domain; they understand how those propositions were derived, what implications they have for other propositions in the domain, and the methods used either to derive or test them. Further, whether someone has this competence is a function of her ability to discharge epistemic activities successfully with respect to these propositions. She is able to form beliefs consistent with the domain, explain different aspects of the domain, and answer questions about the domain. And she has this ability even if she does not display it to any particular person (though many people were likely required to help her obtain this competence). And, of course, this person displays these traits, or at least indicators of these traits, even if her beliefs in this domain are not true.

I call this non-veritistic account of the cognitive competence of experts the *epistemic facility* account:

> (EF2) A subject, S, is an expert in a domain, D, if and only if S (a) understands enough of the terms, propositions, arguments, applications, and aims of D, along with the procedures used to formulate meaningful or useful claims or advice in D, such that (b) S has the ability to successfully demonstrate (a) to some relevant population in the discharge of her epistemic activities.

A subject who has both (a) and (b) has an *epistemic facility with D*, that is, she is well placed in a domain and has the ability to improve others' epistemic placement in that domain. It is this epistemic facility that constitutes for S the authority to speak to, perform in, or give advice regarding issues, problems, or questions that fall within the scope of D, regardless of whether any of the expert's beliefs are true.

I label this account EF2 because it is a revised version of the epistemic facility account I defended in (2018). There, I was focused on invoking a responsibilist theory of justification to underwrite an alternative to truth-based accounts of expertise (see Watson 2017, chapter 2 for my defense of responsibilism). Though I still hold a responsibilist view of justification, I now think expanding epistemic facility in the way I have done here better captures the broad cognitive competence of experts.

By "discharge of one's epistemic activities" I mean the expert's ability to engage productively with their domain. I use "epistemic" to encompass both *knowledge-that*, what philosophers refer to as propositional knowledge, or knowledge of specific claims, and *know-how*, which refers to the ability to do something.[26] You might, for example, know how to make a fried egg without knowing many claims about doing so. So, engaging with one's domain is not restricted to reporting about it or giving advice to others, and can include carrying out domain-specific tasks, like knowing how to use a tool to test water quality or knowing how to replace a carburetor on a '66 Mustang. The notion of "success" in condition (b) is pragmatic, that is, it is a function of the needs and expectations in a domain, for example, the ability to pose and answer questions about the subject that facilitates further understanding of it or the ability to troubleshoot and solve the most common problems in the domain.[27]

Consider that accountants may understand how to use accounting software, but if they cannot explain why the software produces the results it does, recognize those occasions when it does not produce the needed results (more often than you might think), and resolve those problems, then it is unlikely they are sufficiently competent in accounting to be an expert, or they are, at best, weakly experts (further down the competence continuum than specialized or general experts, but still perhaps experts in a weak sense).

Condition (b) does not require that S contribute new propositions to D, only that she understands D well enough to contribute to meaningful conversations about D. For example, a medical doctor who is a general practitioner (GP) need not have a facility for medical research or be able to form new beliefs about the course of a disease or treatments. She relies heavily on drug representatives, medical journals, and medical conferences for such information. Nevertheless, she does not simply regurgitate her medical school training; she successfully discharges it in a variety of cases. Her understanding of her domain allows her to diagnose and treat on the basis of answers to old questions, even if it does not allow her to contribute new propositions to that domain. This is consistent with people Collins and Evans (2007) call "interactional experts," that is, people who can engage meaningfully with a specialized domain but not contribute to it.[28] We will look at interactional expertise closely in Chapter 6.

There are a number of questions to ask about EF2, including how EF2 renders expert testimony epistemically authoritative, how it avoids the criticisms of veritism, and whether any current account of "understanding" is sufficient for EF2. I address some of these in Watson (2018), but here it is enough to highlight that Turner's social account of scientific authority and EF2 are non-veritistic ways of explaining the cognitive authority of expertise that do not entail epistemic relativism.

3.6 Summing Up

Truth-based accounts are intuitively compelling because they connect one of our central interests in experts (the desire to be in an objectively better epistemic position) with a clear condition for pursuing that interest (a reliable connection with true claims). On inspection, though, there are serious obstacles to formulating and defending a successful veritistic account. And while there are ways of addressing these obstacles, there are also alternatives that maintain veritism's commitment to objectivity without slipping into relativism or reputationalism. Ultimately, though, given the vast and growing literature on expertise, we have to decide whether pursuing a purely cognitive account of expertise is constructive, even for epistemologists. It may be that the cognitive elements we are interested in are simply better captured by performative accounts.

4 PERFORMANCE-BASED ACCOUNTS OF EXPERTISE – PART 1

The Philosophy of Expert Performance

[Socrates said it is] extravagant to go and consult the will of Heaven on any questions which it is given to us to decide by dint of learning. As though a [person] should inquire, "Am I to choose an expert driver as my coach[driver], or one who has never handled the reins?" "Shall I appoint a mariner to be skipper of my vessel, or a lands[keeper]?" And so with respect to all we may know by numbering, weighing, and measuring. To seek advice from Heaven on such points was a sort of profanity. "Our duty is plain," he would observe; "where we are permitted to work through our natural faculties, there let us by all means apply them."

(Xenophon, *Memorabilia*, 1.1.9, trans., H.G. Dakyns, 1897)

In this chapter, I introduce the widely discussed performance-based account developed by Hubert and Stuart Dreyfus (4.2–4.4). They argue that expertise is the largely subconscious ability to perform at a high level of competence that emerges over time through extensive practice. After watching dozens of novices become experts, they claim that, after a novice does anything for some period of time, the activity becomes part of their whole body rather than something they know in their head. Becoming and performing as an expert are not purely mental activities. Therefore, even asking an expert to explain what they are doing yields misleading answers since, by definition, they can speak only to those aspects of the practice they can think consciously about. I then explain a number of objections to the Dreyfuses' view, some of which are less serious than others (4.5). I close with the idea that approaching expertise from the perspective of experts rather than novices promises an account of expertise that avoids the major objections to the Dreyfuses' account (4.6).

4.1 Why Performance-Based Accounts of Expertise?

Outside of philosophical contexts—that is, in domains like psychology, neurology, exercise science, and education research—discussions of expertise focus, almost exclusively, on types of performance: chess playing,[1] violin playing, taxi driving, surgery, radiography, sports, and so forth. Experts can *do* things, either things that others cannot (perform surgery, fly a plane) or things that others can do, only better (play chess, play the violin). And we turn to experts—when we choose them for Olympic teams, contract with them to fix our plumbing, hire them to prestigious law firms, and consent to let them treat our cancer—precisely because of their competence over others.

This is not to say that researchers who defend performance-based accounts discount the importance of extensive domain-specific knowledge for expertise; they are unanimous that extensive knowledge is essential. They simply situate the role of knowledge—at least propositional knowledge—differently than defenders of truth-based accounts, and differently from one another depending on the domain. As we will see in this chapter, philosopher Hubert Dreyfus and his brother, industrial engineer Stuart Dreyfus, argue that the knowledge relevant for expertise is *know-how* as opposed to *know-that* and thus, reject the account presented in the last chapter, which states that at least some types of expertise are grounded in propositional knowledge. In the next chapter we will see that psychologist K. Anders Ericsson contends that knowledge is a "by-product" of expertise, by which he means experts learn the propositional knowledge necessary for their domain as they practice it, whether in order to make an improvement or through the practice itself (2016: 130–2).

4.2 What Computers Can't Do?

What might it mean to have or develop the ability to perform a task expertly? In 1986, after extensive research in computer learning and artificial intelligence, and after evaluating people who performed at various levels of competence in a variety of domains—"airplane pilots, chess players, automobile drivers, and adult learners of a second language" (20)—the Dreyfuses concluded that all of these domains share a common path from novice to expert. They claim that expertise is a kind of competence in performing in a domain and that this competence develops with practice through a series of five stages. Significantly for their account of expertise, they argue that the sort of learning necessary for achieving the later stages is not possible for computers.

1. Novice

A novice spends time learning the basic facts and features of a performance. If it is driving, they will learn what the ignition switch is, the difference between the pedals, what gears are, how to accelerate and decelerate, etc. They will practice applying this knowledge, tracking their progress by how well they follow the rules they are learning. (Press the brake pedal when shifting from Park into Drive; do not change from Drive to Reverse while the car is in motion; etc.).

2. Advanced Beginner

The advanced beginner learns more complex rules and situational cues, and starts incorporating them into their performance. Continuing with the driving example, they will learn when to start braking and how hard to depress the brake pedal when they see brake lights ahead of them on the highway. They will learn to use their mirrors to judge other cars' location and speed.

3. Competent

The competent performer can do more than follow rules; they can use those rules to make and execute plans. The competent driver chooses efficient routes from point A to point B, "chooses [that] route with attention to distance and traffic, ignores scenic beauty, and as [they] drive select[] [their] maneuvers with little concern for passenger comfort or courtesy. [They] follow[] other cars more closely than normally, enter[] traffic more daringly, and even violate[] the law" (24).[2]

4. Proficient

If a competent performer finds that they don't enjoy the challenge or find success in the domain rewarding, it is unlikely that they will maintain emotional investment long enough to advance further. The proficient performer still finds unfamiliar situations and decisions somewhat frightening, still focuses on errors, and has to work hard to correct them. But their emotional investment in the performance pushes them to continue performing, continue practicing. During this stage, training becomes easier, rules are left behind, and the performer develops a sense of ease (even excitement) with unfamiliar problems to solve. The proficient driver gets around town without conscious thought but has to mentally prepare for long trips or navigating new cities.

5. *Expert*

After the proficient performer has been immersed in a domain for a while, new and unfamiliar situations are experienced without hesitation or conscious reflection. "Thanks to [their] vast repertoire of situational discrimination, [they] also see[] immediately how to achieve [their] goal" (2006: 205). The expert enters into a "flow" state (1986, 2005), a concept richly developed by the Hungarian-American psychologist Mihaly Csikszentmihalyi[3] (1975, 1988, 1990), though the Dreyfuses do not mention his work. The body's training unconsciously processes all relevant contextual features, which "allows the immediate intuitive situational response that is characteristic of expertise" (2006: 205).[4]

The non-rule-following aspects of performance that emerge in the proficiency stage become apparent when, after much practice and very unlike a computer, humans think less and less about the rules of practice but start doing the task more quickly and effortlessly than ever before. Whereas AI researchers seem to think that expertise is simply a matter of following rules faster and more accurately, human experts start performing better than they did when they were following rules. Unconsciously, their brains and bodies have hit upon a way of doing the task that fills in pieces that the rules do not, and arguably cannot, include—pieces that depend on the details of complex contexts, specific body types, differences in mental processes, and so on. The result is an unconscious and effortless performance. The body is doing things of which the mind is not aware. The act is not perceived as effortful by the expert; in fact, it is not perceived at all. Thus, when performing as an expert, the expert enters into a sort of mystical state.

The boundaries between these levels of competence are fuzzy, and whether one could distinguish the advanced beginner from the competent practitioner, and so on, in any particular domain and whether it would matter are open questions. Is someone who is merely a good doctor, who has to work hard to be good, only proficient and not an expert? What about the climate scientist who has never experienced a flow state but regularly publishes in the top journals in her domain? The point of the Dreyfus model seems to be simply to highlight some common features of the highest levels of competence. Whether this taxonomy is useful for explaining other aspects of expertise is not especially clear. It does, however, constitute a jumping off point for their explanation of how expertise is acquired.

The Dreyfuses argue that what transforms the ability follow rules into expertise is something that computers, in principle, cannot have, namely, *embodiment*. Computer programming, even in its most complex forms, with the development of "artificial neural architecture" and capacities for "deep learning," is limited to propositional and situational information. But expert practices involve bodies and, more specifically, bodies with knowledge distributed throughout them in forms that are neither propositional nor situational, such as interpretations of ambiguous background information, anticipation, ratiocination, and significance.[5] The Dreyfuses draw on arguments from classic phenomenologists like Edmund Husserl and Maurice Merleau-Ponty to substantiate their point. With respect to *significance*, for example, Merleau-Ponty writes of someone who acquires a skill:

> [They do] not weld together individual movements and individual stimuli but acquire[] the power to respond with a certain type of solution to situations of a certain general form. The situations may differ widely from place to place, and the response movements may be entrusted sometimes to one operative organ, sometimes to another, both situations and responses in the various cases having in common not so much a partial identity of elements as a shared significance. (1945: 142)

If the Dreyfuses are right, computers cannot be experts because expertise is an embodied state, and that state requires a particular kind of body.

In this book, I am interested less in what computers can't do than in what makes someone an expert. So, regardless of whether computers could be experts, could the notion of embodiment adequately account for expertise?

4.3 Expertise as Embodiment

There are three key elements to the Dreyfus account of expertise. The first is that expertise is essentially *know-how* rather than *know-that*. This distinction drawn by philosopher Gilbert Ryle in 1945, but the Dreyfuses use "know-how" in a very narrow sense, referring only to the type of embodied performance of experts:

> When we speak of intuition or know-how, we are referring to the understanding that effortlessly occurs due to discriminations resulting from previous experiences. We shall use "intuition" and "know-how" as synonymous .... *Intuition or know-how ... is neither wild guessing nor supernatural inspiration, but the sort of ability we all use all the time as we go about our everyday tasks.* (1986: 29, italics theirs)

This implies (contra Ryle) that simply knowing how to wire a three-way electrical switch is not "know-how," even if I know how to do it. I can do it, but I have to think about it. It is certainly not intuitive. It is worth noting that other accounts of *intuition as know-how* do not tend to imply anything with respect to expertise.[6] I am not sure how the Dreyfuses would categorize one-off instances of knowing how to do something, or why they do not want to call them know-how, but I will set that aside and focus on *expert* know-how. The point here is that expertise is embodied in the sense of effortless competence, rather than merely a function of cognitive processes or one-off knowledge. And this kind of embodiment excludes the possibility that expertise is truth-based according to the accounts in the last chapter.

The second key element of the Dreyfuses' account is also included in the quotation above, namely, that expertise is performance at the upper end of a continuum of experiences, and those experiences are no different from our everyday experiences. This means that, if you do something long enough, like walking and driving, you will become an expert at it.

The third key element is that expertise is non-cognitive and arational. Once someone reaches a point where they are no longer relying on rules, they cannot express what they are doing in propositional terms. "The fact that you can't put what you have learned into words means that know-how is not accessible to you in the form of facts and rules. If it were, we would say that you 'know that' certain rules produce proficient bicycle riding" (16). By "arational," they mean "action without conscious analytic decomposition and recombination" (36), or, in other words, without a conscious, step-by-step strategy for how to do something. This means an expert cannot analyze each piece of their performance and explain it as a whole. It is neither rational nor irrational. "Competent performance is rational; proficiency is transitional; experts act arationally" (36).

The idea seems to be that when experts perform as experts, they aren't consciously thinking about a set of rules. If there are rules, they've left them behind. And the Dreyfuses argue that expert performance is inherently embodied such that there are no rules that can be formulated. So, there is a combination of muscle memory, know-how, and conscious intention to do something. When these come together to perform a task, the result is expert performance. Of course, not all expertise is "performative" in an overt sense. Art history critics and mathematicians are no less experts on the Dreyfuses' view. It's just that, while we think of mathematics as this conscious, intellectual activity, more often than not, expert mathematicians don't *do* calculations, they *see* the implications of a formula. This ability to intuitively see mathematical relationships is a way of exhibiting expertise.

We have to be careful here. It is not quite right that a bit of knowledge is know-how rather than know-that simply because *you cannot put it into words*. Perhaps you simply lack a vocabulary rich enough to express what you understand. Your knowledge may be propositional knowledge even if you lack the linguistic tools express it as such. Consider two arguments:

If Jonah is taller than Obadiah,
And Obadiah is taller than Jeroboam,
Then Jonah is taller than Jeroboam.

If Jonah loves Obadiah,
And Obadiah loves Jeroboam,
Then Jonah loves Jeroboam.

One can know that the former argument is a "good" argument while the latter isn't even if one doesn't know the words "transitive," "valid," or "deductive." Further, a case can be made that many cases of know-how can be formulated propositionally. Consider the instructions, "To remove the bottle's cap, press it down and turn it counter-clockwise." To be sure, I have to know how to coordinate both hands, elbows, and wrists in order to comply with the instruction, and I may not be able to express this propositionally, but the instructions adequately express motions sufficient for performing the action. This is not to say that the Dreyfuses are not onto something important. It is just important to note that the distinction between knowledge-how and knowledge-that does not turn, strictly speaking, on whether one's actions can be expressed as propositions. Rather, the key seems to be that the expert need have no conscious knowledge of what those propositions might be even if they could be formulated. Their muscles and brain work together to do the work so that no conscious reflection on the process is needed, and, in fact, would slow them down and make them less expert performers.

To support their three key elements, the Dreyfuses offer two lines of argument. First, they contrast incredible demands on human intelligence with what they take to be the upper limits of computer programming. Computers can do things that humans cannot. But that is a matter of degree, not kind. Humans can do things that are inherently unachievable by programming; it is a difference in kind, not degree. Thus, expertise is something over and above mere computational proficiency. The relevant difference, they claim, is having a body of a certain type that is immersed in a practice over time.

Second, they (and other researchers following them) have compiled extensive phenomenological testimony from people as they transition from novice to expert. The consensus seems to be that, as you become more experienced with a task, the number of elements you must pay attention to in order to do the task better and faster become overwhelming. And if you paid attention to each one, you could never do it faster—that is, you couldn't improve to the level of expert competence. Conscious attention is just too slow and clunky for that. And yet, if you ignored them, you would never improve, either. So, what people report is a transition from rule following to "just doing" that becomes, eventually, unconscious as one masters the activity.

4.4 A Notable Implication of the Dreyfus Account

Perhaps the most significant implication of the Dreyfus account of expertise is what it means for experts' role in society. If experts perform in ways that prevent them from being able to accurately express their expertise in natural language (that is, propositionally), then asking an expert to comment on their performance is bound to be, at best, inaccurate and, at worst, incoherent (think of the inane commentary of athletes who try to explain how they played in post-game interviews). In essence, they are being asked to rationalize, retrospectively, what is inherently arational: "Examining [an expert] becomes a futile exercise in rationalization in which expertise is forfeited and time is wasted" (1986: 196). In fact, according to the Dreyfuses, only experts who share the same background experiences can successfully communicate with one another about their domain:

> There is surely a way that two expert surgeons can use language to point out important aspects of a situation to each other during a delicate operation. Such authentic language would presuppose a shared background understanding and only make sense to experts currently involved in a shared situation. (Dreyfus 2000: 308)

Recall from the last chapter that Goldman says that a central reason why novices seek out experts is that they are more likely to be right than novices in their domain, in other words, experts can put them in a better epistemic position. If the Dreyfuses are right, this reasoning is wrong-headed: Experts can advance their domains and perform as experts, but they cannot make novices epistemically better off.

Evan Selinger argues that this implication raises a *"recognition problem"* for the Dreyfusian account (2011: 29), which is the problem of how novices, who know little about a domain, can identify or assess the merits of experts. According to Selinger, Dreyfus "leaves no grounds for understanding how an expert might be legitimately challenged (or instructed, for that matter, as in the case of sensitivity training, nonexpert review panels, etc.)" (2011: 29). No account may give us sufficient tools to solve the recognition problem, and it may be a problem we have to live with no matter what, but this is an unfortunate implication of the Dreyfuses' account, especially if other at least equally plausible accounts are available.

4.5 Objections to Embodied Expertise

The Dreyfuses do not offer a scientific account of how expertise develops (that is, they do not offer a psychological, neurological, or biological explanation for expertise), though Hubert Dreyfus (1999a, 1999b) does argue that his view is confirmed in the neurological work of Walter Freeman. But even without strong empirical support, the Dreyfus view is not an isolated or idiosyncratic way of thinking about the embodied nature of performance. Anecdotally, Dreyfus's view of how the mind loses itself in bodily performance tracks the way many expert performers talk about their abilities. Psychologist Mihaly Csikszentmihalyi calls it "one of the most universal and distinctive features of optimal experience" (1990: 53). Barbara Montero (2016) highlights no less than a dozen examples of people who report the "nonminded" or "unconscious" nature of expert performance, which she calls the "just do it" principle. And a recent version of Dreyfus's embodiment thesis is endorsed in philosopher Mark Rowlands's (2015) Rilkean theory of memory.

Rowlands argues that when the consciousness of a memory's content is lost, the memory may still live on in an embodied form. Building, like the Dreyfuses, on the phenomenological tradition, Rowlands takes this particular type of embodiment from the German poet Rainer Maria Rilke:

> And yet it is not enough to have memories. You must be able to forget them when they are many, and you must have the immense patience to wait until they return. For the memories themselves are not important. Only when they have changed into our very blood, into glance and gesture, and are nameless, no longer to be distinguished from ourselves—only then can it happen that in some very rare hour the first word of a poem arises in their midst and goes forth from them. ([1910] 1985: 14)

Exercise physiologist Arturo Leyva (2018) applies Rowlands's Rilkean memory to competence in sport. Athletes practice until their activities become part of their "very blood." Leyva takes this competence to be a kind of competence distinct from either know-how or know-that: "It is not procedural (knowing how), declarative (knowing that), or a combination of both because it requires the learning or embodiment of content" (12). I am not convinced that Leyva is offering something distinct from what Dreyfus or Ryle would consider "knowledge-how," because both describe knowledge in embodied terms, though Ryle is less explicit than Dreyfus about this.[7]

Nevertheless, every element of the Dreyfus view has been challenged. Here, I am less concerned with whether the Dreyfuses are right or wrong than with how the objections can help us formulate a better account of expertise. Even if we ultimately set aside their view for a more powerful account, I think there is much to be learned from studying it.

4.5.1 The Domain Problem

One concern with the Dreyfuses' view is that the examples of performance around which they construct their view vary so widely that it is unclear whether they are tracking a consistent phenomenon across domains. They talk about walking, riding a bicycle, and driving alongside piloting an aircraft and nursing. While the latter seem clearly to be domains of expertise, it is unclear that the former should count. This raises, yet again, the question of how we should circumscribe domains. What counts as a domain in which expertise can be developed? Is riding a bike one of those domains? Is what you had for breakfast such a domain?

Philosopher Evan Selinger argues that treating walking and driving as types of expertise is simply inconsistent with ordinary usage and should be dropped from their account: "We do not call licensed drivers 'experts'—nor driving enthusiasts or competitive amateurs—even when they have an intuitive relation to operating their vehicles. Rather, we reserve the word for drivers who belong to professional driving organizations, participate in certain kinds of competitions, and so forth" (2011: 23). This objection is not particularly strong. There are plenty of philosophical concepts that are inconsistent with regular use and for good reason. For example, the concept of "knowledge," as philosophers use it, differs dramatically from many colloquial uses. But this reflects the poverty of colloquial usage, in particular its lack of technical nuance. Recall that David Coady claims to be an expert on what he had for breakfast. And while Coady admits that "this sounds like a strange thing to say," he rightly points out that "that does not mean it is false" (2012: 31). So, are there other reasons to reject walking and driving as types of expertise?

In response to the idea that experts should be identified relative to how well others perform, Barbara Montero (2016) simply stipulates that, even if mundane activities are types of expertise, they are not the ones she is interested in:

> Given that I aim to identify a conception of "expert" according to which someone who drives for her daily commute to work would not typically count as an expert while the Indianapolis 500 driver would, this

relativistic criterion for expertise is inadequate since it might lead us to count someone with quite ordinary abilities as an expert. Take the skill of shirt buttoning (among adults in cultures where button-down shirts are a common mode of attire). Perhaps if tested on some sort of time and accuracy trial (how many buttons can you fully fasten in five minutes) we would find a normal distribution with some people emerging in the top 99 percent, yet, for the purposes of arguing against the just-do-it principle, I don't want the ordinary shirt-buttoner to count. (61)

This stipulation captures an intuition (*of course we don't want to count them as experts*), but it is ultimately question-begging: Why *shouldn't* we want the ordinary shirt-buttoner, walker, and driver to count? Is there a principled reason for carving them out of our taxonomy of expertise?

Perhaps a better question is: Is there any place for them in our taxonomy of expertise? They are clearly not one-off instances of knowledge. Walking is not "one-off," and it does require some work, as eighteen-month-old children and people who have been bedridden for several weeks demonstrate. Ericsson and Pool (2016: 66) say that *reading* is an instance of expertise precisely because it requires thousands of hours of very specific practice to master.

Could walking and driving (and perhaps reading) be instances of what sociologists Harry Collins and Robert Evans (2006, 2007) call *ubiquitous expertise*? This refers to the "talents of ordinary people" (2007: 16), but not just any talents, and they don't mean "talents" in the sense of inherited abilities (as when some people say, "You really have a talent for music," when they mean something like, "You have a natural gift"). They mean a skill that requires significant training. But they also don't mean a *specialized* skill because everyone has a number of ubiquitous expertises. These are the skills needed "to live in a human society" (2007: 16). "Fluency in the natural language of the society is just one example of a ubiquitous expertise. Others include moral sensibility and political discrimination. These are abilities that people acquire as they learn to navigate their way through life" (16). Interestingly, Collins and Evans reject the idea that driving is a ubiquitous expertise. They argue that, even in cultures where driving is prominent, it is not ubiquitous because driving "is not learned integrally with learning to live in society but needs specialist training and the specialist tacit knowledge that goes along with it" (2007: 18, fn. 4).

By this reasoning, walking wouldn't be a domain of expertise, either, since walking is not necessary for navigating human society. Reading, however, might be, since an inability to read makes it extremely difficult to get around in society (much like not knowing the local natural language). What else is ruled out on the Collins/Evans view? "One might have huge experience of lying in bed in the morning, but this does not make one an expert at it (except in an amusing ironic sense). Why not? Because anyone could master it immediately without practice, so nothing in the way of skill has been gained through the experience" (2007: 17).

I don't intend to settle this debate here, but one way of nudging it along is to introduce the notion of *localized expertise*. Walking, bicycle riding, and driving do fall along a continuum of competence, albeit at the weak end. Models, stage and film actors, and politicians not only practice walking but get better at walking, not to mention the training required for the Olympic sport of race walking. What establishes these as specialized types of expertise is the structure given by the *purpose* of the activity. This purpose helps determine the minimum standard of performance in the domain. The sport of race walking, for example, establishes a standard both of form and of speed by which to evaluate competitors. Runway walking sets similar expectations. Everyday walking falls *so far* outside these sorts of practiced competence, and lacks the structured purpose of specialization; it is, at best, a type of localized expertise and, thereby, carries very little epistemic authority.

However, if we do allow that normal walking and bicycle riding are types of expertise, the Dreyfus account faces another concern. In some domains, what the Dreyfuses call *competence* and *proficiency* are better regarded as *degrees* of specialized expertise than as competence that *falls short* of expertise. Consider a second-year resident physician—this is a physician two years out of medical school who is still in training and is not licensed. They are still learning, and their learning is slow and frustrating (nowhere close to non-minded). And yet, they are highly trained, they see patients (under the auspices of a licensed physician), they write chart notes (usually co-signed by a licensed physician), and they are far better placed in their domain than anyone who has not gone to medical school. When they walk into a patient's room, they rightly identify themselves as "doctor." Resident physicians are far from the Dreyfuses' conception of expert, and yet they are all competent to a substantive degree, and many are proficient, especially by their fourth or fifth year of residency. Other examples of competence and proficiency that are rightly regarded as expertise include many local musicians and artists, minor league athletes, new accountants and attorneys, and so on. These performers do not experience nonmindedness, but they have skills that far exceed those of someone without their training and experience.

The Dreyfuses attempt to handle this concern by drawing a distinction between "*crude skills*, like walking and driving, and *subtle skills* like music, sports, and ... surgery" (2005: 788, italics theirs). They contend that crude skills are easier to master and have large margins of error, whereas subtle skills require "subtle discriminations" because small changes or errors can make big differences in outcome. This could help explain how a daily commuter could be an expert in driving while a medical resident is not an expert in medicine. But even this distinction does not help distinguish the everyday commuter from the stock car driver, or someone who can walk from a race walker.

While the Dreyfuses seem to be right that the development of expertise falls along a continuum, their taxonomy cuts across examples in unhelpful and seemingly unprincipled ways. Their category of "expert" includes people who can walk and drive to work and excludes resident physicians and some professional musicians. Without a more nuanced and principled way to explain the development of competence, their five-stage model seems to fall short of an adequate account of expertise.

4.5.2 Problems with Embodiment

A second concern with their view regards their notion of embodiment. Whereas the Dreyfuses argue that expertise requires the sort of bodies that humans typically have and immersion in the work of an expert, Harry Collins and Robert Evans (2007) argue that this sets the bar too high. They argue, in contrast, that expertise requires only the minimal amount of embodiment necessary for understanding the language in a domain. Collins and Evans agree with the Dreyfuses that computers—at least on current technology—cannot become the sort of experts that humans can: "We do not believe any existing computers have or could acquire human fluency in language" (77). However, while Dreyfus thinks that the development of expertise occurs primarily at the level of the individual, Collins and Evans argue that it occurs socially, through interaction with people of various skill levels (78). We will explore Collins and Evans's view in detail in Chapter 6, but for now, it is enough to note that *how* someone interacts with a community is a key element of their account of expertise:

> The only way to become a fluent English speaker is to be embedded in the English language-speaking community and absorb the ability. The only way to maintain that ability is to remain embedded as normal English usage changes. ... [T]he crucial thing which prevents computers from becoming and remaining fluent English speakers is our complete lack of understanding of how to make them into regular members of English-speaking society. (78)

Their key criticism of the Dreyfus view is that whether one can become an expert and to what degree is determined, in large part, by the degree to which they can become "linguistically socialized" in that domain of expertise. And this goes for any domain: physicists must learn the language of physics; football players must learn the language of football and football training; musicians must learn the language of music. "Insofar as a body is required to participate in a linguistic community, then it must include some physical structure that allows it to open itself to the social world of that community" (85). Rather than treating embodiment as an all-or-nothing affair, as the Dreyfuses seem to do—Collins and Evans contend that language is powerful enough to allow some degree of mastery in many domains of expertise.

Recall that Hubert Dreyfus argues that surgeons can only successfully share their expertise with one another because they share the same background experiences, namely, their performance as surgeons. And he dismisses people he calls "kibitzers," commentators on sports and other types of expert performance when they have never performed at the expert level. With respect to "chess kibitzers," he says they "have not committed themselves to the stress and risks of tournament chess and so have no expertise" (Dreyfus, Spinosa, and Flores 1997: 87). Collins and Evans disagree that such commentators could not be experts of a sort.

To support their claim, they give the example of psychologist Oliver Sacks's patient Madeleine, who was born blind and unable to use her hands to read braille.[8] Through extensive engagement with Sacks and with books being read to her, Madeleine not only learned to use her hands, but became fully proficient in language skills. "She has learned the language through immersion in the world of language alone rather than immersion in the full-blown form of life" (82). In contrast, Collins and Evans argue that people who are prelingually deaf—born profoundly deaf or go deaf before beginning language acquisition—lack thorough linguistic socialization in a natural language. While "it is not impossible for the prelingually deaf to learn ordinary language, ... it can be done only with an immense effort and with the aid of teachers who will spend hours a day, using lip movement and other non-natural cues, to substitute for the bath of speech in which the infant is normally immersed" (83). Because they missed out on "early language socialization," Collins and Evans argue that they "do not learn to master the natural language with any degree of fluency" (84).

Further, Collins, though a sociologist by profession, has spent a large part of his career studying gravitational wave physics, with the aim of being able to talk meaningfully with gravitational wave physicists about their domain. Not only did Collins succeed, he participated in blinded experiments where he answered gravitational wave physics questions alongside a real gravitational wave physicist (2007: 104–9). Participants had to guess, based on the answers, who was the "kibitzer" and who was the physicist. Most couldn't tell the difference. Collins will fully admit that he cannot contribute to the domain of gravitational wave physics (and he has not become gravitational wave physicist). Nevertheless, his linguistic socialization has given him what he calls "interactional expertise" in that domain, in other words, he understands enough of the language associated with gravitational wave physics that he can have meaningful conversations with other experts in that domain, and he is so fluent in their language that they would not immediately suspect that he was not a practicing gravitational wave physicist himself. He does not *do* gravitational wave physics, as the Dreyfuses argue is necessary, and yet, he has good evidence that he knows what he is talking about.

Collins and Evans's point is simply that one need not be fully bodily immersed in a domain—they need not be full practitioners—in order to have a non-trivial degree of expertise. So long as someone has the bodily capabilities for linguistic socialization in a domain, they can at least achieve interactional expertise in that domain. We will explore interactional expertise in Chapter 6. For now, it is enough to note that it constitutes a type of competence that the Dreyfus account seems unable to accommodate.

4.5.3 The Continuum Problem

A related problem is that the Dreyfuses extrapolate *how to become* an expert from examples of how people become competent with mundane activities. Their account includes no principled distinction, for example, between the types of experience and practice required for a normal commuter to be a competent driver and an Indy 500 competitor to be a competent driver. Their assumption seems to be that one has simply been *doing it longer*. The problem is that this assumption is inconsistent with decades of empirical research on expertise. K. Anders Ericsson and colleagues have studied expert performers in numerous domains and found that the *type* of practice, not just the *amount* of practice, is an essential factor in developing expertise. "Research has shown that, generally speaking, once a person reaches that level of 'acceptable' performance and automaticity, the additional years of 'practice' don't lead to improvement" (2016: 13). Even psychologists who argue that there is a substantive genetic component to expert competence (see sections 5.3.1 and 5.3.2) tend to agree with Ericsson and colleagues that a specific type of practice is necessary for expertise.

A different problem related to how one progresses through the Dreyfuses' stages is Collins and Evans's argument that the Dreyfus account is too individualistic. There is a difference between performing an action—say, riding a bicycle—and performing it under certain conditions—riding in traffic. Riding in traffic requires a much broader background of tacit knowledge about how others move in the world—cars, buses, traffic laws, rush hour, middle fingers, jingly bells, etc. Developing expertise, then, is not simply about mastering a particular activity, it is mastering it in a context that gives the activity meaning. Certain actions "depend on social understanding"; they "require that behavior fits changing social circumstances, and they cannot be mastered by machines failing a way of making machines that fit as smoothly into social life as humans" (2007: 27). The Dreyfuses' inability to distinguish everyday drivers from stock-car racers seems to be a function of this sort of narrowly individual notion of performance.

These arguments are not inherently inconsistent with the Dreyfuses' account. They could, it seems to me, incorporate these insights into the second key element of their account without giving it up altogether. They could allow, for example, that what facilitates the transition from competent to proficient performer, and subsequently, from proficient performer to expert is the amount of what Ericsson calls "deliberate practice" someone puts in, and also allow that deliberate practice takes place against a rich social background. In fact, Gloria Dall'Alba (2018) sketches what she calls a "lifeworld perspective" on expertise in the Dreyfusian spirit that does something very close to this. But an adapted account that incorporates deliberate practice wholesale would require an explicit commitment, as noted in the previous concern, to reserving the term "expert" for superior performers, that is, those who perform significantly better than others in a domain. This, of course, runs contrary to the Dreyfuses' contention that everyday walkers and drivers are experts, since these people (presumably) have not engaged in the deliberate practice necessary for superior skill.

This suggests that the Dreyfus account faces a dilemma: proponents must either commit to accepting the empirical evidence that underwrites deliberate practice and incorporate this practice into their stages but give up the idea that mundane tasks can be types of expertise, or keep the mundane tasks and reject the evidence supporting deliberate practice. Since mundane tasks are easily accommodated with categories like *persons of experience* or *localized expertise*, I think the choice is easy.

4.5.4 The Problem of Nonmindedness

Of course, incorporating deliberate practice into the Dreyfus view raises a further concern about embodiment, namely, whether deliberate practice results in the sort of nonmindedness the Dreyfuses claim. This leads us to our final objection. While the claim that expert performance is inherently nonminded and unconscious does seem to map onto a large number of experts' stated experiences, there is a worry that the experts do not have (or at least do not use) the technical vocabulary necessary to track the sort of distinctions that philosophers and psychologists draw in a way that substantiates the claim. For example, when I play a song I know really well on the guitar, I don't have to think very hard to play it. I certainly do not have conscious thoughts like: *Put your index finger on the third fret of the low-E string; put your middle finger on the second fret of the A string*; and so on. I literally "just do it." And I just do it through the whole song. I rarely even think about what chords to play; I *know* what chords to play, in the Dreyfuses' sense. The Dreyfuses cite martial artist Taisen Deshimaru on this point: "There can be no thought, because if there is thought, there is a time of thought and that means a flaw .... If you take the time to think 'I must use this or that technique,' you will be struck while you are thinking" (1986: 32).

But Barbara Montero (2016) points out that there is an ambiguity in claims like "I don't have conscious thoughts [when I am performing]" and "there can be no thought [when performing]." They could be referring to any number of conscious states, including:

- Thinking self-reflectively
- Planning
- Predicting
- Deliberating
- Paying attention to my actions
- Monitoring my actions
- Conceptualizing my actions
- Controlling my actions
- Trying
- Putting in effort
- Having a sense of self
- Acting for a reason (41ff)

Montero argues that even if some of these aren't present when I play a song that I know well, at least one of them likely is. And when pressed, even expert performers admit this. If this is right, then expert performance is not completely nonminded.

Anders Ericsson, in his research on expertise, finds that many experts lack this sense of flow, especially as they advance from weaker to stronger expert competence. In fact, when experts stop advancing in their skills and fall back on what they "know," they are in danger of "arrested development" (Ericsson 2009).

As we will see below, Ericsson's deliberate practice approach is used by experts and burgeoning experts alike to continually improve their abilities. Whereas the Dreyfuses treat expertise as a sort of completable end stage of a process, Ericsson has found no particular upper bound to performance development. So, even if there are times when experts perform at or below their current abilities (and in those moments experience effortless flow), when they are working to improve their abilities or are competing against others for the very upper end of superior performance, they tend to experience this as conscious, effortful, and sometimes frustrating.

So, why do the Dreyfuses think nonmindedness is a necessary element of expertise? They suggest that it is necessary for explaining three phenomena: (1) the effortlessness of expert performance, which happens too quickly for the clunky human mind; (2) the widely shared view that "thinking" gets in the way of expert performance—in the Dreyfuses' words, that it "produces regression to the skill of the novice or, at best, the competent performer" (36)[9]; and (3) the widely shared feeling of "flow" when one is performing as an expert, that is, the sense that their conscious self is somehow disengaged from the performance, and the performance is "just happening."

Montero argues that all these phenomena are unsubstantiated assumptions. We don't need nonmindedness to explain them because they don't exist to need explaining. For example, while some types of expert performance seem effortless to the observer, they are anything but effortless to the performers, especially in high-stakes performances like the Olympics, surgery, and cooking competitions (like Top Chef). Even the best novelists regularly report that the process of writing a novel is grueling and hard, even in cases where the finished book reads effortlessly (see also Kellogg 2018 on professional writing expertise). And Montero spends an entire chapter of her book (2016: ch. 4) debunking research that supposedly shows that thinking interferes with performance. She argues that in some cases, the experiments do not match the conditions under which experts actually perform; in other cases, the task they are asked to perform conflicts with their expert performance; in still others, the experiments are done on novices and simply extrapolated to expert performance. If Montero is right, while some kinds of thinking get in the way of some kinds of performance, skill-focused thinking (much like Ericsson defends as part of deliberate practice) is not only possible with expert performance but beneficial to it.

4.6 Summing Up and Moving Forward

The embodied expertise account captures some intuitive aspects of expertise—the seeming ease with which experts perform, the continuum of progress from novice to expert that happens with practice.

Unfortunately, it does not capture other details that are just as important. For example, some ways of being an expert are not effortless, even if they seem that way from the outside (novel-writing, high-stakes competition). And even if experts don't have conscious thoughts about every aspect of their performance, many do say they have conscious thoughts about some aspects of it, especially when they're working hard to perform even better. And there are better ways of categorizing everyday performances like walking and bicycle-riding than "expertise," ways that help us talk more effectively about the authority of epistemic agents under various conditions.

Happily, some researchers have addressed these concerns by approaching the problem differently. Instead of starting with everyday activities and expanding to expert performance, some researchers start by studying expert performers and try to connect similarities in training, genetics, and social background. These approaches have resulted in several performance-based accounts of expertise that are different from and seemingly more powerful than the Dreyfuses'.

5 PERFORMANCE-BASED ACCOUNTS OF EXPERTISE – PART 2

The Psychology of Expert Performance

> *You would fain be victor at the Olympic games, you say. Yes, but weigh the conditions, weigh the consequences; then and then only, lay to your hand—if it be for your profit. You must live by rule, submit to diet, abstain from dainty meats, exercise your body perforce at stated hours, in heat or in cold; drink no cold water, nor, it may be, wine. In a word, you must surrender yourself wholly to your trainer, as though to a physician.*
>
> (Epictetus, *The Golden Sayings of Epictetus*, CIV, trans. Hastings Crossley, 1909–14)

In this chapter, I turn to Anders Ericsson's research on "deliberate practice" as the key to explaining expert performance (5.1). Ericsson argues that a certain type of practice creates thousands upon thousands of mental representations of an act performed correctly. As the expert performs, they draw on these representations subconsciously, which allows them to perform the activity quickly and smoothly—unlike a novice. Ericsson's account has proved powerful across a number of domains, and it is, arguably, the current dominant psychological theory of expertise. But that does not mean it is without its limitations. I take a brief aside in 5.2 to assess whether Ericsson's research contradicts psychologist Mihaly Csikszentmihalyi's work on the concept of "flow." Taking cues from psychologist Angela Duckworth, I conclude that they are best understood as offering complementary explanations for different aspects of expert performance. In section 5.3, I discuss some important criticisms of Ericsson's deliberate practice approach, highlighting research that suggests genetics plays a much larger role in superior performance than Ericsson and colleagues acknowledge.

In the final sections (5.4–5.5), I review work on expertise by psychologists Robin Hogarth, Philip Tetlock, and Gary Klein. Although most researchers largely accept Ericsson's findings, the work of these three suggests reasons to think that, for some types of expertise, deliberate practice must be supplemented with additional training strategies. For example, the sort of skills that Tetlock helps people develop go well beyond the limits of what Ericsson and colleagues acknolwedge for deliberate practice. And few of Tetlock's training strategies meet the strict demands of deliberate practice strategies. Klein, on the other hand, is less concerned about the strict demands of deliberate practice and more with its general form. He suggests ways to extend the spirit of deliberate practice into largely unstructured domains.

5.1 Deliberate Practice

Among psychologists who study expertise, there are optimists and pessimists. Pessimists purport to show evidence that expertise is very rare and most people whom we think are experts are not. Optimists, on the other hand, purport to show either that expertise is quite plausible, even if the demographic of experts is rather small, or that it is more widespread than we typically acknowledge. Pessimists draw on research like the heuristics and biases literature that shows how even experts are subject to irrational belief-forming processes and work that shows how often experts get it wrong, such as Philip Tetlock's (2005) research showing that financial advisors choose stock options with a success rate no better than dart-playing chimps.

Optimists, on the other hand, point to the success stories—people we know are experts, such as chess grandmasters and Olympic athletes—and study how they got to be experts. They then take these findings and try to replicate them in other domains to see if they've hit upon the right combination of criteria.

Despite their disagreement, optimists and pessimists tend to agree on at least three general points that can help point us in a constructive direction:

1 Expert performance (and for most, even expert judgment) exists in the world (even if rare), but it takes a long time to develop and is hard to come by.

2   Heuristics and biases affect everyone, but some people (almost miraculously) seem to overcome them.

3   Developing expertise and overcoming erroneous heuristics and biases involve a significant amount of experience and practice.

This consensus raises the question of what kind of experience and practice cultivates expertise. There are plenty of people who have been playing music for many years (like me) who are just mediocre (ahem). And there is evidence that some people—even putative experts—perform worse as they gain more experience (Choudhry et al. 2005). Interestingly, there is almost unanimous agreement among optimists and pessimists alike that the most successful approach to developing expertise, when it is possible to apply it, is what psychologist K. Anders Ericsson calls *deliberate practice*.

In the 1980s, Ericsson and colleague William G. Chase conducted some experiments on memorizing numbers (Ericsson, Chase, and Faloon 1980; Ericsson and Chase 1982; Ericsson 1985). At the time, psychologists thought that eight or nine digits was about the most someone could hear and then repeat back immediately. Over the course of two years, one of their test subjects learned to hear and repeat back eighty-two digits. These results have ballooned into international competitions, where competitors routinely memorize over a thousand numbers.

Ericsson was convinced that the "nature" view of talent is mistaken. He hypothesized that no matter what your genetic endowment, with the right kind of training, you can become a superior performer. Further, he suspected that there is no inborn limit to how much you can improve. If you continue to apply the principles of deliberate practice, there is no reason you cannot keep improving over your entire life. So, he expanded his research from memory exercises to musical instruments and dance.

For the sake of experimental design, Ericsson and colleagues construct an operational definition of expertise as "superior performance." What "superior performance" means has varied somewhat over the years. In a 1994 study, admittedly for the sake of identifying a metric, Ericsson and Neil Charness stipulated that expertise is performance that is "two standard deviations above the mean" in a domain or, in other words, somewhat fewer than the top 1 percent of performers in a domain:

> Some type of metric is of course required to identify *superior performance*. The statistical term *outlier* may be a useful heuristic for judging superior performance. Usually, if someone is performing at

least two standard deviations above the mean level in the population, that individual can be said to be performing at an expert level. In the domain of chess (Elo 1986), the term *expert* is defined as a range of chess ratings (2000–2199) approximately two to three standard deviations (200 rating points) above the mean (1600 rating points) and five to six standard deviations above the mean of chess players starting to play in chess tournaments. (731)

Ericsson and Robert Pool (2016) leave the concept of "superior" much vaguer, allowing reading, novel writing, poetry writing, and medicine to count—domains for which there is no way to establish competence of two standard deviations above the mean. Importantly, though, Ericsson and colleagues need not be committed to any strict criterion. Their aim is to demonstrate that, through deliberate practice, anyone can ascend to some of the highest levels of performance in almost any domain. And according to them, regardless of what counts as the "highest levels," there is no upper limit on how much you can achieve.

In 1993, with a slightly vague notion of expertise as superior performance, Ericsson and two other colleagues conducted two groundbreaking studies on violin and piano that changed the way psychologists—and most of the world—talk about expertise (Ericsson, Krampe, and Tesch-Römer 1993). In their primary experiment, they carefully curated three groups of violin students—the best, the good, and the just good enough—from a music conservatory. They found many similarities in their backgrounds—all had started taking lessons around eight years old (374), all decided to be musicians around age fifteen (374), and they all spent about fifty hours a week in music-related activities (playing for fun, playing with others, taking lessons, giving lessons, etc.) (375). But the top two groups practiced on their own around twenty-four of those hours, while the bottom group practiced just over nine hours on their own (375–6). But what really separated the top two groups was the amount of practice each student had accumulated *before coming to the conservatory*. By age eighteen, the best violinists accumulated an average of 7,410 hours of practice, while the good and good enough groups accumulated only 5,301 and 3,420, respectively. By twenty, the best violinists had put in around ten thousand hours of practice—exactly what Simon and Chase said it took to be a grandmaster at chess, though, as we will see below, Ericsson and Pool (2016: 110) note that these twenty-year-old violinists were not yet masters.

Nevertheless, these findings were so influential that they broke the boundaries of academic research and inspired journalist Malcolm Gladwell to make Ericsson's findings a central theme of his 2008 book *Outliers*, in which Gladwell coined the now-famous "ten-thousand-hour rule" of expertise. Gladwell interprets Ericsson as arguing that just about anyone can become an expert at something if they spend at least ten thousand hours doing it. But Ericsson and Pool (2016) correct Gladwell, pointing out that the specific amount of time is not the key to becoming a superior performer. Gladwell apparently focused on a rather arbitrary figure in Ericsson and colleagues' (1993) conclusion:

> [He] could just as easily have mentioned the average amount of time the best violin students had practiced by the time they were eighteen—approximately seventy-four hundred hours—but he chose to refer to the total practice time they had accumulated by the time they were twenty .... And, either way, at eighteen or twenty, these students were nowhere near masters of the violin. (2016: 110)

Ericsson and Pool say that the number of practice hours necessary for expertise varies from domain to domain: "I don't know exactly how many hours of practice the best digit memorizers put in today before they get to the top, but it is likely well under ten thousand" (2016: 110).

Based on his own experiments and his review of others, Ericsson came to the additional conclusion that it is not merely practice that develops expertise, but a specific *type* of practice. Rather than ten to fifty thousand hours of *practice*, as Simon and Chase hypothesized, expertise requires some thousands of hours of *deliberate* practice.

To get a sense of how deliberate practice works, consider two tennis players. One is a hobbyist we'll call Elena. Elena goes out on the court a couple of times a week with a friend. She plays hard and wants to improve, and her friend is slightly better than she is, so she often feels challenged. She takes a few lessons from the local tennis coach and watches a few YouTube videos on techniques. But mostly she plays with her friend. Every now and then, she makes a marvelous stroke and returns an especially difficult serve. Her backhand improves some, as do her returns close to the net. She now feels comfortable with her game. Elena wins some and she loses some, and despite experimenting with different grips and swings, and doing exercises to increase her strength, this is roughly how things continue for Elena. Ericsson calls this kind of practice "purposeful."

The second, whom we'll call Asali, practiced the way Elena did for a while. Then she started taking lessons from a local coach. She learned some swings that worked for her and started practicing them four to five times a week. If she didn't have a partner, she would rent a machine to serve to her. She started taking videos of herself to watch her movements, and she made slight adjustments when something didn't look right. Then she joined a league and started playing with people who were slightly better than she. Asali watched their footwork and tried to imitate it. Every time Asali noticed a problem area—with her forehand or serve—she focused on getting better in that one area for a few weeks until she improved. Several months later, she was regularly beating the people who used to be better than her in her league. She is now considering training for a local competition.

Note that both Elena and Asali practice; they put in the time. They are also both determined; they want to get better and take steps to improve. Elena, though, hits a plateau and can't seem to break through it. Asali adds something that Elena doesn't, namely, a strategy for getting feedback on specific aspects of her game and then working to improve those specific aspects, a little at a time. Whereas Elena tries to improve her whole game at once, Asali figures that this is too vague of a goal. She knows the game is made up of a lot of little skills that add up to the whole performance. Ericsson says that Elena's purposeful practice works, but only up to a point. Asali, on the other hand, is engaged in "deliberate practice," and this is what Ericsson argues is the key to superior performance, that is, to expertise.

5.1.1 The Principles of Deliberate Practice

According to Ericsson and Pool, there are two key ways deliberate practice differs from purposeful practice. First, the domain must be "well developed," by which Ericsson means that there is clearly a domain of practice in which some people have excelled and others have not, such as "musical performance …, ballet and other sorts of dance, chess, and many individual and team sports" (Ericsson and Pool 2016: 98). What doesn't count? Domains where either excellence cannot be directly linked with performance or there are "no objective criteria for superior performance" (98). "Pretty much anything in which there is little or no direct competition, such as gardening and other hobbies, for instance, and many of the jobs in today's workplace—business manager, teacher, electrician, engineer, consultant, and so on" (98).[1]

Second, unlike purposeful practice, deliberate practice requires a teacher, trainer, or coach. This means that, not only must the domain be well-defined, but there must be a long enough history of practice in the domain that there are teachable techniques for improvement. These two features draw "a clear distinction between purposeful practice—in which a person tries very hard to push himself or herself to improve—and practice that is both purposeful and *informed*" (98, italics theirs). What does deliberate practice look like? Ericsson and Pool offer seven principles.

Deliberate practice:

1. Develops skills, using known techniques, that other superior performers are already employing
2. Happens outside your comfort zone, requiring "near-maximal effort, which is generally not enjoyable"
3. Has well-defined goals that can be achieved by improving isolated parts of the performance (rather than "some vague overall improvement")
4. Requires "full attention and conscious actions"
5. Requires feedback from a trainer or coach and changes in behavior based on that feedback
6. Produces and depends on effective mental representations (which I will explain in more detail below)
7. Involves "building or modifying previously acquired skills by focusing on particular aspects of those skills and working to improve them" (99–100)

On the face of it, this is an odd list. Principle 6 seems to be more about how deliberate practice *works* than what it *is*. For example, if it turned out that Ericsson were wrong about the mechanism by which deliberate practice works, it seems he could still defend it as a strategy by which people become superior performers. Principle 7 seems part of 3, so I am not sure why it is a separate "principle." And 5 seems too restrictive (and perhaps implausible, since there are ample examples of people who became superior performers without formal coaching or training). And it is especially odd given that Ericsson and Pool allow a range of mechanisms for getting the necessary feedback for improvement. In one section of their book, they explain how to train if you don't have a teacher, and they give an example of how Benjamin Franklin became a great writer by constructing exercises for himself that continuously pushed him out of his comfort zone. Further, they acknowledge that there are ample training opportunities available at the click of a mouse:

> Fortunately, we live in a time when it is easy to go to the Internet and find training techniques for most of the common skills that people are interested in and quite a few that are not so common at all. Want to improve your puck-handling skills in hockey? It's on the Internet. Want to be a better writer? On the Internet. To solve a Rubik's Cube really fast? Internet. Of course, you have to be careful about the advice—the Internet offers just about everything except quality control. (157)

Ericsson's point, it seems, is not so much about having a teacher as it is about getting the right kind of feedback and knowing how to use that feedback to inform future practice.

Principle 2 is emphasized throughout Ericsson and his colleagues' work. In contrast to the idea that expertise involves nonmindedness, all the subjects in Ericsson's studies report conscious, concentrated effort, much of which isn't fun when they are engaged in deliberate practice. Notably, as we will see below in 6.9, this near-maximal effort occurs while people are in the process of becoming experts and when experts push themselves to greater degrees of competence. They did not ask participants what they experienced when playing for fun or when they were performing pieces they knew well.

Note that nothing like the "ten-thousand-hour rule" is on this list. Ericsson is dedicated to breaking the myth that it's the hours that matter. Some people will improve immensely long before ten thousand hours; for others, it may take a bit longer.

5.1.2 Deliberate Practice and Mental Representations

How does deliberate practice work? In contrast to the Dreyfus account, which is largely grounded in the phenomenology of expert performance, Ericsson and colleagues offer a psychological theory of the development of expertise. But like the Dreyfus account, deliberate practice does result in something similar to what the Dreyfuses call embodiment. Deliberate practice encourages the brain to form *mental representations* of a performance that are stored in long-term memory. Mental representations are chunks of related information that are meaningful in the course of an activity.[2] They are immediately recognized as meaningful when they are encountered.

The importance of mental representations is demonstrated in experiments where grandmaster chess players encounter different chess boards arranged in different ways, some standard arrangements that would result from normal game play and some non-standard arrangements. When shown standard arrangements and asked to make a move, the grandmasters can move within seconds. But when shown a board where the chess pieces are arranged randomly, in a way that the rules of chess prevent, or a standard chess arrangement that is turned 90°, grandmasters are reduced to novice-level decision-making (Chase and Simon 1973; Gobet and Charness 2006; Bartlett, Boggan, and Krawczyk 2013). They take longer to move, and they make more mistakes. This suggests that the grandmasters typically draw subconsciously from millions of on-demand images of boards to make lightning-fast moves.

Building on early chess research by de Groot and Simon and Chase, Ericsson and colleagues argue that mental representations accumulate over time and become accessible at speeds faster than conscious reflection—they become, in effect, intuitive, or what Daniel Kahneman calls the result of System 1 cognitive processing. However, unlike the "natural" intuitions Kahneman describes, which are often biased or faulty, these System 1 processes accumulate through intentional training, and are thus less subject to the sorts of errors for which Kahneman and colleagues are famous (see Stichter 2015).

Mental representations also allow experts to plan complicated procedures, like surgeries, rock climbing routes, and musical performances. Not only do experts perform better than novices, they plan better. With a rich fund of background information and mental representations to draw from, experts form more detailed plans and handle unforeseen obstacles better than novices (Ericsson and Pool 2016: 72–6).

5.1.3 Limitations of Deliberate Practice

Ericsson and colleagues admit a number of limitations of deliberate practice. First, your ability to form high-quality mental representations changes with age. While Ericsson and Pool say "there are relatively few absolute limitations on what is possible for people who begin training as adults ... [they admit] expertise in some fields is simply unattainable for anyone who doesn't start training as a child" (2016: 194). These domains usually involve physical activity, such as distance running, ballet dancing, and baseball pitching (195–6). Further, "with increasing age we lose flexibility, we become more prone to injury, and we take longer to heal. We slow down. Athletes typically attain their peak performance sometime in their twenties" (194–5). But we also know that adult brains are less "plastic" than child brains, so that learning cognitive domains, like other languages and mathematics, can take much more time and energy (45).

Second, deliberate practice in one type of task can lead to loss of competence in other tasks. "In many cases people who have developed one skill or ability to an extraordinary degree seem to have regressed in another area" (45–6). This emphasizes the "domain specific" nature of deliberate practice (60) and also explains why chess expertise drops off when experts are presented with non-standard arrangements.

Third, you must keep up deliberate practice or you will lose your skill level. Dozens of experiments, from medicine to sports, show that people who stop improving—even if they maintain their current level of practice—usually lose competence in their domain (46–7; 132–7; 195).

And fourth, Ericsson and Pool admit that the majority of benefits of deliberate practice are limited to a narrow set of domains (2016: 136–7). If a domain does not have a well-developed body of knowledge and skills which are available, and which a teacher could use to help an aspiring expert excel, deliberate practice will not produce the results it does in, say, tennis or chess. Further, deliberate practice is not possible in domains that require complex judgments, such as business management, fiction writing, and political forecasting. Nevertheless, they seem to allow that there are experts in some of these domains. They argue that, even when deliberate practice cannot be strictly followed, the principles of deliberate practice do offer some benefit to anyone in any domain: "This is the basic blueprint for getting better in any pursuit: get as close to deliberate practice as you can" (2016: 103). This may strike us as surprising given their criticism of Gladwell. If there are other routes to expertise, perhaps the ten-thousand-hour rule is not "off the mark" so much as "another path."

5.2 Has Ericsson Stopped the *Flow*? The Ericsson-Csikszentmihalyi Debate

Before we look at objections to the deliberate practice account, it is worth considering what seems to many an implication of the view, namely, that it flatly contradicts the Dreyfuses' claim that expert performance is something you "lose yourself in," where your actions seem to place outside your conscious attention. A foremost proponent of nonmindedness in expert performance is psychologist Mihaly Csikszentmihalyi. Over decades of studying and working with experts, Csikszentmihalyi (1975, 1990) developed a theory of expert performance around what he calls, interchangeably, "autotelic experience," "optimal experience," and "flow":

> The autotelic experience is one of complete involvement of the actor with [their] activity. The activity presents constant challenges. There is no time to get bored or to worry about what may or may not happen. A person in such a situation can make full use of whatever skills are required and receives clear feedback to [their] actions; hence, [they] belong[] to a rational cause-and-effect system in which what [they] do[] has realistic and predictable consequences. (1975: 36)

Although the Dreyfuses talk about nonmindedness in terms of "flow," they do not elaborate on the rich psychological processes involved. Csikszentmihalyi, on the other hand, offers a robust account of it.

In the flow experience, there is a sense that your skills are adequate for coping with the challenges presented by a goal-directed, rule-bounded performance that provides clear cues as to how well you are performing. The phenomenon that the Dreyfuses call nonmindedness enters the picture as an indication you have entered the flow state: "Perhaps the clearest sign of flow is the merging of action and awareness" (Csikszentmihalyi 1975: 38).

In contrast, we have seen that deliberate practice is rarely nonminded, it is always challenging, and it is not always enjoyable. So, on one side there are decades of research showing that expert performance is nonminded and pleasurable, and on the other, decades of research suggesting the opposite. What do we do with this tension?

In 2006, Ericsson and Csikszentmihalyi gave a joint presentation at the University of Pennsylvania, where each outlined their perspectives in light of the other's comments. Here was a prime opportunity to sort out some of the details. But, in typical scholarly fashion, they did not reach a compromise. Psychologist Angela Duckworth, who helped organize that event, found the conclusion anticlimactic:

> Somehow, the dialogue I hoped would resolve this conundrum played out as two separate presentations—one on deliberate practice and the other on flow—spliced together. ... I found myself a little disappointed. It wasn't the drama I missed, it was the resolution. I still didn't have an answer to my question: Is expert performance a matter of arduous and not-so-fun-in-the-moment exertion, or can it be effortless and joyous? (2016: 130)

However, something important did come from this event. Duckworth began gathering data in light of her own research on a concept she calls "grit" (the degree of determination and direction you have in pursuing a goal) and assessing it in light of Ericsson's and Csikszentmihalyi's findings. Her conclusion? They are not incompatible views; they simply describe two different aspects of the process of expert performance.

> There's no contradiction here, for two reasons. First, deliberate practice is a behavior, and flow is an experience. Anders Ericsson is talking about what experts *do*; Mihaly Csikszentmihalyi is talking about how experts *feel*. Second, you don't have to be doing deliberate practice and experiencing flow at the same time. (2016: 131, italics hers)

Reading their accounts side-by-side, it is surprising that they did not make this point explicitly in their presentation. Ericsson describes performance that helps experts improve, that pushes them from less to more competence. As Duckworth explains it, "You're in 'problem solving' mode, analyzing everything you do to bring it closer to the ideal ... You're getting feedback, and a lot of that feedback is about what you're doing wrong" (131–2). And some experts are engaged in that sort of practice all the time (e.g., Olympic runners and swimmers), so there is little opportunity to enter the flow state.

Csikszentmihalyi, on the other hand, describes performance at the level of your competence—the challenge meets you where you are but doesn't goad you to improve. "Though you are concentrating one hundred percent, you're not at all in 'problem solving' mode. ... You're getting feedback, but because the level of the challenge *just meets* your current level of skill, that feedback is telling you that you're doing a lot right" (132, italics hers). When the goal is just performance and not competitive, as when musicians play a normal concert and dancers do a routine they've perfected, there is much less need for deliberate-practice-style performance. Experts are free to enjoy the moment without the pressure to improve.

Of course, as research shows, if experts shoot only for the flow state, they can lose their expertise or stagnate at their current level of performance. But this is no indicator that Csikszentmihalyi is wrong about how expertise facilitates the flow state.

But we should be a bit careful here about blessing Duckworth's happy marriage. Flow states do not only occur in expert performance. They can occur any time a challenge is sufficient for your current level of competence, and Csikszentmihalyi (1990) gives some unusual examples, such as "the feeling a father has when his child for the first time responds to his smile" (3), solitude and spending time with friends (164–91), and your everyday work: "In theory, any job could be changed so as to make it more enjoyable by following the prescriptions of the flow model" (154). Surely, no one is an expert at playing with their children or hanging out with friends. This raises some questions about the relationship between flow and expertise beyond the scope of this book. But it also opens Csikszentmihalyi to a version of a critique posed for the Dreyfuses. The Dreyfuses seem to think that flow is necessary for expertise, and we saw evidence that that is not so. Csikszentmihalyi seems to present flow as a sufficient condition for expertise, but these examples belie that. At best, we can say that flow states tend to occur in expert performance when that performance is at the upper limits of their competence, but it also tends to occur at the upper limits of anyone's competence, irrespective of whether they are an expert. Flow seems to be something distinct from expertise.

5.3 Objections to the Deliberate Practice Account

As we should expect with any account, the deliberate practice approach faces a number of criticisms. And again, rather than assessing whether the whole account stands or falls, I am interested in the bits that uncontroversially survive criticism. While most scholars agree with the broad outlines of Ericsson and colleagues' findings (that many hours of structured practice improves performance), there is significant disagreement over some of the details, including whether the performance improvement offered by deliberate practice is sufficient for superior performance, that is, for expertise as Ericsson and colleagues define it. Here, I will sketch three concerns about deliberate practice, two based in the idea that biology has a non-negligible role to play in expert performance and one based on the limited scope of benefits offered by deliberate practice.

5.3.1 The Objection from Genetics, Part 1: Minds Are Born Different

Although researchers have long left behind the idea that "genius," "talent," and "expertise" are gifts from God, many researchers still argue that biological inheritance plays a significant role in expert performance. Some argue, for example, that there are genetic bases for musical expertise (Mosing et al. 2018; Tan et al. 2018), some that there is a role for personality traits in explaining drawing expertise (Drake and Winner 2018), and still others that there are genetic connections between autism and child prodigies (Ruthsatz et al. 2018).

Drake and Winner (2018), for example, define what they take to be artistic "procosity" in children as having a drawing ability that is about two years ahead of their peers (competence with shapes, fluid ability to merge shapes into complex images, ability to create the illusion of three dimensions, etc.), they have a compulsion to draw (and therefore practice), and they share many biological characteristics with savants (are left-handed, have visual–spatial strengths, have linguistic deficits, all of which are known to have genetic bases). They then conclude that exceptional drawing in children cannot be explained by deliberate practice because children have not engaged in deliberate practice.

Unfortunately, their findings do not constitute evidence against the deliberate practice account. First, they admit that none of the children in their study were experts or superior performers, and they did not correlate precocity with expertise or superior performance in adults. Further, their results are consistent with the claims of proponents of deliberate practice that no one starts as a master (even savants), and with evidence that kids who are behind in childhood may catch up in adolescence or adulthood. The only relevant piece of evidence is that there may be a genetic component to the *willingness* to put in more effort, or grit, to overcome plateaus and obstacles to superior performance. But Ericsson and Pool (2016: 165–79) acknowledge this potential variable and argue, along with Angela Duckworth (2016), that "grittiness" can be trained, as well.

Some attempt to undermine deliberate practice by showing that IQ scores—which are stipulated to be biological and not a result of deliberate practice—also predict expertise. Ericsson and Pool admit that higher IQ makes some difference in how quickly people develop chess skill, but they find that once a person masters the game, differences in IQ do not predict performance, and a higher IQ does not predict advantage over players of lower IQ (2016: 230–1). Philip Tetlock and Dan Gardner (2015) present similar evidence with expert political forecasters. "Although superforecasters [their term for expert political forecasters] are well above average [70–80 percent above average], they did not score off-the-charts high and most fall well short of so-called genius territory, a problematic concept often arbitrarily defined as the top 1%, or an IQ of 135 and up" (109).

However, psychologist Jonathan Wai and education researcher Harrison Kell present evidence that people in the top 1 percent of intelligence are highly likely to be successful, hold positions of power, or work in "elite" careers or as "professional experts." Further, they argue, contra Ericsson and Pool, that there is no threshold of success correlated with IQ, rather the higher one's IQ, the more successful they are likely to be.

Unfortunately, there are a number of problems with these conclusions. First, even if people with high IQs occupy positions of power or prestige, this does not show that they are experts (many psycho-social factors are responsible for socioeconomic standing and educational privilege— moral corruption may be as strongly correlated with positions of power, we just don't know). Further, of those who are experts, their research does not show that they did not engage in deliberate practice. Further, Wai and Kell do not assess their sample against the base rate of people in these elite positions. They only say "roughly half of the people in these positions of leadership and power were in the top 1% in ability" (79). Is that better than chance? What about the remaining 50 percent? How did they achieve their status as powerful if not by intelligence? And, of course, all this ignores the many studies showing that IQ tests are invalid instruments (see Hampshire et al. 2012, for just one of these).

As of right now, this sort of genetic argument against deliberate practice doesn't seem promising. But this is not the only type of "nature" view of expertise in the offing. Irrespective of how genetics might affect performance directly, there is at least one indirect way it seems to affect it significantly.

5.3.2 The Objection from Genetics, Part 2: Body Types Affect Ability

One of Ericsson's central claims for deliberate practice is that it defies the traditional assumption that there is a predetermined biological limit to what individual humans can achieve (apart, of course, from his and Pool's concessions to age). His original experiments with number memorization have inspired others to excel even further. In 2016, Alex Mullen became the first person ever to memorize over 3,000 numbers in an hour (International Association of Memory). And whereas most people can do 40 to 50 pushups with practice, and maybe 100, Minoru Yoshida did 10,507 nonstop in 1980. In 1993, Charles Servizio set the world record for pushups, doing 46,001 in 21 hours and 21 minutes. There are even people, like Jan Kareš, who can do more than 4,600 pull-ups, suggesting that we drastically underestimate what the body can do (Ericsson and Pool 2016: 34). But do all activities admit of this extreme degree of excellence? Could these people just be special in some biological/genetic sense?

Consider Olympic foot racing. In 1904, the winner of the Olympic marathon finished in just under three hours and twenty-nine minutes. In 2012, the winner finished in a hair over two hours and eight minutes, almost an hour-and-a-half faster. Have new types of training made all the difference? Journalist David Epstein (2014a, 2014b) says no. In 1936, Jesse Owens ran the 100-meter dash in 10.2 seconds. In 2013, Usain Bolt finished in 9.77 seconds. According to Epstein (2014b), Owens would have still had fourteen feet to go after Bolt crossed the finish line. Has human performance improved that much over seventy-seven years? Consider that:

> Usain Bolt started by propelling himself out of blocks down a specially fabricated carpet designed to allow him to travel as fast as humanly possible. Jesse Owens, on the other hand, ran on cinders, the ash from burnt wood, and that soft surface stole far more energy from his legs

as he ran. Rather than blocks, Jesse Owens had a gardening trowel that he had to use to dig holes in the cinders to start from. (Epstein 2014b)

Biomechanical analysis suggests that, if Owens had been running with the same advantages as Bolt, "he wouldn't have been 14 feet behind, he would have been within one stride" (Epstein 2014b).

This suggests that, in some types of activity, deliberate practice (for that's what Olympic athletes engage in if anyone does) still operates within certain structural limitations of human beings. In the case of advancements in running, the differences seem to be more technological than anything. And in this book, we have seen how technology (expert systems) can enhance performance. The same goes for technologies like running surfaces and training tools. In some cases, the key to improved performance is more about training techniques and equipment than the time spent. For example, in the 1200s, Roger Bacon argued that it would be impossible to learn all of mathematics in less than thirty or forty years. But all of known math then was roughly equivalent to what is taught in one high school calculus class, and the only method for learning in Bacon's time was self-study. Today, students have teachers and strategies and calculators, and they can learn it in one year.[3] This doesn't mean students are smarter. The much more likely conclusion is that our tools for learning are better.

But there's more to the story. Once upon a time, sport scientists thought the "average" body type (literally, the bell curve average of all body types) was the ideal body type for all sports. It turns out, that is drastically mistaken. As sport scientists got savvy, the "average elite shot putter is now 2.5 inches taller and 130 pounds heavier than the average international high jumper" (Epstein 2014a: 116) and over "the last thirty years, elite female gymnasts have shrunk from 5'3" on average to 4'9" (2014a: 117). And these changes are found across all athletic sports. Basketball players got taller, the forearms of water polo players got longer, swimmers got longer torsos and shorter legs, and runners got longer legs and shorter torsos. This shouldn't have been surprising—the guy with the thick chest in the gym can always out-bench-press the thin-chested guy, no matter how much the thin-chested guy trains. Nevertheless, body-type-specific selection for competitive sports has become so widespread that sport scientists Kevin Norton and Tim Olds (2001) dubbed it the "Big Bang of Body Types." This suggests that genetics has as much or more to do with superior performance in some domains than deliberate practice.

5.3.3 The Scope Problem: Deliberate Practice Defines Expertise Too Narrowly

All of Ericsson and colleagues' research has been lab-based (not all was technically in a lab, but lab-style, with surveys given under controlled observations). Ericsson has been explicit that deliberate practice is limited to well-defined domains where techniques for training are well known. And yet, there are training programs that purportedly help firefighters and military commanders develop expertise, despite the fact that they work primarily in novel situations. Further, Epstein (2019) offers a dozen or so examples of superior performers who did not follow the deliberate practice model, including Duke Ellington, Roger Federer, and Dave Brubeck. What should we make of examples of expertise that do not follow the deliberate practice model?

As careful scientists, Ericsson and Charness (1997) note that they "will … not seriously consider anecdotes or unique events, including major artistic and scientific innovations, because they cannot be repeatedly reproduced on demand and hence fall outside the class of phenomena that can be studied by experimental methods" (5), and this is admirable. However, given that there do seem to be experts in these natural environments, and given that such expertise seems to be acquired on a fairly reliable basis, there are reasons to think that the competence deliberate practice cultivates is too narrow to capture even what Ericsson and colleagues regard as expert performance.

5.4 Kind Worlds and Wicked Worlds

The limitations of deliberate practice (those that Ericsson and colleagues acknowledge and those they don't) remind us that expert performance takes place in a messier world than we can replicate in a lab. With tasks like playing the violin, playing chess, and feats of memory, the task itself is not dependent on any particular environment; the activities are well-defined (i.e., we know what it means to play the violin well and the techniques it involves), the goals of the activities are well-defined, and success is easily measured. To be sure, adding some environmental factors, like high-stakes competition or different climate, can affect performance. But once the basics of the activity are mastered, an expert can then deliberately practice in stressful environments. Cognitive psychologist Robin Hogarth (2001, 2010) calls environments like these "kind learning environments," environments where the "feedback [that one gets from a performance] links outcomes directly to the appropriate actions or judgments and is both accurate and plentiful" (Hogarth, Lejarraga, and Soyer 2015: 379). In his (2010), Hogarth describes kind environments as "those where the information tacitly processed leads to valid inferences, for example, when the sample of instances the person has encountered is representative of the environment in which the ensuing intuitive judgment is applied. Feedback is neither missing nor distorted, and so on" (343). Laboratory experiments, to the degree that they are well-constructed, are paradigm cases of kind environments. Most of the extenuating variables have been controlled so that outcomes are linked (hopefully causally) with the target behavior.

In contrast, Hogarth calls "wicked environments" "situations in which feedback in the form of outcomes of actions or observations is poor, misleading, or even missing" (Hogarth, Lejarraga, and Soyer 2015: 379). In these cases, "samples of experience are not representative and feedback might be missing or distorted. Worse still, mistaken beliefs can lead to dysfunctional actions in the form of self-fulfilling prophecies" (2010: 343, citations removed). Consider "survivorship bias," which is a fallacy that occurs by studying only the population that has achieved some target, such as celebrity status, while ignoring those who didn't make it. If you only focus on successful cases, you can miss relevant factors that impeded the success of countless others (or miss the fact that luck played a much bigger role than anyone realized). Without a way to control for success conditions, trying to learn from, say, business gurus across a diversity of businesses in a diversity of markets is likely to be an exercise in confirmation bias.

Further, intuitions that are developed and work well in kind environments are likely to fail in wicked environments because of their inability to handle novelty (as when grandmaster chess players are reduced to novices when the board is turned 90°). As Hogarth (2010) explains, "Our naive human learning processes are remarkably well adapted to the regularities of the environments that we encounter. From the viewpoint of establishing valid intuitions (in a predictive sense), this is both a great strength and a source of weakness" (343).

But even if the benefits of deliberate practice are limited to kind environments and the world is largely wicked, that doesn't mean there is a problem for deliberate practice. Perhaps there simply are no experts outside of kind domains. Perhaps their success conditions are just too fuzzy to develop anything like the competence we associate with expertise. Or maybe there are experts, but because we cannot study them in laboratory conditions, we cannot be certain who they are or how their expertise developed. Some suggest the famous "mystery" surrounding chicken sexing (distinguishing male and female chicks before obvious traits appear) is an example of what we might call *inscrutable expertise* (it has been described as a mystery as recently as Ray 2019). Chicken sexers have a 98 percent accuracy rating over about 1,000 chicks, but they seem unable to explain their methods. Without any explanation of chicken sexing success, deliberate practice can't get off the ground. Further, in domains like teaching and counseling, where variables outside the domain of practice are often far more influential than variables inside the domain of practice,[4] it is difficult to figure out what works and what doesn't. Sometimes we think we know *who* successful teachers are, but we cannot say *why*. The same seems true for domains like internal medicine, where any particular patient's complex array of conditions is unlikely to be found in a journal article and their idiosyncratic response to certain medicines is unknown. In these cases, decision-making proceeds by trial-and-error, making little changes within acceptable limits of risk with the aim of finding a combination of treatments that works. As sociologists Harry Collins and Trevor Pinch (2005) point out, bodies are "largely self-repairing entities" (7). "One never knows whether it is the last medical intervention that gave rise to the cure or whether the body would have cured itself anyway" (7).

5.5 Beyond Deliberate Practice: Additional Elements of Expert Performance

But the situation is not so dismal. There are also strategies for studying expertise in wicked environments. Despite the persistent air of myth surrounding chicken sexing, there have been teachable indicators since at least 1987 that, with practice, improve novice performance to almost expert competence (around 82 percent accuracy) (Biedermann and Shiffrar 1987). And, as noted earlier in this chapter, some psychologists have found ways to improve expert performance in firefighting and military command. So, if the deliberate practice account of expertise accurately describes expertise in kind environments, our world is largely wicked, *and there are uncontroversial examples of developing expertise in wicked environments*, then deliberate practice is insufficient as a general theory of expertise. But just because it is insufficient on its own does not mean it cannot be supplemented with tools that expand its general assumptions in ways that effectively explain expertise in wicked environments. In this section, we will look at two attempts to supplement deliberate practice to explain and develop expertise in wicked environments.

5.5.1 Philip Tetlock: Foxes, Hedgehogs, and Dispositions for Expertise

In 2005, psychologist Philip Tetlock concluded a multi-decade study of political and financial forecasting. He was interested in what he calls "good political judgment," by which he means the ability to predict events like who will win an election, how a foreign leader will react to a new policy, and the likelihood that one nation will attack another. His overall findings were dismal. Evidence showed that political and financial forecasters were no more accurate than chance (recall that Mizrahi [2013], appeals to this evidence, as we saw in Chapter 3). Tetlock's description—that they were no more accurate than monkeys throwing darts at a dartboard—became a popular jibe against financial advisors and election analysts.[5] As other psychologists had found, statistical prediction rules fared much better than the best experts in Tetlock's research (see Bishop and Trout 2005, for a brief history). But Tetlock didn't stop there.

Digging into his data, he found that some groups of forecasters did marginally better than others. People who thought in big-picture models, that is, principle-based reasoners who analyzed evidence in light of their understanding of a situation, did much more poorly than the other subgroup. He calls these big-picture reasoners "hedgehogs," following philosopher Isaiah Berlin's (1953) distinction between *hedgehogs*, who "know one big thing," and *foxes*, who "know many things." The fox group didn't approach a problem with a preconceived notion of how the world works. They took the evidence on its face, focused on the details of the situation, and then drew inferences from there. Fox-thinking outstripped hedgehog-thinking time and again, though it still didn't come close to the performance of the decision tools. But this got Tetlock thinking about how to improve fox-like thinking.

In 2011, Tetlock and Barbara Mellers started the Good Judgment Project to try to improve the forecasting of both military leaders and political forecasters (Tetlock and Gardner 2015). With a team of self-selected non-professionals, Tetlock faced off in a government-sponsored tournament against four teams of top intelligence researchers, including teams from MIT and University of Michigan. By the second year, his team outperformed the professional groups by margins between 30 and 78 percent (2015: 17–18). His work paid off. He not only discovered a group of people who could be trained into "superforecasters," he figured out how to train them. And their success wasn't correlated with IQ or a penchant for political trivia, but, much like Ericsson discovered, with a type of training.

Unlike Ericsson's environments—controlled laboratory experiments in well-defined domains—Tetlock's domain was the real, messy world of politics and business. Feedback was rarely immediate, and even when it was, it was hard to trace back to specific decision points. What Tetlock needed to find was a set of strategies that work to develop expertise in environments where deliberate practice doesn't.

This work culminated in eleven strategies that, when combined, improve performance in wicked environments (Tetlock and Gardner 2015: Appendix). For the sake of brevity, two of those are sufficient to demonstrate expert training independent of deliberate practice. The first is a strategy called "balancing the outside and inside views," first developed by Kahneman and Dan Lovallo (1993). "An inside view forecast is generated by focusing on the case at hand, by considering the plan and the obstacles to its completion, by constructing scenarios of future progress, and by extrapolating current trends" (1993: 25). In contrast, the outside view "ignores the details of the case at hand ... [and] focuses on the statistics of a class of cases chosen to be similar in relevant respects to the present one" (25). An example of taking the outside view is considering the base rate of an event rather than trying to assess its likelihood based on circumstantial clues. You may feel confident that your child will score highly on a standardized test, but if most children are average, the chances are good that your child is average, too. Learning the base rate should lead you to lower your confidence in your initial prediction by some percentage points.

This doesn't mean that the inside view has nothing to offer. If you're trying to predict whether someone will go to the movies tonight, you might start with the base rate: how many people go to the movies on nights like this? But if you have some inside information, such as that the person broke their leg today, that inside information trumps your base rate assessment. You can confidently predict that the person won't go to the movies no matter how high the base rate. Camerer and Johnson (1991: 204–5) call this kind of insider reasoning "broken-leg cues."

The point is that it is a mistake to take only the outside or the inside view. Forecasters do best, according to Tetlock and Gardner, when they start with the outside view (to prevent certain kinds of bias, like anchoring) and then move to the inside view, balancing the two against one another (what they call the "outside first" strategy).

A second strategy for improving forecasting expertise is to constantly update your judgment in light of new evidence, a strategy that Tetlock and Gardner call "perpetual beta." "Beta" is the term computer programmers use to describe a program that is still being developed and tested. Perpetual beta is the state of being in constant development and testing (2015: 174–90). The willingness to update and the tendency to update with fine-grained probabilities was a better indicator of accurate forecasting in every one of their test cases (192). The biggest difference between hedgehogs and foxes, they found, is that hedgehogs try to protect their pet theories while foxes trash them in light of contrary evidence. But they don't trash them wholesale. They are careful updaters, upgrading in small increments, taking the new evidence seriously while not forgetting the weight of the old. The key here is the disposition to keep your conclusions, beliefs, hypotheses, and guesses at arm's length, always subjecting them to new evidence, and always revising them as more evidence comes in.

Of course, a necessary component of perpetual beta is getting enough evidence to update with. Some types of decisions and evidence are so far removed from their effects that updating is almost impossible. Voters, for example, never *really* know whether a policy they vote for has the effects they want because the subsequent observations are not immediately tied to policy—there are innumerable variables that can make a policy seem successful that have nothing to do with the policy. Tetlock and Gardner give the example of police officers who become confident that they can tell whether a suspect is lying long before enough evidence could accumulate as feedback on their judgments (180–1). Their confidence increases independently of any evidence that they are actually better. Even in wicked environments, feedback is necessary for improvement.

How do these additional strategies work? Is there a psychological mechanism that underlies them, as we saw with deliberate practice? Like the Dreyfuses, Simon and Chase, and Ericsson and colleagues, Tetlock accepts that expert knowledge is largely tacit (i.e., abilities that either are not or cannot be expressed as propositions or rules). He also accepts the idea that practice trains intuitive (System 1) thinking, and that deliberate practice is the appropriate type of training for kind environments.

But here is where things get interesting. Tetlock suspects that intensive training engages slow, System 2 thinking, and that this slow, deliberate training is what conditions System 1 intuitions. "My sense is that some superforecasters are so well practiced in System 2 corrections—like stepping back to take the outside view—that these techniques have become habitual" (Tetlock and Gardner 2015: 236). Recall the thousands of unpleasant hours of deliberate practice. If Tetlock is right, then each practice session is engaging System 2 thinking, and in the process, forming mental representations. During a performance or competition, the expert is no longer working to improve but focused on performing in the environment they've trained for. This allows their intuitive, System 1 processes to take over and become the sort of nonminded expert performance that the Dreyfuses describe. More on this in Chapter 7.

Despite these additional training strategies, one might still wonder whether they are all just dependent on whether one is *genetically predisposed* to use them or not, that is, whether one was *born* a fox or a hedgehog. Perhaps these are biologically determined personality traits that are recalcitrant to training. That may be. Tetlock and Gardner admit that "not every superforecaster has every attribute" of a fox (192). However, they say there are "many paths to success and many ways to compensate for a deficit in one area with strength in another" (192). They agree with Ericsson and Pool and Duckworth that grit can be enhanced even if you start with a low store of it.

5.5.2 Gary Klein: Natural Decision-Making

A different alternative to deliberate practice was developed by psychologist Gary Klein, who spent many years studying decision-making in the wicked environments of firefighting and military commanding. Unlike Tetlock, Klein's strategies do not depart so starkly from Ericsson's. Klein employs four key elements of deliberate practice to explain and develop decision-making in wicked environments: tacit knowledge, mental models, the indispensability of feedback, and the benefits of good coaching (Klein 2003).

Like other psychologists who study this domain, Klein accepts that expert knowledge is largely tacit, and that intuitions are trained through experience. Unlike Ericsson and Tetlock, however, Klein is suspicious of the idea that training deliberative System 2 processes is involved in all types of expertise. "My own research suggests that people with experience rarely engage in the process of choosing among several options. Using their intuition, the patterns they have acquired, they usually identify an effective option as the first one they consider, based on the pattern-recognition process (Klein, Wolf, Militello, and Zsambok 1995; Klein, et al. 2010)" (Klein 2015: 165). It is unclear whether Klein thinks this is only true *after* an expert has acquired expertise or whether it also applies to the *process of developing* expertise.

Regardless of what he thinks about System 2 deliberation, Klein thinks intuitive accuracy can be strengthened through domain-specific exercises called "Tactical Decision Games," which include providing written responses to cases, role-play, team-based problem-solving, and on-the-job learning (where participants observe other experts, ask questions, and get feedback, much the way medical residents round with attending physicians in hospitals) (2015: 166-7). These games create an environment for practice and immediate feedback, which he argues builds "recognition" of scenarios. Then, when someone encounters a similar situation in real life, their intuition is primed to recognize it—what Klein and colleagues call "Recognition-Primed Decision Making" (Klein, Orasanu, Calderwood, and Zsambok 1992).

In addition to intuition, evidence shows that people who have explicit and thorough mental models of their task tend to perform more consistently than those without a thorough model (Yates et al. 2011). And we saw with deliberate practice that expert surgeons and rock climbers engage in more and better planning than novices. Klein thinks mental models can also be enhanced using tools such as "Cognitive Task Analysis" to help experts make explicit "the kinds of relationships and concepts that a person has a mental model about" and techniques to capture spatial and temporal relationships (Klein 2015: 167).

The idea seems to be that training can be designed in low-stakes environments that mimics the relevant decision-points and evidence encountered in high-stakes environments well enough to develop expertise in those high-stakes environments. This is similar to case-based education in medical schools, where students in controlled environments like simulations, role-play, case discussion, or rounds, are faced with low-stakes decisions about patient care. If the feedback on these cases itself matches reality in the relevant ways, medical students eventually develop into medical experts.

5.6 Summing Up

The central strength of performance-based accounts of expertise is that they have an extensive and largely consistent fund of empirical research findings that help define, explain, and train expertise in a wide variety of domains. These findings reveal two important insights: (1) domain-specific training and knowledge are crucial to expert-level performance, and (2) an explanation of expert authority requires much more than simply evidence that an expert is competent in a domain, it requires an explanation of why they are competent, that is, an account of the process by which they developed that competence.

Of course, empirical research on expertise is only as good as its analysis of relevant concepts. Despite a seeming agreement across researchers, definitions of what counts as "superior performance" vary widely, and whether any particular set of practices is "deliberate" over and above the way, say, athletes and musicians typically train, is not always clear. No one thought we needed decades of research to tell us that extensive, intense practice is correlated with better performance (even Aristotle made his case for training virtue by drawing an analogy with training for the Greek games!). But empirical research has enhanced our understanding of why this training works and also serves as a check on accounts that place too much emphasis on the cognitive aspects of expertise (knowledge, belief, justification, etc.) or too much emphasis on rule-based decision-making (i.e., expert systems).

An increasingly palpable gap in our discussion so far, apart from an emphasis on good coaching, is the role of society and expert communities in developing, enhancing, and identifying experts. Are domains essentially isolated from the society in which they exist? Is their validity immune from acceptance or rejection by others in their social context? Who determines what amount of accuracy or ability counts as expertise in the first place? To address these questions, we turn to social-role accounts of expertise.

6 SOCIAL ROLE ACCOUNTS OF EXPERTISE

> My dear Mrs. Alving, there are many occasions in life when one must rely upon others. Things are so ordered in this world; and it is well that they are. Otherwise, what would become of society?
>
> (Pastor Manders in Henrik Ibsen, *Ghosts*, Act One, 1881/1888, trans. William Archer)

In this chapter, I introduce the role of society in shaping both our understanding of expertise and experts' role in directing our lives. After distinguishing reputational from objective accounts of expertise (6.2), I review three social role accounts that purport to be objective: the "constructivist" account of Neil Agnew, Kenneth Ford, and Patrick Hayes (1994) (6.3), what I call the "public influence" account of Stephen Turner (2014) (6.4), and what Harry Collins calls the "social acquisition of tacit knowledge" account (2014: 61) (6.5). After exploring some criticisms of Collins's account (6.6), I close by highlighting how insights from social role theories might inform a general theory of expertise.

6.1 What Does Society Have to Do with Expertise?

So far, we have discussed expertise in largely individual terms—someone's cunning intelligence, someone's knowledge, someone's superior performance. But there is an important sense in which our epistemic community (people both inside and outside a domain) shapes what it means to be an expert and how expertise develops. There are at least two senses of "shaping expertise" at work here, and it is important to keep them separate.

In one sense, because some scholars treat "expert" and "professional" synonymously, what counts as expertise is artificially determined by whatever arbitrary profession someone defines—administrative assistant, associate vice president, social impact and community engagement coordinator, and so on. On these views, being able to do the job of an administrative assistant is tantamount (because one is a professional in that domain) to being an expert administrative assistant. The implication is that society shapes expertise by defining expertise in terms of being able to do a certain set of tasks. This is a rather minimal sense of "shaping expertise," as it does little more than define a domain. But it is also misleading, since simply being able to do one of these jobs is different from being highly competent in them. And not all of these jobs admit of expertise (because some tasks do not admit of expertise—walking the dog, getting the mail, etc.). To equate expert with professional undermines the distinction between basic and advanced know-how. Thus, this is not what I mean in this chapter when I say that society shapes expertise.

In another sense, domains become domains of expertise precisely because humans pay attention to them. Who would have thought that using brooms and buckets to make noise could be a domain of expertise? And yet the performance group STOMP has made it a specialized art. The implication of this is quite subtle. It means that domains are not made up solely of claims, practices, and methodologies; they also include how experts talk about their domain, what they find interesting or meaningful. How they weigh the significance of some of those claims. Harry Collins explains that he had this realization when he was spending time with physicists trying to learn gravitational wave physics:

> I can vouch for the fact that when physicists talk to each other, or when they sit on decision-making committees, they are not doing calculations and they are not doing experiments. They are talking the kind of talk that I learned to talk from hanging around: that is what feeds into their decision-making. … [And even when it comes to standard practices in physics] [I]t is mostly words that teach what is to be seen as the salient pattern. The world as it first impacts on the outermost layers of our senses is confused and featureless, but we use talk with others to learn how to break it up into the discrete objects that become the currency of the community of experts. (2014: 72–3)

And this talk can look different depending on where you are placed in the domain. Philosophy graduate students are taught to focus their research on projects that are "hot," meaning what certain subsets of philosophers are interested in reading and working on, and, therefore, what is more likely to get published. So, even though the question of say, whether universals are *ante rem* (as Plato thought) or *in re* (as Aristotle argued) is a perennial one, if philosophers at a time happen to be more interested in the ontology of color, the domain of metaphysics in philosophy will reflect that interest by making the latter debate more prominent in the literature than the former. As the landscape of the domain shifts, different philosophers become the gatekeepers for what counts as good philosophy.

There are similar influences outside domains. For example, which academic departments get or keep funding (several philosophy programs are cut each year), and which government agencies or organizations are willing to fund research on what topics. Furthermore, government restrictions on what kinds of research can be done under what contexts shape what it is possible to understand in a domain. And then, of course, public support for, or antagonism against, a domain (such as climate research, breast cancer research, marijuana research) can significantly boost or undermine the apparent credibility of researchers in those domains, irrespective of their actual education, training, and competence.

Further still, many domains of expertise depend for their success on other domains of expertise in which they are not and, if for no other reason than lack of time, could not be. Philosopher John Hardwig (1985: 346–7) gives an example of an experiment that required fifty work years just to gather the data, another sixty work years, over five geographic locations and forty physicists and technicians to interpret it, and ninety-nine total authors from various different specialties to complete. "Obviously," Hardwig says, "no one person could have done this experiment" (347). Philosopher Stephen Turner (2014) gives another example of what was called the "Homestake" experiment in South Dakota in the 1960s. "The knowledge relevant for the experiment was distributed among many people, with specialist knowledge and perhaps tacit knowledge that was not possessed by other members of the team working on the experiment" (267). Call this sort of mutual trust among experts to accomplish a complex task the phenomenon of *expert coordination*. Recall from section 3.4.3 that philosopher Moti Mizrahi's argument against appealing to experts was grounded partially on the claim that experts do not trust experts simply because they are experts. This is evidence that, not only is that not true, but expert coordination is essential to scientific research, and the ability to coordinate experts is itself a type of specialized expertise (recall "theoretical directing" expertise from 2.1).

It is in this second sense—that the way humans inside and outside expert domains pay attention to those domains affects those domains—that I mean society shapes expertise. But how does all this social influence inform an *account* of expertise? Does it make defining and developing expertise an essentially social phenomenon, such that all talk of knowledge and ability reduces to the subjective judgment of people who are themselves the products of stochastic social processes? Or is the social dimension of expertise simply a matter of how objective expertise is understood and received by society at large, and therefore, independent of whether someone is actually an expert or what it means, objectively, to be an expert?

6.2 Reputational vs. Objective Social Accounts

There is a widespread notion that the concept of expertise is overblown. Rather than being an objective state of competence in the world that deserves respect, expertise is often viewed as a term invoked to make some people seem more trustworthy than they are. There is a worry that we manufacture credentials and degrees in order to bolster our preconceived notions on a topic.

This suggests that expertise is nothing more than a manufactured social phenomenon. As philosopher Matt Stichter jokes, "If someone loudly declares 'I'm an expert', then we can always reply 'Only if we say you are'" (2015: 126). Political scientist Ben L. Martin (1973: 159) claims that "expertness is an ascribed quality, a badge, which cannot be manufactured and affected by an expert himself, but rather can only be received from another, a client."

Alvin Goldman (2018) calls this the "reputational" view of expertise: "A person is an expert only if s/he has a reputation for being one" (3). Sociologists Harry Collins and Robert Evans (2007) call it the "relational" view: "Relational approaches take expertise to be a matter of experts' relations with others. The notion that expertise is only an 'attribution'—the, often retrospective, assignment of a label—is an example of a relational theory" (2–3).

If expertise is purely reputational, that is, merely a "badge," as Martin puts it, this raises serious problems for the idea that expertise is "authoritative" in any objective sense—that is, in a way that suggests we should trust doctors and climate scientists because they are objectively competent rather than because society has granted them the role "doctor" and "climate scientist." Computer science researchers Neil M. Agnew, Kenneth M. Ford, and Patrick J. Hayes (1994) argue that "snake oil salesmen *are* experts on this view. Expertise is not synonymous with knowledge. Expertise, unlike knowledge, does not reside in the individual, but rather emerges from a dynamic interaction between the individual and his physical/cultural domain" (67, italics theirs). If expertise is grounded on nothing but reputation, then expertise carries only pragmatic authority, the authority people let other people have in order to accomplish certain goals. The authority that people give others because it is convenient or useful or expedient to do so, for example, the authority of a university president or police officer. A university president has no "authority" over anyone who is not voluntarily a part of that university. Becoming a part of that university involves acknowledging the president's "right" to make decisions. But that right is grounded in nothing more than the university board's pronouncement, "We are giving you this ability," and the board could revoke that ability at any moment.

But as we saw in section 3.4.5, the idea that expertise is objective only if it is grounded in truth or knowledge and is completely subjective otherwise is a false dilemma. There, I gave Stephen Turner's account as an example, and we will explore his view in more detail in this chapter. First, consider another possible route to grounding expertise in social roles.

6.3 A Constructivist Account of Expertise

Agnew, Ford, and Hayes argue that while expertise is not grounded in knowledge, not every type of expertise is tantamount to snake oil selling. They reject the idea that a social role account implies wholesale relativism. How do they substantiate this claim? They begin with a critique of the objectivity of science. The idea that science is objective faces a number of obstacles, such as those discussed in section 3.4.2. They argue that science turns out to be a largely instrumental project, aimed at certain social and institutional goals and must fight continually against human bias and moral corruption in the conduct of research and the presentation of findings. They then ask, "How ... are we to maintain confidence in modern knowledge and expertise, given the limitations of our knowledge-making and expertise-selecting methods as portrayed by the history and philosophy of science?" (1994: 224).

6.3.1 Expertise as Social Selection

Following philosopher D.T. Campbell (1977), Agnew, Ford, and Hayes propose an evolution-inspired "selection theory" of how knowledge is distributed through society. "Selection theory is based on the notion that a variation-selection-and-retention process is fundamental to all inductive achievements, to all increases in knowledge, and to all increases in the fit of system to environment" (1994: 221). Much like natural selection, the beliefs, reasoning strategies, methodologies, and practices that "work" to address some social need survive. Those survivors then help determine the "fitness" of new beliefs, reasoning strategies, etc. Whatever survives is considered "knowledge." "Selectors" operate like environmental conditions, favoring or disfavoring information and activities. Some selectors are general, "cross-cultural," and "selecting for 'fit' to larger space/time frames than those selectors serving more local contexts" (224). Further, these selectors do not simply hit on knowledge that works and aggregate all other findings around it. Rather, they also "give competing variations and hypotheses a chance" (225), which allows for novel discoveries and paradigm shifts.

Interestingly, this kind of selection can apply broadly to any practice that can be imitated. When the ancient guilds would pass down standardized practices to their protégées, they were packaging those practices in a way that ensured that they would be replicated over time, and the privileged access to guild training protected the practices against competing practices and corrupting influences. A package of practices or information that can be imitated by others and transmitted through culture is called a "meme," a term coined by biologist Richard Dawkins (1976) in his book *The Selfish Gene*, taking from the Greek word for imitate, "*mimema*" (μίμημα), though it has now been transformed yet again to refer to culturally recognizable pictures with captions for the sake of entertainment or political satire.[1]

Importantly, Agnew, Ford, and Hayes argue that their view does not discount the significance of individual "cognitive competence." They allow that cognitive competence is often what emerges from certain types of social interaction—that is, it is the product of selection. But the process of selection, they maintain, is social. "Expertise, along with painting, poetry, and physics, can be seen as a product of the interplay between cognitive and cultural/social processes" (225), and this can be studied from the perspective of individual development (as, say Ericsson and colleagues do) or from the perspective of the society in which they emerge as experts (which Agnew, Ford, and Hayes purport to do).

How do these selectors work to ensure objectivity as opposed to "anything goes" social dynamics? They argue that "reality" plays an important role in the selection process, by limiting what sort of competencies address which needs in which contexts:

> That someone's view of a tree is something idiosyncratic constructed in [their] mind and that the very concept of 'tree' has arisen from social intercourse and takes its authority ultimately perhaps from faith in arborists—all of this does not entail that the tree is not real or that it is inaccessible to discussion. (228)

The idea seems to be that the more stable a set of competencies are for addressing needs in various contexts, the more confident we can be in those competencies. But context makes all the difference: "Today's experts become tomorrow's endangered species" (222).

What emerges from the selection process, they argue, are two types (or "levels") of expertise. While "all experts have been selected by their constituency," some expertise is more "reality-relevant" than others (236). By "reality-relevant" they mean processes that let stable perceptions of the natural world arbitrate information, such as controlled scientific experimentation. "Level 1 expertise is personally constructed and socially selected—but not necessarily reality-relevant. As may be expected, Level 1 experts include those who are subsequently labeled as con artists, quacks, delusional, sincere but misguided, etc." (236–7). But these are not the only members of Level 1 expertise. Some who pass the test of their constituencies in non-reality-relevant ways can look quite respectable: "doctors, lawyers, accountants, coaches, teachers, technicians, etc. ... [T]hese experts sometimes pass extensive domain entry hurdles and keep passing domain-specific performance tests" (237). Level 2 expertise, on the other hand, is reality-relevant. "We grant the accolade of reality-relevance to knowledge claims which continue to pass the tightest empirical tests that our culture can devise" (236).

6.3.2 Objections to the Constructivist Account

The constructivist account has clear affinities with relativist views such as that of Steven Shapin and Simon Schaffer, who argue that "it is ourselves and not reality that is responsible for what we know" (1985: 344). But Agnew, Ford, and Hayes attempt to carve a path between veritism and relativism. Their account purports to offer an account of expertise that is consistent both with the celebrated accomplishments of people with specialized training and with the role that society plays in choosing which of those people to champion. This account has the added benefit, they contend, of making experts easy to identify, thus, solving the recognition problem (the problem of how novices identify experts). On their view, experts are simply those people whom constituencies trust.

But there are some conceptual problems that threaten to undermine the account's plausibility. First, in calling Level 1 expertise "expertise," the constructivist account conflates the descriptive "people we do trust" with the normative "people we should trust." Perhaps they would reject the idea that there is some objective standard by which we "should" trust some people over others, reducing all such claims to subjective interests and preferences. (For example, they might offer some practical advice like, "If you are interested in 'reality-relevance,' you should trust those in Level 2.") But if that is the case, then the difference between Level 1 and Level 2 has nothing to do with "reality" relevance. This is because the notion of "reality" on that view is just what counts as "stable" according to a relatively wide set of interests and preferences. It is still appealing to social agreement; it is just appealing to the fact that agreement on topics in Level 2 is more stable than agreement on topics in Level 1. Saying, "if you are interested in 'reality-relevance'" is tantamount to saying "if you are interested in what a lot of people have found useful over a long period of time." And that notion of reality cannot escape relativism.

Further, saying that interest in science is more stable than interests in the lower level is an empirical claim without much support. Note that they place scientific expertise in Level 2, and regard it as having a much broader hold on "reality" than religion (they don't mention what level religious belief is in, but in a diagram, they show that it is less "reality-relevant" than science). Yet, only about 40 percent of Americans trust scientists. And a much larger portion of the world has accepted, for example, Buddhist metaphysics over a much larger period of time than those who are committed to the naturalism of science. So, why is scientific expertise more reality-relevant than Buddhist wisdom? This seems an assumption of their view that is not supported by their view.

There is also a self-defeat concern lurking here, because they take their selection model from the scientific concept of "natural selection." If that concept is itself merely "knowledge" that has been selected by a range of interests and preferences, then it is not clear whether it has authority to be descriptively adequate, despite their regarding it as a Level 2 expertise. The theory of evolution is relatively young, and a large portion of the world has rejected it for a long time, suggesting that non-evolutionary views might also be Level 2, and thus, just as (or more) legitimate than evolution. Someone might respond that those non-evolutionary views have not passed "the tightest empirical tests that our culture can devise." But notice that proponents of those putatively Level 2 views could simply counter that "empirical" tests do not track what they regard as "reality." But if that's right, then their "selection theory" of expertise is merely one way among many to explain expertise, and thus we are back to relativism.

Another concern is that, while attempting to ground expertise in the "interplay between cognitive and cultural/social processes," they lose any way to distinguish Level 1 from Level 2 expertise.[2] In allowing that Level 1 experts "pass extensive domain entry hurdles and keep passing domain-specific performance tests" they open themselves to conflating "professionals" and "experts." For some types of employment—accounting, administrative assistant, program manager—the "tightest empirical tests that our culture can devise" are domain-specific performance tests. Thus, anyone who meets those minimum requirements—which are the requirements for becoming a professional in those domains—counts as a Level 2 expert in those domains. Tests for expertise are difficult for any account of expertise, but the constructivist account offers no mechanism for distinguishing degrees of expertise, and it cannot help adjudicate disputes among experts at either level. In fact, there is no room for normative judgments about whom we should trust on their view. Without any conception of epistemic placement in a domain or epistemic authority, their view is simply a description of whom we happen to trust in society at a time that invokes a theory that is itself subject to selection pressures, rendering its objectivity questionable. Thus, it seems the constructivist view attributes far too much influence to social processes to avoid relativism.

6.4 The Public Influence Account

Not every social role account falls prey to these concerns, though. Recall from section 3.4.3 Stephen Turner's (2014) account of the epistemic authority of scientists in a democratic society:

> The cognitive authority of scientists in relation to the public is, so to speak, corporate. Scientists possess their authority when they speak as representatives of science. And the public judgments of science are of science as a corporate phenomenon, of scientists speaking as scientists. (23)

Turner seems to be saying that when scientists speak publicly, on behalf of their shared commitment to a certain epistemic process, their collective voice carries presumptive epistemic authority. This presumption is legitimated for their community by successful advancements in science and engineering that are perceived by that community as beneficial. So, while not grounded in truth per se, the epistemic authority of scientists is legitimated by a process of gathering and assessing evidence that is at least partly independent of public opinion, and so, does not reduce to mere reputation.

Like the constructivist account, Turner's is largely descriptive. He aims to explain how expertise is distributed in society, how it differs from social or political power, how it aggregates knowledge (for better or worse), and how it might more effectively solve knowledge-based social problems. The only normative dimension is the last, and his normative suggestions are grounded in historical examples of when expertise aggregated knowledge in a way that met a social need effectively. Also like the constructivist account, Turner approaches expertise from the perspective of whom people in a society tend to trust and why.

Turner's primary goal is to engage with the classic concern that expertise is incompatible with democracy. The idea is that, if democracy presupposes that political problems can only be solved by widely distributed knowledge that is aggregated through voting, then allowing experts to influence the democratic process, either as politicians, advisors to politicians, or political checks on the public understanding of scientific issues, renders expertise is inconsistent with democracy. Turner agrees that some types of expertise can pose problems for democracy, but he ultimately concludes that they are not incompatible.

6.4.1 Five Types of Expert

To show that the worry applies to only some types of expertise, he begins his discussion with a five-stage taxonomy of social trust in experts:[3]

- **Type I Experts:** The ideal or paradigm case of "legitimate cognitive authority." These experts are "democratically acknowledged," by which he means they're accepted as authoritative by society at large (irrespective of any particular individual's views of or trust in science). This acceptance legitimates their authority, according to Turner. Physicists are Type 1 experts on this account.

- **Type II Experts:** These experts have an audience that is restricted by the beliefs of a particular community. The people who count as experts are those that a community of belief accept as consistent with that community of belief. The audience is "predetermined" or "pre-established" on Turner's view (25) because the community's sectarian beliefs constitute the standard by which the expert's claims are legitimated.

- **Type III Experts:** These experts create their own following. They are trusted to the extent that people perceive they are helpful for achieving their ends: People paid for their services, like massage therapists, personal trainers, self-help gurus. Their authority does not extend beyond those who seek their services, nor need it do so. "Some people do not benefit by massage therapy, and do not find the promises of massage therapy to be fulfilled. So massage therapists have what is, so to speak, a created audience, a set of followers for whom they are expert because they have proven themselves to this audience by their actions" (25).

- **Type IV Experts:** These are experts whose authority is created by paying them to "speak as experts and claim expertise in the hope that the views they advance will convince a wider public and thus impel them into some sort of political action or choice" (27). This social role "appears at the end of the nineteenth century in the US, and developed hand-in-hand with the development of philanthropic and charitable foundations" (27). These are people who likely have some Type I expert training, but who are paid to support a particular side of a social issue, as when organizations like the Sierra Club hire experts to report on policy matters.

- **Type V Experts:** These experts are administrators. They are accepted as experts only by other administrators, but they have substantial discretionary power. "The legitimacy of the cognitive authority exercised by these individuals is not a matter, ordinarily at least, of direct public discussion, because they deal with issues … that are not discussed in newspapers until after they become institutional fact" (30). Historically, this social role was created by professional public administrators, who trained "municipal workers" to do what they do (to enter their "profession"), who then subsequently teach other administrators (31). Their audience is thus a default of the role itself. But this role has expanded to any person who works behind-the-political-scenes who has what I call "administrative authority." "No foreign policy expert is obligated to demonstrate the validity of [their] views on foreign policy by producing an unambiguous success, like curing cancer or constructing atomic weaponry" (33).

Turner thinks Types I and II pose no real problems for democracy. The authority of physicists is legitimated by "rational belief in the efficacy of the knowledge they possess" (35). We might say, it is legitimated in a non-political way, for example, by the fact that we have jet engines, lightning fast internet speeds, and antibiotics. Type III causes problems only when governments ignore their expressed neutrality on sectarian issues. The state should not subsidize, say, religiously grounded policies, but it often does. Types IV and V, however, present "more serious problems" (35), according to Turner, because by definition, they screen off evidence and expert reasoning from public scrutiny.

While Turner's highly detailed treatment of this question is worth working through, here we are only concerned with his account of expertise. Like Agnew, Ford, and Hayes, Turner thinks that expertise is primarily legitimated by its audience. Also like them, Turner takes scientific expertise to be the paradigm case of expertise and grounds the authority of that expertise in a non-veritist type of "knowledge." But unlike the constructivist view, Turner attempts to avoid relativism by construing knowledge as successfully addressing social needs in ways rationally acceptable to the public at large.

Traditional accounts of knowledge, according to Turner, are too restrictive. Rather than treating knowledge in terms of true propositions that one acquires in a non-accidental way, we can look to see how people actually come to "know." "What is true is that the people who carry out routines often have a very limited perspective on the whole, and that what they 'know' is shaped by experiences that are themselves limited. But it is also true that they know things that must be known for the institution to work" (7). What this suggests is that knowledge in a domain is actually the product of a complex social arrangement of people with limited but diverse knowledge.

For Turner, this suggests that a "theory of knowledge" just won't do the job. "Knowledge is, in my view, a much too diffuse and confused concept to yield to 'analysis' in the traditional philosophical sense. At best, we can work with a functional notion of knowledge: A routine can do things for us that a justified true belief can do; and instruments can do what a trained body can do;" and so on (7). What's important for Turner is that this "functional" account of knowledge does not reduce to the merely pragmatic "what will work in a given context according to a given audience," as Agnew, Ford, and Hayes seem to imply. The very practice of knowledge-seeking implies some checks and balances on what counts as acceptable for addressing any particular need.

Does this appeal to functional knowledge stave off relativism concerns? Not by itself, for reasons we noted with the constructivist account. Different communities will find different knowledge projects sufficient to different degrees for addressing social needs. Rather, functional knowledge that has gained the approval of all of society does seem to have a better hold on reality than mere problem-solving ability. When we compare science to, say, religious claims, it becomes apparent that the audiences vary for interesting reasons. "In the case of theological knowledge we do see something that was perhaps not so clear in the case of the cognitive authority of science, namely that the audiences for authority claims may indeed be very specific, and may not correspond with the public as a whole" (24). What emerges from this realization, according to Turner, is a sort of upturning of the traditional veritist picture of expertise. Rather than saying it is the wide consensus among scientists that they possess knowledge obtained through reliable practices that establishes the authority of scientists as experts, it is, instead, the publicly accepted demonstrations of science as authoritative that legitimate the practices thought to establish the products of science as "knowledge," and thereby, scientists as experts. Thus, though Turner gives no specific name to his approach, I have dubbed it the "public influence" account because its key insight is that expertise is determined (ideal, Type I expertise, anyway) by the degree to the public as a whole perceives certain people to exert appropriate rational influence on their beliefs and behaviors.

To further help the public accept the authority of science, scientists themselves engage in what Turner calls "bonding" activities (as in a guarantee of work, not relationship-building). The possibility of being "wrong" according to scientific standards of wrongness is mitigated by distributing the risks of being wrong through mechanisms that check for errors, bias, fraud, etc. These mechanisms include joining accrediting organizations, systems of peer review, protocols for conducting experiments, IRBs to protect research participants, and so on. Bonding is "an act in which an agent pays for an assurance (in this case an assurance by other scientists) that the agent will act in accordance with a principal's interests in a situation of information asymmetry" (188). Thus, there are means of retracting bad or fraudulent research, ousting perpetrators from the domain of legitimate authorities, and public accountability for the institutions and journals that perpetuate these problems.

6.4.2 Some Concerns about Turner's Account

One concern is simply with Turner's taxonomy. As we have analyzed the concept of expertise in this book, neither holding an administrative office nor serving in a professional social role is sufficient for expertise. As we can distinguished epistemic from administrative authority, the authority to compel behavior is different from the legitimate authority to compel behavior. And the legitimate authority to compel behavior depends on more than epistemic competence, it also requires a consent on the part of the governed.

Further, the fact that people do trust religious figures (like Jim Jones or Sun Myung Moon) does not indicate anything about these people that overlaps with historical or contemporary elements of expertise. We trust people who are not experts, like our parents and significant others, so trust alone is not sufficient. We obey people who are powerful for fear of reprisal, not because they have epistemic standing in a domain, so power is not sufficient for expertise. Thus, people who meet the criteria for Type II, IV, or V expertise are only "experts" in any meaningful sense if they are also highly competent practitioners in a Type I or III sense. The fact that a foreign policy "expert" is not required to demonstrate competence to anyone is a moral and epistemic travesty, not a distinct type of expertise.

With respect to Turner's defense of the objectivity of Type I expertise, I have two concerns. First, that broadening the scope to public approval is insufficient to establish the authority of "science" writ large, and second, that doing so fails to establish the authority of specialized sciences. With respect to the first, non-scientists tend to have little idea what scientists actually do, so even when Turner says they accept the products of successful science, they often have no idea (a) which "science" produced them, or (b) what sort of practices led to them such that they should approve of them.

With respect to (a), David Coady (2012) shrewdly points out that there are no experts in "Science," as if it had a capital S; rather, science is a "kind of loose baggy monster" (54). "I submit that no one is so well-informed about it that they should be treated as an expert on it." There are so many specialties and subdisciplines of science that an expert in one can be "quite ignorant of what scientists working in other branches of science do, or who wrongly think that the methods of their branch of science characterize science as a whole" (54). So, if scientists themselves either can't (because it's too unwieldy), or are not motivated to (because they want to focus on their own areas of interest), keep up with what counts as "Science" or "scientific methods," relying on a public full of non-scientists is not an obvious way to ensure objectivity. With respect to (b), some domains of science are so stigmatized (e.g., gene-edited babies and posthumous reproduction) that they would never be regarded as experts by the public at large even if scientists working in them cured cancer.

But even if the public could understand a particular science well enough to grant it legitimacy, there is still a worry that the claim that they are doing so because the science seems "reasonable" is not enough to escape an unacceptable degree of relativism. Consider that natural languages emerge, are maintained, and develop by similar social checks and balances. Philosopher Michael Polanyi writes: "The combined action of authority and trust which underlies both the learning of language and its use for carrying messages, is a simplified instance of a process which enters into the whole transmission of culture to succeeding generations" ([1958] 1962: 207). Polanyi is drawing an analogy between the transmission of culture and the transmission of language to make a point about culture; but notice the implications for language. When we are young, we are enculturated into a certain way of speaking, for better or worse. From then on, the only way of communicating, or even of critiquing that way of speaking, is to use that way of speaking. Thus, someone can authoritatively say that it is objectively true that "'could've' is an acceptable formulation in English, but 'could of' is not." And yet, that fact—for it is a fact as of right now—tells us something only about the world we have decided to create, namely, the world of English. It could have just as easily been the opposite (hence, the torrent of objections about the "singular 'they'" despite its extensive pedigree in English history[4]).

My second concern is that grounding the legitimacy of expertise in public approval will not work for domains that are so specialized the public don't know they exist or that have no impact on their lives. I once had dinner with an astrobiologist who worked for NASA. At the time, I had never heard of astrobiology, but it turns out they study the conditions for and possibility of living organisms on astronomical objects outside of Earth's atmosphere. It was fascinating to talk with him, but I cannot imagine that much of the public would understand what he was attempting to do, much less why their tax dollars were funding his research. His research program was not explicitly accepted as a domain of expertise by the public at large and would not likely be if they knew about it. One might reply that it inherits its legitimacy from the broader public acceptance of "biology," but if there is no such domain as "Science," then, given the vast diversity of specializations in biology, there is no such domain as "Biology."

A reviewer pointed out that, in fact, the public may view the case quite differently. Given our predisposition with intelligent alien life, maybe they would welcome the opportunity to fund these Star-Trek-like adventurers.

Perhaps they would be much less sanguine about a philosopher who writes on expertise or consults on the ethical dimensions of medical decisions in a hospital. The reviewer could be right. But my concern remains: If the public does not know my job as a clinical ethicist exists, or is indifferent to it, who could legitimize it on Turner's view?

While Turner's account is distinct from both veritism and normative reputational relativism, I do not think it is adequate for a general account of expertise. To escape the clutches of relativism, something more substantive than public acknowledgment must do the work of distinguishing novices from experts and weak experts from strong.

6.5 The Social Acquisition of Tacit Knowledge

In contrast with the constructivist account and the public influence account, Harry Collins has developed one of the most influential accounts of expertise in the literature. And while it is a social role account, it locates the social conditions on expertise in its development and distribution rather than in its account of epistemic authority. Collins ultimately accepts Ericsson's performance-based, process account of epistemic authority, and this preserves its objectivity. But as a sociologist, he focuses his account on exploring the social aspects of expertise development. He describes his account as a "'social theory' of the acquisition of expertise: it comes through mixing with other experts—it comes from social contact" (2014: 61).

In collaboration with colleague Robert Evans, Collins argues that the key to developing expertise in technical domains is *linguistic socialization*. To get a sense of what they mean by that, I start by reviewing Collins and Evans's response to the Dreyfuses' performance-based view (6.5.1). I then review what they call the "periodic table of expertises," explaining their distinctions between default and substantive expertises and ubiquitous and specialized expertises (6.5.2 and 6.5.3). Collins's most significant contribution to the expertise literature is what he calls *interactional expertise*. In 6.5.4, I review this concept and contrast it with the more traditional view of expert competence that he calls *contributory expertise*. And finally, in 6.6, I turn to some common concerns about Collins and Evans's account.

6.5.1 Social Acquisition and Tacit Knowledge: The Response to Dreyfus

It is worth noting that Collins and Evans (2006, 2007) primarily restrict their discussion of expertise to the sciences and technology. Though they identify some non-technical types of expertise, such as what they call "beer-mat knowledge" and "popular understanding," they view their research as enacting a Third Wave of Science Studies as a corrective to the overconfidence of the First Wave and the skepticism of the Second Wave. So, while they do think their discussion can be extended to the expertise of accountants, musicians, and pogo-stick jumpers, they take the competence exemplified in the specialized domains of science and technology as paradigmatic of expertise. This should not affect our broader discussion except to note that their view aims to justify the legitimacy of the scientific domains rather than attempting to defend that legitimacy. Because of this restriction, however, their view does raise a question about the role of *practice* in the social acquisition of expertise in domains outside of the sciences, such as athletics and musical performance. I will explore that question in 6.6.

Recall that Hubert and Stuart Dreyfus argue that expertise is a matter of knowledge-how, that is, tacit knowledge that becomes part of one's body in performing a set of tasks. It requires mastery of an entire form of life, rather than merely a set of cognitive activities. Collins and Evans agree with the Dreyfuses that the knowledge involved in expertise is largely tacit and, like them, are interested in the limits of computer technology in replicating human abilities. But rather than concluding that computers cannot approximate human expertise because they lack bodies, Collins and Evans argue that they cannot approximate expertise because they lack the opportunities for relevant socialization in our language (2007: 77). Note that the Dreyfuses' claim is that computers cannot even in principle approximate the lives necessary to mimic human expertise. Collins and Evans's claim is more modest: Computers, as they currently exist in the world, cannot engage in the sort of linguistic socialization necessary for human expertise. If computers could be similarly immersed in language acquisition, they very well could achieve something akin to human expertise. Collins and Evans present evidence that expertise is less a matter of having a certain kind of body and more a matter of having a body sufficient for understanding the linguistic content of a domain.[5] So, rather than defending "embodied expertise," what Collins and Evans call the "social embodiment thesis," Collins and Evans defend what they call the "minimal embodiment thesis."

The Dreyfuses' social embodiment thesis, "holds that the particular language developed by any social group is related to the bodily form (or practices) of its members because bodily form affects the things they can do in the world" (2007: 79). Taking an example from Wittgenstein, Collins and Evans say that "a community of speaking lions ... would not have the equivalent, or near equivalent, of 'chair' in their language because they do not sit down in the same way. ... Thus, here, a difference in the physical joints of the lions corresponds nicely to a difference in the conceptual joints" (79).

However, Collins and Evans argue, while this might be true if lions acquired their language independently of English-speakers, if a speaking lion were "snatched from its cradle and brought up alongside humans in the same way as are domestic dogs and cats, [they] would acquire human language, including the word for chair, even though it, as an individual, could not sit" (79). So, even though a lion cannot experience the same form of life as a human, their being socialized into how human language is used is sufficient for understanding the meaning of concepts and experiences it cannot fully experience, such as sitting in a chair, writing with a pen, somersaulting, and so on. Collins and Evans think this suggests that a less robust type of embodiment is sufficient for many types of expertise, namely, the *minimal embodiment thesis*: "Though bodily form gives rise to the language of a community, only the minimal bodily requirements necessary to learn any language are necessary to learn the language of any community in which the organism is embedded" (79). Since a large part of becoming and being an expert is learning a way of talking about a domain, someone who is linguistically socialized into that domain has a degree of expertise in that domain. In addition to this thought experiment, recall from section 4.5.2, Collins and Evans offer two examples of people who lack the ability to fully engage with a domain in the Dreyfuses' sense (Oliver Sacks's Madeleine and Collins himself), and yet have sufficient linguistic skill to be competent in that domain, and a third (people who are prelingually deaf) of people who lack a minimum necessary bodily ability for understanding a domain. If Collins and Evans are right, then the Dreyfuses' claims about embodiment are overstated. Even though the knowledge required for expertise is tacit and cannot be expressed as rules stated as propositions, that knowledge is still a function of a way of talking and thinking about a domain, and therefore is still a largely cognitive endeavor.

6.5.2 Default and Substantive Expertises

Collins and Evans think that competence with language accounts for a number of different types of expertise—what they call "expertises" (to the consternation of spell check). However, not all linguistic competence is enough. One might think, for example, that the vast store of information on the internet provides sufficient resources for ordinary citizens to be competent at engaging with those who practice in any domain. It gives people "the sense that every citizen is part of the ball game of science and technology because there is no difference between us and the ball players" (Collins 2014: 15). Collins calls this leveling of the playing field "default expertise," the ability of anyone, because of the epistemic advantage granted via technology, to know as much as the "experts." This sense, combined with the harsh critique of science by many postmodernists (see Barnes and Bloor 1982), leads some people to dismiss the authority of experts wholesale.

But therein lies a problem:

> In a sense, a default expert is not really an expert at all because their sense of being an expert comes only from the fact that there are no real experts. The supposed experts have been defined as experts because of the way they fit into social life—the relational theory—but the default expert sees through it. (Collins 2014: 49)

Understanding why "default expertise" is not really expertise helps point us to what Collins calls "substantive expertises," which are competences that explain why some people perform better than others in a domain and how some people become those people who perform better. Substantive expertises are the answer to those who naively assume there are no differences in performance or who chalk up any apparent differences to reputation.

What, then, count as substantive expertises on Collins's view? Collins takes Ericsson's "ten thousand hours of effortful practice" as a starting point (though we understand from Chapter 5 this is not exactly Ericsson's view). But he thinks that Ericsson's view leaves out a number of rather remarkable abilities that don't quite fit that model. For example, there are dozens of activities that allow us to live our lives in our respective cultures

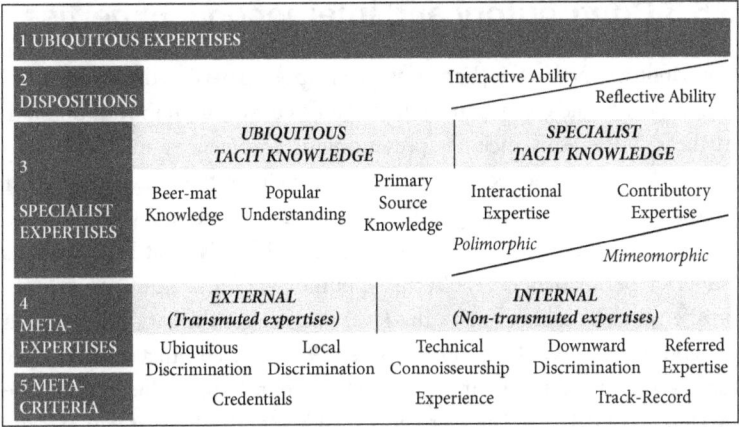

FIGURE 6.1 Harry Collins's Periodic Table of Expertises, Collins and Evans (2007: 14). Reproduced with permission from University of Chicago Press. Versions of this Table are featured in Collins (2014: 62); and Collins (2018: 6).

and that do not require any conscious effort at all, but that would not be useful in other contexts. He includes activities like speaking your native language, table manners, moral sensibility, and political discrimination, and calls these *ubiquitous expertises* because they extend throughout our culture (Collins and Evans 2007: 16; Collins 2014: 53). (See Figure 6.1, row 1.)

The more acculturated you are, the broader your range of ubiquitous expertises. Collins and Evans suggest that as we move beyond the general fund of ubiquitous expertise we all have, we pass through *beer-mat knowledge* (trivia we pick up from different contexts), *popular understanding* (information we glean from the news and popular media), and, with a little conscious effort, we can read the primary literature in a domain and acquire *primary source knowledge* (Figure 6.1, row 3).

These substantive expertises make up the category that Collins and Evans call "ubiquitous tacit knowledge." As you gain competence beyond primary sources knowledge, you progress into the category of "specialist tacit knowledge," which includes *interactional expertise* and *contributory expertise*. Specialist expertises form a continuum, and Collins and Evans explain that "there is a transitive relationship between the five levels of the ladder. If you possess one of the higher levels you will possess, at least in principle, all of the lower levels but not *vice-versa*" (2007: 36, italics theirs).

6.5.3 Contributory and Interactional Expertise

Contributory expertise is the prototypical type of expertise, the competence to do research and contribute to the ongoing conversation in your domain. In the sciences, this includes presenting at conferences and publishing your findings. On the technology side, this includes the Dreyfuses' fighter pilots and Ericsson's chess grandmasters (who contribute by establishing and adding to statistics and by breaking records). It is what Ericsson calls "superior performance." The terms "polimorphic" and "mimeomorphic" on the periodic table refer to the level of social understanding required for competence (Collins and Evans 2007: 26–7). Driving on an empty racetrack is more mimeomorphic in that your primary focus is on the mechanics of driving. There are no stoplights, no traffic, just you and the car. You don't need a high degree of understanding of the world around you since it is largely fixed. Driving in LA traffic, on the other hand, is highly polimorphic (your behavior has to fit changing circumstances). You have to drive the car, but you also have to account for the traffic laws, other drivers, and the occasional political activist. You need a high degree of understanding of the world around you in order to drive well in those conditions.

Interestingly, according to Collins, contributory expertise makes up only a fraction of the expertise in science and technology. Consider gravitational wave physics, the domain Collins has studied for decades. According to Collins:

> There are around a thousand physicists working in the international, billion-dollar field of gravitational-wave detection. Each of them belongs to a sub-specialism within the area, such as working out the wave forms that will be emitted by various cosmic catastrophes, designing the lasers that are used in the laser-interferometer detectors, working on the principles of the detection apparatus, ... and so on. In the main, no person from one subgroup could step in and do the work of a person from another subgroup—at least not without a long apprenticeship. If that were not so, they would not be specialists. And yet all these people have to coordinate their work. The way they coordinate their work is by sharing a common language. (2014: 69–71)

So, while each specialist is a contributory expert in their subdomain, they also interact effectively with other experts from other subdomains.

This is another example of what we called *expert coordination* at the beginning of this chapter, and this suggests that interactional expertise is key to such coordination. But this interaction requires far more understanding of gravitational wave physics than any person off the street or undergraduate physics major. In addition, then, to people who contribute to a domain as contributory experts, there are others who can interact meaningfully with that domain through a shared language, some of whom are contributory experts in another domain. Collins calls this ability to meaningfully speak the language of a domain *interactional expertise*.

Interactional expertise is important for two reasons. First, it explains how large, complex groups of experts—like those who build skyscrapers and passenger jets—are able to work together to complete highly specialized projects. And second, it explains how scientists are able to check and safeguard one another's work.

> Interactional expertise is the key to most of what happens in science. ... The much-hyped "peer-review" process for the vetting of journal articles and the award of grants works via interactional expertise because it will almost never be the case that the reviewers have actually done work that is identical to that which they are reviewing. ... Even learning to become a contributory expert in a narrow technical domain is mostly a matter of acquiring interactional expertise because it is through talk that one learns how to act in practical matters. (Collins 2014: 72)

Interactional expertise is still tacit, in that its competence cannot be expressed as strict rules. But neither is it purely performative. It may actually do a better job of explaining how coaching or performance training works than a psychological theory like deliberate practice. "The human coach can teach some things through the medium of spoken language because the coach shares some of the nonexplicit skills of the student: the shared linguistic skills can transfer mutually understood tacit meanings" (2007: 30).

6.5.4 Meta-Expertises

So far, we have only explored rows 1 and 3 of the periodic table. Row 2 refers to the sorts of dispositions that allow one to excel under different social conditions. As your specialist expertise increases, you need an increasing amount of reflective ability to be able to address domain-specific needs on your own. Whereas, with a lesser degree of specialized expertise, you need to be able to interact efficiently with others in the domain.

Rows 4 and 5 list the abilities needed to identify and assess the merits of expertise. These abilities are not competence *in* a domain, rather they are competence *about* a domain, typically from the perspective of a novice in that domain. *External* meta-expertise refers to the ability to evaluate expertise based on an understanding of the *domain*. It asks whether the expert is in a domain that generally fits with our understanding of the acceptable domains in a society. What Collins calls *ubiquitous discrimination* is a function of our ubiquitous expertise. It involves using the same sort of judgments about "friends, acquaintances, neighbors, relations, politicians, salespersons, and strangers, applied to science and sciences" (Collins and Evans 2007: 45). We know that physics is widely acceptable but astrology is not, so we discount claims to astrological expertise and give credence to claims of physics expertise.

By "transmuted," Collins and Evans mean that social knowledge is transformed into technical judgments, that is, an evaluation of a technical domain, like engineering or climatology. By "non-transmuted," they mean that people possess some measure of expertise in the domain they are judging.

What Collins and Evans call *local discrimination* is a matter of having a certain degree of specialized expertise in a domain where other experts attempt to claim authority. For example, imagine you are a localized expert with your company's copy machine—you know its basic functions and its idiosyncratic tendencies. If an expert in copy machine repair were to give you advice, there is a normative presumption that you should take it. You have enough local discrimination to believe you should trust the copy machine repair person.[6] But if an electrical engineer tried to give you advice about how to operate your company's copy machine, even though the person is a specialized expert in a domain that overlaps with the basic operation of the copy machine, you have enough local discrimination of the idiosyncratic workings of your machine to give less credence to the engineer.[7] However, Collins and Evans say that external meta-expertises are typically "very unreliable because of the temptation to read too much into stereotypical appearances and stereotyped behavior" (51). Recall my critique of Turner's reliance on public opinion to approve of different scientific domains. The picture the public has of scientists and what they do is often colored by their value commitments.

Internal meta-expertise refers to the ability to evaluate expertise based on an understanding of *experts* in a domain. Collins and Evans call these *non-transmuted* expertises because they require some degree of expertise in the domain they purport to judge (though see footnote 6). *Technical connoisseurship, downward discrimination,* and *referred expertise* are different degrees of interactional expertise in a domain. Connoisseurs can recognize certain technical proficiencies that non-connoisseurs cannot. Downward discrimination is the sort of meta-expertise exhibited in the peer review process, where, while the reviewing expert may not be an expert in the particular problem that the author is working on, they have a greater degree of expertise in the same domain (think: the relationship between a senior scholar and a junior scholar, hence "downward"). And referred expertise is a meta-expertise where a contributory expert in one domain is sufficiently expert enough in another domain that they can, by drawing analogy with the methods and background assumptions, judge the expertise in another domain. The meta-criteria in row 5 (credentials, experience, track record) are strategies for judging expertise.

6.6 Strengths and Weaknesses of the Socially Acquired Tacit Knowledge Account

Collins has helped further the domain of expertise studies in a number of important ways. First, he has demonstrated important limitations on the Dreyfuses' account. According to Selinger and Mix (2006), Collins shows, for example, that "a sociologist who does not have any direct experience practicing surgery, but who, nevertheless studies surgery from a third-person perspective ... would be quite capable [contra the Dreyfuses] of acquiring 'authentic' surgical language" (2006: 304). Second, the concept of interactional expertise explains the legitimate epistemic authority of less superior performers. And third, his account of meta-expertise offers a strategy for solving the recognition problem—how novices can identify experts—by suggesting how novices can assess the credibility of an expert's claim while lacking expertise in that domain.

Some scholars, however, have raised concerns about Collins's account. Here, I will review three of those. The first is that Collins's defense of the "minimal embodiment thesis" is an empirical claim without empirical support.[8] His examples of Madeleine, himself, and the prelingually deaf are at best anecdotal and speculative. How people are socialized to use language, what role the socialization plays in their linguistic development, and what sorts of understanding different forms of embodiment allow are all empirical questions for which we don't have answers. Therefore, to simply say that Collins's interactional expertise with gravitational wave physics arises from his linguistic socialization ignores the possibility that Collins has a special sort of intelligence or photographic memory that allows him to make sense of gravitational wave physics (much the way Saul Kripke was able to publish a completeness theorem for modal logic at age 19) or that he practiced solving theorems in gravitational wave physics for an extensive period of time (much the way chess grandmasters learn to "talk" about chess). Further, some of his examples of how people learn to engage with a domain (Madeleine and the prelingually deaf) are not examples of expertise. So, even if *learning* requires only the minimal capacity for linguistic socialization, it is not clear that *expertise* is developed largely through linguistic socialization. A certain type of practice (as we saw defended by Ericsson and Tetlock in Chapter 5) may be the most important element of developing expertise, and this is more consistent with the Dreyfuses' social embodiment thesis.

Another element of this critique is to ask whether Collins's claims, even if empirically supportable for scientific and technical domains, would extend to expertises that are primarily performative, such as Olympic swimming or sharpshooting. Collins (2004) makes a telling claim: "Madeleine could acquire a pretty good ability to talk tennis talk even though she will never walk the tennis walk, she probably would not be as good a tennis talker as Martina Navratilova because Navratilova does a lot more tennis talking in the normal course of things" (137). Selinger and John Mix (2006) point out that this is problematic because "it assumes that Martina Navratilova is as good a talker as she is a tennis player. But what evidence licenses this inference that 'talking it' is a necessary consequence of 'walking it'?" (308). Again, Collins is making an empirical claim about the development of expertise through linguistic socialization that is not (yet, anyway) supported empirically.

A second concern about Collins's account is that he misconstrues the phenomenological tradition he is rejecting when he rejects the social embodiment thesis. While the Dreyfuses are using "embodiment" in a phenomenological sense of a "holistic interrelation ... between an organism and its environment," Collins "conflates 'embodiment' with 'bodily features,'" and "acts as if he has established that moveable limbs, eye sight, and hearing are not necessary features that a human needs to possess to learn a language" (Selinger and Mix 2006: 311). If Collins is misrepresenting embodiment the way Selinger and Mix claim, then his objections to the social embodiment thesis miss their mark. Further, his examples of minimal embodiment focus narrowly on sensory faculties rather than on the holistic interaction between a body and its environment. So, not only is his rejection of the social embodiment thesis unmotivated, according to Selinger and Mix, his defense of the minimal embodiment thesis is too minimalist to capture the richness of learning tacit knowledge. In fact, interactional expertise might be a more powerful explanatory tool if it included a richer sense of embodiment (317).

The final concern is a weakness more than an objection. While Collins and Collins and Evans have given us some insightful tools for understanding degrees of expertise, these tools do not seem to have much to say about epistemic authority or the sort of competence that constitutes expertise. Though Collins (2014) gives a nod to Ericsson's approach, he never elaborates on the sort of experience necessary for processing from ubiquitous expertise to contributory expertise. Perhaps he is assuming something like deliberate practice in the background, or perhaps he is indifferent to how competence is established in various domains, allowing them to set their own standards of linguistic socialization. Because he never specifies and focuses solely on the social elements of the development and distribution of expertise, the social acquisition of tacit knowledge theory is incomplete.

6.7 Summing Up

Social role accounts constitute a needed check on studies of expertise that depend largely on operational definitions. They remind us that the contexts in which expertise is acquired—even the most highly regarded and well-supported types of expertise—are primarily social contexts, where people—some more fallible than others, some more virtuous than others—hold the keys to the gates of domains. Public image, public pressure, funding sources, hot topics, strong personalities, racism and sexism, and so on play a much bigger role in determining who is authorized to speak or advise in a domain than we would like to admit.

Nevertheless, giving too much credit to social elements causes serious problems that call us back from wholesale skepticism of expertise. Instead of giving up, we are forced to do the hard work of explaining real differences in competence in a messy world where normative ideals (like truth) prove too optimistic and impracticable and where overly narrow operational definitions (like deliberate practice), while successful, do not fare well outside their research programs. These are the challenges of formulating an adequate general theory of expertise. And I think the insights gleaned over the past four chapters point us in a constructive direction, namely, the subject of Chapter 7.

7 THE COGNITIVE SYSTEMS ACCOUNT OF EXPERTISE

The more the imagination or the poorest talent is exercised, the more it gains in embonpoint, *so to speak, and the larger it grows. It becomes sensitive, robust, broad, and capable of thinking. The best of organisms has need of this exercise. … If one's organism is an advantage, and the preeminent advantage, and the source of all others, education is the second. The best made brain would be a total loss without it …. But, on the other hand, what would be the use of the most excellent school, without a matrix perfectly open to the entrance and conception of ideas?*

(Julien Offray De la Mettrie, Man a Machine, 1748,
Translated Gertrude Carman Bussey, 1912)

In this chapter, I develop a novel account of expertise. I open with some conceptual foundations needed for my account (7.1). Then, combining insights from the accounts discussed in Chapters 2–6 with psychologist Daniel Kahneman's dual-process account of decision-making, I suggest that expertise is competence in a domain that develops along one of two cognitive pathways, and I call this the *cognitive systems account of expertise* (7.2–7.4). In 7.5 and 7.6, I consider some objections to the cognitive systems account and subject it to some test cases. I close the chapter by reviewing the remaining big questions about expertise (7.7).

Parts of this chapter are adapted from Watson (2019).

7.1 Picking up the Pieces

In this section, I highlight some points from earlier chapters that serve as a sort of ground-clearing for developing a new account of expertise. They are points that I think everyone who approaches expertise studies should accept in some form or another, though I realize that is rather optimistic for academics. But even if not everyone accepts them, they are accepted widely enough to stand as a useful starting point for many debates regarding expertise.

7.1.1 Expertise Is, in an Important Sense, Relative

In the preface, I stipulated that expertise is a high degree of competence in a domain. Yet, I argued in Chapter 3 that veritism has trouble linking expertise to any particular objective criterion of competence (like truth) because, given the social dynamics of human belief-formation, that criterion is likely to change. What was "known" in Newton's day, for example, is not "knowledge" today. And what counts as knowledge today may not count 500 years from now. Upon reflection, we can see that any objective account of expertise faces this concern. What counted as "superior performance" in the 1960 summer Olympics is not sufficient today. Were those athletes not experts?

It seems we must be committed to some sort of relativism about expert competence in order to accommodate such historical examples. But we need not be committed to the relativism of purely reputational accounts of expertise. What justifies our trust in experts is evidence that they have a certain type and degree of competence in a domain. And whether that type and degree are sufficient for expertise are determined by the state of competence of the practitioners in that domain at a specific time.

For example, for some types of expertise, the current set of practitioners (people who comprise the domain at that time) will determine that having a certain amount of information combined with having the ability to use processes aimed at truth, such as experimentation and statistical analyses, are sufficient for expertise at that time. People who demonstrate such competence through, say, a Ph.D. thesis or research program, may be admitted, by other experts, to the ranks of experts in that domain.

For other types of expertise, the domain at that time will determine that performing at a certain skill level, such a ballet or chess, is sufficient for expertise at that time. People who demonstrate sufficient skill may be admitted to the ranks of expert by those in charge of a prestigious dance troupe or simply by virtue of achieving the minimum elo score in chess.

A domain-at-a-time is the state of accepted understanding (note, not necessarily knowledge) or level of performance as determined by the practitioners in that domain at whatever time we are asking the question of who or what counts as an expert. This allows us to say that Newton was an expert on physics when he was alive but wouldn't be if he were alive today.

This implies that expertise is relative rather than absolute. Instead of comparing a person's understanding or performance to some context-independent measure to which we have no reliable access, such as the entire set of truths in a domain, or to an implausibly small minority of superior performers, it compares them with the understanding or performance of those who are performing at the objective standard of competence in a domain at a time. It is not, therefore, subjective or reputational. Rather, it is an objective comparison of the abilities of a person in a domain with those who do what constitutes the state of practice in that domain. In philosophy, for example, we would not reasonably doubt Descartes's expertise on the grounds that he did not engage with Gettier problems or arguments for infinitism because those ways of approaching philosophical concepts had not been formulated in Descartes's time, and therefore, did not constitute part of the domain at that time. Descartes did, however, engage with the relevant arguments and concepts that comprised his domain at the time he was writing (and unlike many others, he even published his critics' objections alongside his own work).

What competence means is domain-specific—moving quickly and successfully in chess; playing sufficiently quickly and accurately a wide range of pieces in musical performance; recognizing when to move into or out of a building in firefighting; effectively diagnosing and treating a wide range of illnesses in a particular medical specialty; and so on. But it is also *domain-linked* in the historical sense of tracking relative levels of competence at a time.

Linking expertise to a domain-at-a-time also addresses the concern raised in Chapter 3 about identifying a "reference class" against which to compare expert competence. Many scholars say that experts are more competent than non-experts or more competent than most people, or even more competent than their peers. But rendering expertise relative to other people faces difficult counterexamples, as we saw in 3.2. We can easily imagine someone alone on a planet, but who, through diligent study, develops a reliable new technology, say an airplane or a gun. It seems reasonable that such a person, with further practice and experimentation, could become an expert, irrespective of whether anyone else exists. However, linking expert competence to the current state of performance in a domain captures both the social dimension of expertise while avoiding the possibility that someone stops being an expert just because they're alone.

7.1.2 How Many People Can Be Experts Depends on the Domain

Nothing we have seen in the book so far requires that only the top 1 percent (or even 5 percent or 10 percent) of performers in a domain count as experts. Even those who operationally define expertise as the highest level of performance in a domain admit that this is largely for the purpose of precision in empirical study. Most researchers allow that expertise is exemplified in varying degrees in different ways across a wide range of domains. To be sure, some domains have such exceptionally high access conditions that, if you are able to engage meaningfully with the information and methods in those domains, you are already an expert. Domains like this likely include transfinite mathematics, cosmogony (the physical study of the origins of the universe), and quantum mechanics. But in most domains, people who have arrived at a certain standard level of competence—doctors, attorneys, art historians, etc.—are experts regardless of how many others perform at that level. Given this wide variation in competence and possible competence in domains, I don't think there is an in-principle way to carve expertise according to percentages of competent practitioners.

7.1.3 Expertise Requires Both Understanding and Performing

I find nothing in the arguments I have reviewed in this book that convinces me that performance ability is more fundamental to expertise than understanding or vice versa. The examples encountered over the course of the book suggest that understanding and ability are largely indispensable to the process of developing and exercising expertise. I think we can clearly locate understanding and performance in different places in different types of expertise. Surgeons, for example, must have a substantial fund of background information before they start practicing their first cut. Yet, in order to be an expert surgeon, they must practice cutting. Both philosophers and ballet dancers must practice extensively, engage with peers and other experts, get feedback, and use that feedback in order to become experts and maintain their expertise. But philosophers and ballet dancers must also have an extensive understanding of information, concepts, and methods in order to become experts and maintain their expertise.

7.1.4 Expertise Is Irreducibly Social

There are three reasons for thinking that expertise is irreducibly (though not essentially) social in nature. The first is that expertise is relative to a domain at a time, which means that practitioners in a domain at a time make a difference as to what counts as expertise. To be clear, they do not get to arbitrarily decide who is an expert. In fact, they don't *decide* at all. They simply perform. Their level of performance determines who joins them as an expert and who does not. Nevertheless, if no one is pursuing an activity, there will be no expertise in the domain defined by that activity.

The second is that, in order for someone to achieve expert-level competence, they must get feedback from those who currently practice at the expert level (whether directly or through books, online courses, videos, etc.). This means that other practitioners are almost always necessary for acquiring high levels of competence in a domain—especially domains that have been developing for centuries, like mathematics.

And third, domains make progress by calibrating information across experts and (in the case of expert coordination) across domains at a time. For example, advancements in the pharmaceutical industry change what counts as expert performance in medicine. Similarly, new technologies can change what expert performance looks like in multiple domains all at once.

Because expertise is irreducibly social, a plausible account of expertise must explain not only the roles of understanding and performance, but the role of others in developing and legitimizing their practice in that domain.

Where do we go from here? If expertise is not essentially truth-based, solely performance- or understanding-based, or purely social, is there any way to make sense of expertise as a unified concept? Is a general account of expertise plausible? I think the answer is yes. But before we get there, we need one additional bit of conceptual machinery.

7.2 A New Tool for a Wicked World: Expansive Practice

In Chapter 5, we saw that, in *kind worlds* (as Hogarth [2010] defines them), deliberate practice provides a fairly robust account of expertise. Recall that deliberate practice involves thousands of hours of intensely focused practice aimed at different aspects of a well-defined skill, aided by immediate feedback, preferably from a teacher. It accommodates what we find valuable about knowledge or understanding in a domain, explains the need for a specific kind of practice in order to develop expertise (irrespective of the role of knowledge or understanding), is consistent with other empirically supported psychological theories of memory and intuition, is consistent with the philosophical distinction between knowledge-that and knowledge-how, and its mechanism of mental representations that result in subconsciously fast performance times is consistent with the phenomenon we think of as "nonmindedness," "embodiment," or "flow" in psychological terms. And while it doesn't explain the "social" nature of expertise, it is consistent with a domain-relative standard of expertise and it does depend on interpersonal feedback, as Collins (2014) points out.

Unfortunately, kind environments are rare. Whereas deliberate practice has clear advice for improvement in surgery and certain sports, it is not possible in any specialty where success conditions are unclear, decision strategies are uncertain, and outcomes are not immediately correlated with whatever might retrospectively be regarded as success: for example, nephrology, pulmonology, palliative care medicine, law, business management, psychotherapy, financial advising, and so on.

However, Philip Tetlock and colleagues pick up roughly where deliberate practice leaves off. Tetlock (2005) and Tetlock and Gardner (2015) accept the requirements Ericsson and others set for an adequate test of competence. And their approach starts with elements of deliberate practice such as copious amounts of practice, getting specific feedback, and revising judgments based on that feedback. But these are not sufficient for developing and enhancing forecasting expertise. As we saw in Chapter 5, Ericsson and Pool (2016) acknowledge limitations of their approach, namely, the narrowness of the domain needed for deliberate practice and the ability to isolate, get feedback on, and develop training techniques for discrete aspects of a technique—all of which wicked environments restrict. With respect to continuing medical education, for example, Ericsson and Pool point out that, while deliberate-practice-like strategies, like "role-play, discussion groups, case solving, and hands-on training" (2016: 134), have shown some improvement in diagnostic outcomes, "the overall improvement was small" (134). Further, "no type of continuing medical education is effective at improving complex behaviors, that is, behaviors that involve a number of steps or require considering a number of different factors" (135). This suggests that wicked environments require something more than or different from specialized intuition training (notwithstanding Klein's work on intuition in wicked environments—more on that below).

In looking for tools to develop and enhance forecasting expertise, Tetlock does not take himself to be offering a new or alternative theory of expertise. Yet, through the process, he discovers a distinct set of principles that make a notable improvement in performance in wicked environments. What emerges, I contend, is a distinct path to expertise, one that helps train complex judgment under uncertainty. Unlike strategies for developing intuition-primed decision-making, Tetlock's strategies for enhancing complex judgments slow down reaction time. They introduce ways to make us stop and consider base rates ("balancing outside/inside views"), to break big problems into smaller, more manageable problems, to look for places where our cognitive biases may be getting the best of us, gathering evidence from diverse sources,[1] to update judgments in light of new evidence, to not over- or under-react to that evidence, and to let cases inform theories rather than vice versa,[2] improving complex judgments over time. This series of checks on our judgments forces us to engage our slower, reflective, System 2 cognitive processes. In contrast to deliberate practice, let's call this kind of training *expansive practice*.[3] By "expansive," I mean a broad set of practices and skills that prevent decision-making from falling into habit. Expansive *practice*, then, is training that develops skill with forming judgments about complex information while avoiding the errors associated with natural System 1 processing.

7.3 The Cognitive Systems Model: System 1 and System 2 Expertise

What Tetlock and Gary Klein seem to have found is that experts in all environments make copious use of background information and skills.

Some of the information includes what Gary Klein calls a "generally prepared mind" (2013: 20–1). A generally prepared mind is a type of expertise that develops through certain kinds of specialized experience, allowing a person to register what Klein calls an "insight," a way of seeing something in information that others would miss. And some of these skills include the highly trained, System 1 intuitions, what Klein might call a "specifically prepared mind" (21)—as when an internal medicine doctor can readily call to mind the appropriate dosage recommendations of a specific pain medication for a certain kind of pain.

Klein thinks that special experience is also the key to developing our cognitive mechanisms to make expert-level decisions in a wicked world. And there is no doubt that Klein has demonstrated some success in training experts to engage in "recognition-primed decision making." There are, however, limitations on Klein's research that bear on a general theory of expertise. Klein's research demonstrates that, in high-stakes, time-sensitive conditions, recognition-primed decision-making improves experts' decisions over some baseline, that is, decisions trained by recognition-primed training strategies are better than decisions would otherwise be. He does not, however, show whether those decisions are better than those made by Tetlock's slower strategies if time were available. This is not a criticism, for situations like firefighting and military commanding are inherently time-sensitive—the value of decisions in these contexts is always absolute (better than previous decisions in roughly similar circumstances) rather than relative (better than other strategies under the same conditions) because (a) the situations are not strictly repeatable and (b) there is no comparable environment in which to train that doesn't have the time-sensitive feature. In other words, any situation in which slower, reflective strategies could be tried as a comparison group would not be similar enough to the real conditions under which those decisions are needed. Tetlock and Klein are simply studying different types of decisions under different contexts. But it also means that Klein's work does not constitute a counterexample to expansive practice as an alternative path to expertise. That is, we cannot say: *Well Tetlock's strategies work in wicked environments, but eventually everyone should aim for Klein's recognition-primed decision-making, which is essentially deliberate practice for wicked environments.* Rather, the situation is reversed: Klein's recognition-primed decision-making works, but we know that deliberate practice does not generally improve complex judgments (as Ericsson and Pool pointed out with medical education), while Tetlock's strategies do. So, when complex judgments are at stake or we are making decisions in a wicked environment, and there is time for deliberation, we should pursue training strategies that slow down our intuitions, that is, we should engage in expansive practice.

7.3.1 System 1 and System 2 Expertise

This discussion leads us to a novel conclusion. A high degree of competence in a domain at a time (expertise) is developed differently depending on the demands of the domain. In domains that are well-defined, highly structured, and include ample opportunities for immediate feedback—i.e., kind environments—expertise is efficiently acquired by training System 1 cognitive processes (with deliberate practice) so that performance is subconscious and intuitive. Call this, following Kahneman's distinction in cognitive processes, *System 1 Expertise*.

In domains that are less well-defined, loosely structured, and in which feedback is largely indirect—wicked environments—expertise can be acquired by training System 2 cognitive processes (with expansive practice) so that performance is reflective and careful. Call this *System 2 Expertise*. By "performance," of course, I am including forming judgments, solving problems, formulating arguments, and drawing inferences from evidence. While drawing hard distinctions between categories of expertise may be useful for identifying certain types of neural pathways, conceptually, I think there is little reason to separate cognitive from performative expertise. All expertise requires some background cognitive understanding and conscious training strategies, and all expertise requires performance of some sort, even if only the mental activities of remembering, solving math problems, or appreciating works of art.

I am taking the terms "System 1" and "System 2" from the cognitive processes that Kahneman identifies, but I want to be clear that System 1 and System 2 Expertise are types of expertise that rely on different ways of engaging these processes in order to acquire expertise. Kahneman says that System 1 and System 2 processes can be active in any decision. You may start to make an intuitive, System 1 decision, like pressing the gas pedal when a traffic light turns green. But if you suddenly see a pedestrian start to walk out into the intersection, your intuition is stopped by a reflective, System 2 process, and you press the brake. If this had not happened, you might have gotten to work and wondered, "Did I obey all the traffic signals? I don't even remember." This is because System 1 processes operate subconsciously, and this is (one reason) why cognitive biases are so difficult to catch. But when you almost hit a pedestrian, this drove the decision process into your conscious, reflective thoughts, so you will likely remember it later in the day. Both System 1 and System 2 processes often operate on single decisions.

In contrast, System 1 Expertise is the result of training that predominantly engages System 2 processes over many decisions to produce more accurate and less biased System 1 intuitions within the scope of a domain. As Ericsson and colleagues note, deliberate practice is hard and effortful, a continual forcing of yourself to engage System 2 processing. But this training results in superb performance that can feel, in low-stakes conditions when you are not trying to improve, effortless and nonminded.

System 2 Expertise often depends on a great deal of System 1 Expertise—the ability to intuitively recall vast amounts of information and methods in a domain. For example, interpreting a piece of intelligence gathered about a political regime in a foreign country requires fluid access to a wide range of background information on the geopolitical context from which that information was gathered. And formulating a plan of medical care for an elderly patient with liver failure requires intuitive access to a wide range of information about kidney values, medicine interactions, and standard treatment options along with their likely benefit and risk values. But in both examples, there is no way to train intuition to produce an accurate interpretation or treatment plan without significant risk of bias and error. The details matter. In the geopolitical case, details about who is responsible for the information and what other important events are happening in the region will make a difference to what sort of response is appropriate. In the elderly patient's case, details about the patient's other health problems, psycho-social situation, discharge options, and preferences and values will make a difference to what treatment plan is plausible or likely to be effective.

The following diagram gives a sense of how the relationships between types of practice, types of cognitive process, and types of expertise culminate in a two-path model of expertise (Figure 7.1).

According to this two-path, cognitive systems account of expertise, we take our background assumptions and skills, plus new information, and subject them to either deliberate practice or expansive practice. Deliberate practice intentionally engages System 2 processes to create

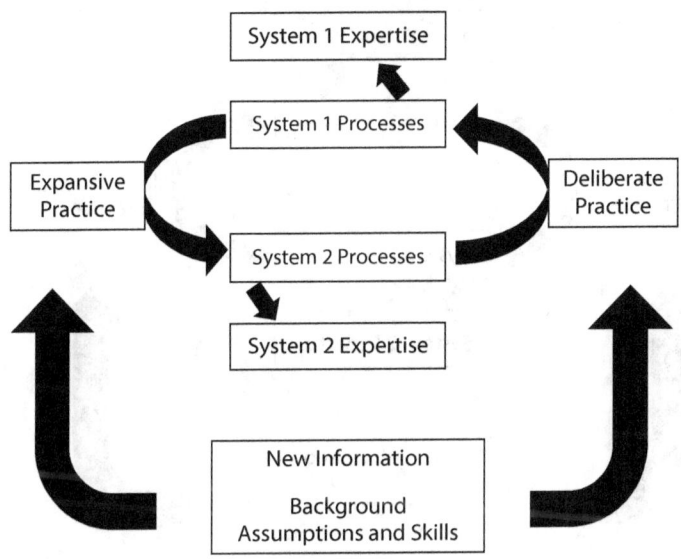

FIGURE 7.1 The Cognitive Systems Account of Expertise.

mental representations and store them in long-term memory. This process makes them available as fast, intuitive, skilled practice that is characteristic of System 1 Expertise. Expansive practice takes our skills and background information along with the products of System 1 processes and slows them down by intentionally engaging System 2 processes to produce the careful, complex judgments characteristic of System 2 Expertise. As a novice engages in expansive practice in light of their study of information, skills, and System 1 expertise in a domain, they train System 1 intuitions to slow down until they become System 2 Expertise.

What is not shown in 7.1 is that some of the information and processes that are included in System 2 Expertise are, as in the cases of intelligence analysis and medical care planning, the products of System 1 Expertise (Figure 7.2).

So far, this account is consistent with our original general definition of expertise from the preface, modified to reflect the domain-relative nature of expert competence:

Expertise*: A high degree of competence in a domain at a time.

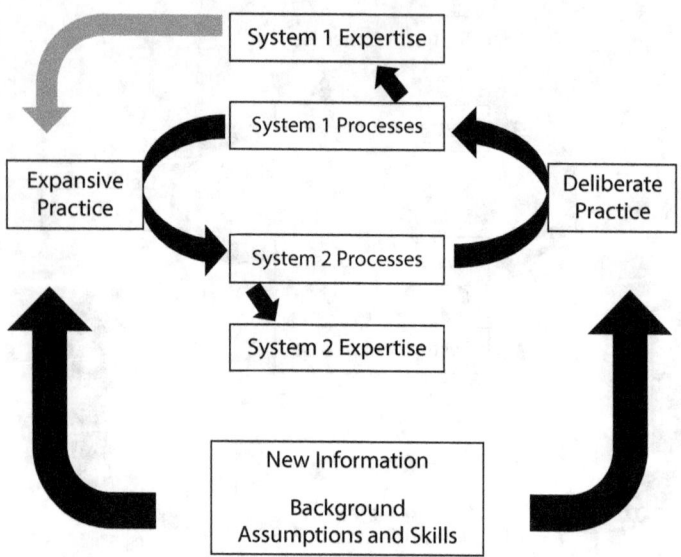

FIGURE 7.2 The Cognitive Systems Account of Expertise, Revised.

Recall that an expert system can exhibit expertise, whether that system is used by a novice or expert user. But the cognitive systems account expands our initial definition of "expert" by including an explanation of why someone counts as an expert:

Expert(cognitive systems): A subject S is an expert in domain D if and only if **(a)** S has a high degree of competence in D at a time that **(b)** is acquired through rigorous training along one of two cognitive systems, and **(c)** that is confirmed to be high enough by the current state of skills and information in D at that time.

The cognitive systems account is broad enough to include understanding or knowledge in a domain, but it is not concerned with specifying their role in the acquisition of expertise; they will play different roles in different domains. The account also explains the ineliminable relative and social dimensions of expertise in that expertise is determined by the current state of a domain, and whether anyone achieves that level of competence will, inevitably, be determined by the community of people who are currently practicing in that domain.

The cognitive systems account is neutral with respect to whether experts should defer to and trust other experts in their domain. While there remain questions about whether relying on peers undermines autonomy, that question is distinct from whether doing so enhances judgment or expertise. There are good reasons to think that when experts engage with other experts, their competence improves (so long as there are safeguards against groupthink and in-fighting; see Tetlock and Gardner 2015, ch. 9). This evidence is also one benefit of team-based medical decision-making (over individual physician decision-making) when hospitals can afford it (Sevin et al. 2009). The cognitive systems account is consistent with whatever strategy improves competence.

Further, this account allows for fine-grained discussions of what constitutes expert placement in a particular domain. In the case of choosing a violinist for an internationally famous orchestra, for example, the primary standard of competence is probably superior performance. In the case of choosing a high-school-level violin teacher, the standard of competence may be medium- to high-quality performance plus a strong facility with the history of the instrument and violin music, music theory, and effective teaching strategies. Epistemic placement can then be used to assess epistemic authority by comparing the degrees to which different people meet the standard of competence.

This account also leaves open what counts as a domain. Whereas some accounts operationally restrict what can count as a domain to what can be studied under certain laboratory conditions (such as practices with known outcomes), or circumscribe them by social processes, such as appointment or social approval (we might feel somewhat incredulous that someone appointed to a vague position like "Risk Management" in a hospital could have expertise in mitigating the vast multiplicity of risks that hospitals face). On the cognitive systems account, new domains can easily count as expert domains, as when behavioral economics emerged from psychology and economics. Idiosyncratic domains, such as games, like Magic: The Gathering, or activities, like pogo-stick jumping, can constitute expert domains.

Importantly, this account does preclude regarding one-off instances of knowledge or acquaintance as instances of expertise. David Coady (2012: 31) claims he is an expert about what he had for breakfast because he knows it better than anyone else. But all he does is *know* it. He has only one isolated experience with it. There is nothing about it with which he has (or could have) developed either understanding or skill. He may have expertise about his *trend* in breakfast *choices* (though simple knowledge of what he has to eat on a regular basis would not count, either), or about breakfast foods, but the cognitive systems account precludes his knowledge of his breakfast as a possible domain of expertise.

7.3.2 A Potential Problem: Hollow Domains[4]

What the cognitive systems account doesn't rule out, on the face of it, are domains that exemplify some of the trappings of expertise, but which are largely comprised, according to other domains, of unsubstantiated or thoroughly discredited claims. Consider acupuncture, which has been around for centuries, has a non-trivial number of practitioners around the world, training schools, a developed methodology, a number of putatively scholarly, peer-reviewed journals supporting the practice, and at least some support from both Western and Eastern physicians. And yet, the benefits of acupuncture, according to many empirical researchers, are debatable (it is unclear whether they outperform placebos), and its metaphysics (*yin*, *yang*, *chi*, and so on) is regarded by most Western scholars as magical thinking. Since my account cannot rule out expertise on the basis of whether putative experts have a substantial fund of truths, I seem committed to the expertise of acupuncturists irrespective of how the debates shake out. The state of the domain, according to its current practitioners, validates it as a domain of expertise. And those outside acupuncture do not, putatively, meet the minimum competence in acupuncture to make authoritative claims about its legitimacy.

Consider also parapsychology. The peer-reviewed *Journal of Parapsychology* is a publication of The Parapsychological Association, "an international professional organization of scientists and scholars engaged in the study of *psi* (or 'psychic') experiences, such as telepathy, clairvoyance, psychokinesis, psychic healing, and precognition." The stated goal of the association is "to achieve a scientific understanding of these experiences" (Parapsychological Association, n.d.) and the group is an "affiliated organization" of the American Academy for the Advancement of Science (AAAS) (AAAS, n.d.). Are parapsychologists experts in parapsychology? Most traditional psychologists think the answer is no. But since non-parapsychologists are, by definition, not experts in parapsychology, it is not immediately clear how they can make pronouncements on the legitimacy of parapsychology.

I think the cognitive systems account can handle this objection. While the cognitive systems account does not explain expertise in terms of truth, per se, this does not mean it is not *truth-seeking*. Evidence is, necessarily, aimed at truth or something close enough to truth. (Elgin [2017: 23–32] points out that, in some cases, instrumental explanations are actually more beneficial than, and preferred over, true ones.) Thus, I don't advocate for any difference in methodology for assessing claims in a domain than truth-based accounts of expertise. For example, whatever evidence veritists would point to in order to evaluate the validity of a domain of expertise, I (and, by extension, my account) would endorse.

But even if this weren't the case, truth-based accounts fare no better in addressing the concern. Acupuncturists and parapsychologists presume to be truth-based enterprises, just as Western medicine and psychology, at least insofar as their explanations that are supposed to reflect the way reality is. Plus, their domains have success conditions and empirical methodologies just like the domains that reject them. Further, some Western doctors accept the legitimacy of acupuncture (its biophysics, if not its metaphysics) precisely because some of the empirical evidence suggests it is beneficial. So, simply appealing to truth-seeking methods cannot resolve disagreements among domains. Further still, there do seem to be people who spend their scholarly lives studying and coming to understand ancient practices and strange belief systems—phrenology, voodoo, alchemy, etc.—and who we have good reason to think are experts in those domains. Even these "hollow" domains are domains, so why shouldn't there be experts in them? The worry is that, once we tie expertise to placement in a domain, we seem dangerously close to another form of relativism.

One attempt to address the problem is to draw a distinction between expertise *in* a domain and expertise *about* a domain. We may allow that there is a domain of acupuncture and allow that some people understand that domain to a high degree, but, based on our understanding *about* it, not accept that there are experts *in* that domain. For example, both Ron Numbers and Thomas Woodward may rightly be regarded as experts *about* Creationism (the belief that natural biodiversity is explained by the direct, creative activity of God in contradistinction to evolution), though the former explicitly rejects Creationism while the latter accepts a version of it.[5] Numbers could respond to questions about creationism with as much authority as Woodward. Similarly, someone might be an expert in some obscure, ancient science, such as the Greek theory of humors, without believing the propositions in that science. While this strategy may be helpful for delineating types of research program in a domain, it does not address the problem at hand because it presupposes that we already know that Creationism and humor theory are hollow domains. It does not help us explain *whether* it is Numbers or Woodward who should give up their beliefs about the matter, or whether acupuncturists should stop practicing as if they were experts.

This raises an interesting question about the relationship among domains. Are domains isolated affairs that preclude assessment by anyone except those who work inside them? The answer is clearly no. There is widespread overlap in the concepts, methodologies, and assumptions across many domains. For example, medical specialties as different as hematology and neurology accept the same claims about the body's biochemistry and drug interactions. Mathematics, engineering, computer programming, and astrobiology share beliefs about how math works. Historians, philosophers (predominantly), geneticists, classicists, and (perhaps to a lesser degree) English professors all accept the basic tenets of logic. If a historian proposes a logically incoherent theory of a historical event, a philosopher has the expertise to reject the historian's claim. And while it is easy to think that the specialists in a domain know best what counts as legitimacy and competence in that domain, specialists can miss important implications that generalists might not (specialists might miss the forest for the trees, so to speak). Thus, a more promising means of addressing the hollow domains problem is to appeal to people who have a grasp of the major overlapping features of multiple domains, that is, to appeal to *meta-experts*.

Recall from Chapter 6 that Collins and Evans distinguish transmuted from non-transmuted meta-expertise, describing transmuted as the ability to take general (non-technical) social knowledge and use it to judge technical expertise, and non-transmuted meta-expertise as having and employing varying degrees of interactional expertise in a domain to judge expertise in that domain. While I think these capture some interesting dynamics between types of expertise, they do not systematically track relationships among experts in domains or different degrees of epistemic placement in a domain. For example, a weak expert in sports trivia is better placed epistemically in that domain than a strong expert in, say American political history. If the history expert makes a claim about, say, Mohammed Ali's conscientious objection to serving in the military, on what grounds could the sports trivia expert challenge her? Would it be transmuted local discrimination or technical connoisseurship or downward discrimination? The key is how well placed the two people are in the overlap between sports and politics. An interactional expert in this overlap can reasonably challenge a contributory expert in this domain by appealing to their understanding of the claims in that domain. Thus, I don't think we need a separate taxonomy of meta-expertises. We simply need a way of explaining how people who are experts in multiple domains can engage with one another on topics in those domains. Borrowing from Collins and Evans's terminology, call this simply *interactional meta-expertise*. On this type of meta-expertise, an expert in one domain is well placed enough (even if they are not a strong expert in that domain) in another domain to judge the plausibility of experts' claims in that domain, and thereby, to help others form responsible beliefs about those domains. This is consistent with Collins and Evans's explanation of meta-expertises without the unnecessary machinery.

Consider the court case of McLean vs. Arkansas Board of Education (1982), which overturned Arkansas's "Balanced Treatment for Creation-Science and Evolution-Science Act" (Talk Origins Archive 1996). The attorneys on both sides of this case were careful not to simply pit evolutionary scientists against creation scientists. Among a number of other physical and social scientists, the attorneys called three people to testify, each of whom had substantive training in both sides at issue in the case. The plaintiffs (those against the Act) called Michael Ruse (a philosopher of science who has a particular research interest in the overlap between religion and science) and Francisco Ayala (a geneticist and former Catholic priest) to testify about the scientific respectability of Creationism as a competitor to Darwinian evolution. The defense called Norman Geisler, a philosopher and theologian, who has written extensively on the relationship between religion and science (*McLean vs. Arkansas Documentation Project 2005*). More than the others, the testimony of these three witnesses, who have substantial research interests in both domains, led to judge William Overton's opinion that creation science is more like religion than science, and thereby, threatens to violate the Establishment Clause of the US Constitution. It is important to note that we have no reason to believe Overton is an expert in religion, philosophy, or science. His expertise is in law, so he presumably comes to these debates as a novice to hear conflicting expert testimony.

In his decision, Overton allows Ruse to set the standard for what is to count as science during the trial. He cites *both Geisler and Ayala* as agreeing that "creation from nothing" is an inherently religious idea. He argues that the case would be stronger if there were, in fact, only two interpretations of the scientific data—Darwinism and Creationism—which even Geisler admits is not true. And he cites Geisler's personal rejection of two of the defense's characterizations of Creationism (catastrophism and young earth theory) as reasons to doubt the strength of the idea that Creationism is good science. He also appeals to Ayala's testimony that many scientists who are religious find no difficulty accepting the Darwinian paradigm, as evidence for the claim that they are not competing *scientific* positions. And finally, he appeals to Ayala's testimony as part of a reason for thinking that evolutionary scientists are not dogmatic in their commitment to Darwinism, allowing that mutation and natural selection do not necessarily account for all significant evolutionary change.

The point is that, though the plaintiffs and defendants brought many scientists and religious thinkers as witnesses, the novice Overton appealed to the experts who had standing in the overlap of these domains—the interactional meta-experts—to draw an informed conclusion about which claim was more plausible. Even if, absent these considerations, each witness's testimony would have been authoritative given his or her epistemic facility with the domain, this authority proves defeasible. Someone who is competent in both domains can help novices adjudicate the conflict. When this sort of expertise is available, the hollow domains problem dissolves; we need not care whether a domain is hollow so long as we have a strategy of determining whether one domain is epistemically preferable to another that is a function of our understanding of expertise.

There are, to be sure, cases where we currently cannot determine whether one is preferable to another. Consider the impasse between classical mechanics and quantum mechanics; neither is sufficient for explaining all physical phenomena and each is sufficient for explaining phenomena the other cannot. In this case, one domain must be hollow (and perhaps both!), but there is no widespread agreement for how to resolve the disagreements. But this is not a problem for either expertise generally or for the cognitive systems account in particular—it is simply a function of human limitations.

So, is a parapsychologist an expert *in* her domain? Given the testimony, not simply of psychologists, but of those who understand the strengths and limitations of experimental procedures (which parapsychologists claim to endorse), I would conclude that parapsychologists of the sort who publish in the *Journal of Paranormal Psychology* and participate in the AAAS are experts *about* their domain, but whose authority to regard it as contributing accurate understanding about the world has been defeated by experts in nearby domains who share competence in the research methods and scientific assumptions that underlie parapsychology.[6] This is where I think the distinction between expert *in* a domain and expert *about* a domain is helpful. Once we've made the judgment that one set of experts' opinions in a domain has been defeated, we may still rightly say they are experts *about* their domain, whether astrology, Creationism, parapsychology, etc. As for acupuncture, while I think there is little evidence to speak for its metaphysics, I think the verdict is still out whether it offers certain kinds of physical benefit over placebo. I am hopeful that some meta-experts will sort it out.

7.3.3 A Tension between Deliberate and Expansive Practice?

So far, I have tried to show that deliberate practice and expansive practice are not only compatible but that they can work together to form different paths to expertise. But there are some red flags that should be taken seriously. Once someone has developed System 1 Expertise, it is very difficult to act outside of one's training. Ericsson (2011: 7) acknowledges this concern when he warns against the "arrested development associated with automaticity" and encourages individuals to "actively counteract tendencies toward automaticity."

There is a sense in which this is inevitable. As we have seen, System 1 Expertise is domain-specific, and the time and energy it takes to develop make it very difficult to acquire System 1 Expertise in multiple domains. And there is a sense in which this is unobjectionable. If you are performing near the upper limit of your domain, shifting practice will most likely lower your effectiveness. But what if evidence arises that your performance is based on a faulty understanding of success in your domain, such that, while you thought the intuitions on which you were relying were successful, in reality, that success was an illusion?

For this example, I'll take aim at some of my own work. Part of my job involves what's called "plain language writing," which is a type of writing and editing of health materials for patients who may have low health literacy. Your health literacy level is how easy it is for you get, understand, and use health information to make important health-related decisions for yourself. It includes how well you understand medical terms, whether you can make sense of risk and benefit language (usually presented as percentages [e.g., 40% chance] or frequencies [4 in 10]), and whether you can accurately fill out paperwork. Plain language writing is full of best practices, from basic grammar (yes, we use the Oxford comma), to numeracy best practices (frequencies are better than percentages), using bullet points for lists, using only 2–3 syllable words when we can, and using the word "to" instead of a hyphen to represent ranges like "2–3" (2 to 3). Once you learn these practices, you can edit a brochure or information booklet pretty quickly. You start to see ways that information in other contexts could be better (direction signs in the hallway, menus). Plain language writing, like other forms of writing, is a developable skill. How many of those best practices are evidence-based? That's a tough question.

When you look at the literature on plain language writing as a way to address low health literacy, there are no controlled experiment studies. How could there be? We can't take a group of people who need important information and divide them into one group that gets information that has been edited using plain language best practices and one that gets dense, jargon-heavy text that reads like a medical textbook. The stakes are too high. And there's a bit of common-sense to it. If you don't know what the word "chronic" means, then a parenthetical note, like "chronic (an illness that lasts more than 12 weeks)," is obviously helpful. But what about bullet points? And the two- to three-syllable words? Is "school" really easier to understand than "education"?

So, where did this list of best practices come from? They sort of emerged through the process of talking about how to make information easier for patients to understand. Clifford Coleman, Stanley Hudson, and Lucinda Maine (2013) surveyed twenty-three health professionals and education experts in an attempt to detect a consensus on a set of best health literacy practices. They discovered unanimity on fifteen of ninety-five practices. More recently, Coleman, Hudson, and Ben Pederson (2017) worked with twenty-five participants to reduce these to eight best practices. The most current systematic review study that tried to determine whether health literacy interventions made a difference was inconclusive (Berkman et al. 2011). What do these studies show? That people who use plain language best practices tend to agree that everyone should use a subset of those practices.

What's the upshot? Even though one can become quite skilled at a set of practices, if those practices do not achieve the goals for which they are performed, performing those practices won't tell you that. I am not sure someone could develop strong System 1 Expertise in plain language writing because it involves a number of critical System 2 processes, but nevertheless, if one simply uses the best practices without reflecting on their efficacy, one could be misled by their seeming success. Happily, in the domain of health literacy, everyone seems to be aware of these limitations. But in domains where there are fewer incentives to check whether a method is working properly or there is a trend toward fad methodologies (as in Six Sigma business strategies, student evaluations of teaching, teaching methods like "think-pair-share," etc.), System 1 Expertise can prevent us from getting much-needed checks on our performance. This suggests that every domain—perhaps outside of music and competitive-Rubik's-Cube solving—would benefit from developing some System 2 Expertise by which to periodically check one's System 1 Expertise.

But we must also be careful not to assume that cognitive errors are restricted to System 1 processes. System 2 processes are subject to their own foibles, for example, decision fatigue and taking either the outside or the inside view at the expense of balancing them against one another. We cannot become so confident in our own judgment that we refuse to use an expert system even when it proves more efficient. Thus, System 1 and System 2 Expertise are not merely two ends of a spectrum that engage System 1 and System 2 processes, but they can also be important checks on one another.

7.4 Is There Evidence for the Cognitive Systems Account?

In developing the two-path model, I have diverged from traditional philosophy in ways some may find disconcerting. I have tied my conceptual analysis to an interpretation of a set of empirical results that may or may not be borne out in the long run. So be it. I think if philosophers want to engage with concepts that will help inform life outside the pages of our books, then we cannot shy away from engaging with empirical work. That said, we must also be honest that empirical research is always shifting and subject to disconfirmation such that arguments based on them are vulnerable in ways besides standard philosophical counterexamples. That said, what evidence is there to support a cognitive systems account of expertise?

I think Ericsson and colleagues have produced an admirable set of evidence for what I am calling System 1 Expertise. Even in light of current criticisms and competing views that attempt to expand the explanation to include some genetic components, I think it will be some time before their theory of how expertise is cultivated and enhanced is eclipsed by something more nuanced and powerful. Therefore, the challenge really lies with identifying evidence that supports the development of System 2 Expertise. And this is not a simple matter.

The disciplines in which System 2 Expertise would likely be found are not siloed, they're not bounded, their results are not typically quantifiable, and they make use of a wide range of experience and knowledge. They include domains like palliative care medicine, journalism, ancient history, politics, and ethics. Tetlock and colleagues' work with superforecasters is probably the most extensive evidence for what I am identifying as this distinct path to expertise. But this is only one research project. If others take up this work and find that Tetlock's decision-making strategies improve judgment in other wicked domains, then the cognitive systems account will be on firmer ground. Happily, I think this work is underway in various forms.

For example, I think there is some important research on medical education that, if it continues to bear out in research, could offer some powerful evidence in favor of expansive practice for developing System 2 Expertise (Norman et al. 2018). Many medical schools now include courses such as Arts and Medicine and Literature and Medicine (as mine does) and medical drawing (as Johns Hopkins's "Art as Applied to Medicine" program does). The thought is that aesthetic experiences and discussion train one's intuition for detail, that is, it has a recognition-priming effect, and then balance that against a bigger picture of what's meaningful. The more attuned you are to noticing and reflecting on detail, the better placed you are to notice subtle symptoms or physical abnormalities and diagnose them (ironically, much like chicken sexing).

And the better you can incorporate those details into the context of a patient's values, preferences, and psychosocial background, the better able you will be to formulate an effective treatment plan. Other attempts to introduce expansive practice into medical school include Readers' Theatre (East Carolina University's Brody School of Medicine; Cleveland Clinic's Lerner College of Medicine), where medical students perform medical plays in various roles, including the role of patient and reflecting writing (Cleveland Clinic), both of which help students understand different narrative forms in order to enhance their empathy and improve their imagination.

Corporations are also finding that people who have a broader set of cognitive abilities seem to perform better in uncertain and unstructured environments like contemporary business (2U 2019). Steve Jobs, for example, said in a 2011 TED Talk, that Apple's understanding that "technology, married with liberal arts, married with the humanities" is what helped make the iPhone a hit (*Technology and Liberal Arts*). Likewise, there are some successful CEOs who claim to have benefited from a liberal arts education (Linshi 2015). To be sure, a liberal arts education is not the same as expansive practice. But it can be part of a broad training strategy in expansive practice. Just as engaging with people who are different from us can reduce bias about those ways in which we are different (Beaman et al. 2009; Qian et al. 2017), engaging with different perspectives can help us think more broadly than our own opinions. And finally, David Epstein's 2019 book *Range: Why Generalists Triumph in a Specialized World* offers copious examples of research suggesting that pursuing a range of diverse interests cultivates skills for operating in dynamic environments.

7.5 What Happens to "Epistemic Facility"?

In Chapter 3, I offered what I thought was the best alternative to veritism called the *epistemic facility* account of expertise:

(EF2) A subject, S, is an expert in a domain, D, if and only if S (a) understands enough of the terms, propositions, arguments, applications, and aims of D, along with the procedures used to formulate meaningful or useful claims or advice in D, such that (b) S has the ability to successfully demonstrate (a) to some relevant population in the discharge of her epistemic activities.

What are we to make of EF2 in light of the cognitive systems account? Is it now obsolete?

I don't think so. In domains where expertise is largely cognitive, involving formulating, evaluating, and debating claims—such as law, physics, philosophy, medicine, and so on—EF2 explains what "competence" means in those domains. In order for a historian, for example, to be well placed in a domain, they must be able to demonstrate to someone that they understand the terms, methods, and arguments in their domain and then use them to produce their own work in the domain (even if it is just teaching materials). On the other hand, in less-cognitive domains, like competitive swimming, sharpshooting, skateboarding, and so on, EF2 doesn't do much work. We wouldn't expect a sharpshooter to know the history of sharpshooting. And if we needed a sharpshooter, that question wouldn't be on the application. For these domains, I don't think we need an analog to EF2 because the outcomes of primarily performative types of expertise are largely sufficient in themselves to determine what counts as "high degree of competence" in those domains.

7.6 Some Test Cases

Any plausible account must be able to address complex situations that, while not problematic on their face, do require some conceptual footwork. In this section, I explore three such situations.

7.6.1 The Boxer and the Coach

In philosophy, it is easy to let our own intuitions about a theory, argument, or counterexample run away with us. Things that seem obvious to those who formulate the idea are not quite so obvious to others (see the extensive literature on lay intuitions about classic philosophical puzzles, such as Weinberg, Nichols, and Stich 2001). In writing this book, I found myself faced with an example of this in Barbara Montero's book *Thought in Action* (2018). She writes:

As some of my undergraduate students vigorously argued, at a boxing match, the old coach in the ring, unable to throw a punch anymore, yet able to impart his great store of information to the boxer is the expert. "Is the coach the expert at boxing theory while the boxer is an expert boxer?" I asked. "Not at all," they responded; on their view, the coach was the only expert in the ring. And my sense is that this conception of expertise while not universally accepted is not idiosyncratic. (2018: 56)

My first reaction was to dismiss the intuitions of "undergraduate students," who, to my mind, simply had not reflected on the nature of the problem. If you wanted to hire someone to fight in a boxing match for you, would you hire the boxer or the boxer's coach who is unable to throw a punch? (If you say, "the coach," dear reader, I respectfully ask that you not mention this to me at a conference. [See how strong my intuition is?])

The only person with the expertise to box is someone who can box.

And yet, when I asked Molly Wilder, a good friend of mine whose philosophical chops are far beyond that of an undergraduate,[7] who the expert in this case is, she also said the coach. While I stumbled on my incredulity, Molly explained that the boxer knows how to *box*, but the coach knows how to *box* and also knows how to *teach boxing*, which involves more competence than simply being able to box.

After discussing, my friend and I agreed that if the coach could also box, then given that she can also teach boxing, she is an expert to a greater degree than the boxer. We also agreed, contra Montero's students, that the boxer is an expert. But someone might make the case that someone who is no longer able to box still *knows how* to box, so the coach still has a higher degree of expertise than the boxer.

The problem, from my perspective, is that the coach can't box anymore. Two questions seem in order, here. First, is it possible to *know how* to do something if you *are not able* to do it? And second, does the ability to teach something demonstrate a superior degree of expertise than being able to do it?

With respect to the first question, Jeremy Fantl (2012) says no:

What is it to know how to ride a bicycle? One natural answer might be this: to know how to ride a bicycle is to have a certain ability—the ability to ride a bicycle. Suppose I am assigning tasks for our start-up pizza business. I ask you, "do you know how to ride a bike?" and, suppose, you say that you do. I might then assign you the task of biking the pizza to the relevant address. If, after the pizza fails to be delivered, you say, "I don't have the ability to ride a bicycle" it seems I can rightly challenge you: "You said you knew how to ride a bike!" This is evidence that knowing how to do something entails the ability to do it. Likewise, it seems that if you have the ability to do something, it follows that you know how to do it. If, when I ask you if you know how to ride a bike, you say, "I'm afraid not," I can rightly be annoyed if later that day I see you tooling around the streets on a bicycle. I can rightly say, "I thought you said you didn't know how to ride!" It would be an odd answer indeed if you responded, "That's right, I don't know how. I'm just able to do so."

This set of examples seems compelling to me until I consider the case of someone who used to ride bicycles but, due to an accident, has become paraplegic. If you ask this person whether they know how to ride a bicycle, would it not be weird for them to say "No"? Don't they still retain the understanding of how to ride a bicycle, even if only tacitly (in their blood, as Rilke says)? What are we to make of this conflict in intuition?

I think the answer is that we are trading on a simple equivocation in meaning in the phrase "know how." If Fantl asked the person with paraplegia if she knew how to ride a bike, and she said, "Yes," he would not be surprised to find that she was not delivering pizzas for him. In the context of hiring a pizza delivery person, the question, "Do you know how to X?" implies "Can you X?" It is a question about ability. But in the context of a person with paraplegia, the question implies, "Do you understand how to X?" where understanding is construed broadly to mean something like, "If I were able, I could."

Does this help the boxer case? I think it does. The boxer knows how to box. The coach knows how to box in the sense that she *understands how to* box, even though she no longer *can* box. If boxing expertise is competence in boxing, then the coach doesn't have as much expertise as a boxer because she can't box. But the old coach surely has something: an understanding of boxing in her mind and blood that would let her, should she miraculously regain strength, box better than most amateurs.

On the other hand, if boxing expertise is competence in what boxing is and means, then the coach surely has boxing expertise, and to a greater degree than the boxer. Consider that world champion swimmer Simone Manuel would be an expert swimmer even if she knew nothing about the history, biomechanics, or physics of swimming. So, the answer to our original question depends heavily on how we carve the domain.

Moving to the second question, let us stipulate that the boxer has expertise in being able to box, and the coach has expertise in understanding how to box. Is the coach more of an expert than the boxer? Consider a different question, if someone who studies the biomechanics of swimming were to teach Simone Manuel about the physiology of how she swims and that improves Manuel's performance, would we say the biomechanics expert is more of an expert than Manuel? That seems like an odd question. They are simply two different—though overlapping—domains of expertise, and that's true even if the biomechanics expert used to be a competitive swimmer. So, in the case of the boxer and the coach, the boxer is more of an expert *boxer* than the coach, and the coach is more of an expert *about boxing* than the boxer. And whether one domain enhances performance in the other depends on the domain. An Art History professor could be a superb teacher of various painting techniques even if she never lifted a brush; and a brilliant painter may be a terrible teacher.

Wrapping up, I don't think there is anything in this case that causes serious problems for accounts of expertise. Once we carve domains according to their performance standards, it seems we can conclude that both the boxer and the coach are experts, only in different domains. Further, it is not obvious to me (though Molly still thinks so) that being able to expertly teach something in a domain renders one more expert than one who merely performs expertly in that domain.

7.6.2 The Lone Ranger Expert

Alvin Goldman (2001, 2018) mentions the possibility of someone becoming an expert independently of an epistemic community. He says, "Someone interested in the history of opera, for example, might become an expert on opera under her own scholarly steam rather than through a series of academic classes" (2018: 4). Given that expertise, on my account, requires specific and extensive training to develop one of two cognitive pathways, is it reasonable to expect a novice to be able to acquire expertise without the substantial support of and feedback from an epistemic community? Could someone be a lone ranger expert, that is, acquire expertise in a domain without engaging with other experts?

I think the answer depends on how we interpret that question. One interpretation is that it is asking whether other experts must be directly involved in a person's training. I think the answer to that question varies depending on the domain. Ericsson and Pool strongly emphasize the role of a teacher in deliberate practice. But their focus is on superior performers, the top 1 percent of people in their domain. And we know that in most domains, more than the top 1 percent are experts even if they would not count as superior performers on their view. Ericsson and Pool also give advice on how to make use of deliberate practice in the absence of a teacher, suggesting that one can substantially improve one's placement in a domain on their own regardless of whether they become a superior performer. And thousands of famous musicians are self-taught, including Django Reinhardt, arguably the greatest guitarist of all time.

But, again, I think the answer depends on the domain. Recall that Harry Collins became what he calls an interactional expert in gravitational wave physics. But he doesn't think he could have done this only by reading books or articles. He had to talk with gravitational wave physicists, ask questions, get feedback. In other words, he had to immerse himself in their linguistic community. Even a veritist would have to admit that learning a domain as specialized as gravitational wave physics is not merely a matter of learning the claims in that domain and the relationships among them. It requires understanding how gravitational wave physicists talk about those claims, how they use them, how they weigh them, and how they regard their significance for other domains of physics.

So, could someone become an expert on opera history without a personal teacher? Probably. Could they learn to *sing* opera on their own? Perhaps a few could. We shouldn't restrict such possibilities *a priori*. But opera singing is like the gravitational wave physics of music. Without a skilled vocal coach, it is very difficult to make progress.

On the other hand, someone might interpret the question as asking whether other experts must be involved in any way, directly or indirectly, in a person's training. A "no" answer to this question is less plausible. The opera buff has books and websites to learn from. She has indirect expert training. How could one learn the history of opera without testimony from people who were there? Even the self-taught guitarist has models to try to mimic in the form of other guitarists. People who learn to play music by ear spend countless hours watching and listening and trying to mimic what they observe. But put a child and a guitar alone on an island, and ask them to start practicing from scratch, and even apart from constant worries about food scarcity, they would likely make little progress. Again, I don't want to rule out empirical possibilities without evidence, but there is no question that technology and the distribution of expertise through books and other media make expertise significantly easier to acquire. So, even if there were no necessary social condition for expertise, in practice, almost all expertise is acquired in and through an epistemic community.

7.6.3 The New Domain Problem[8]

What about new domains? If there is no developed domain to practice, then it might seem that my account implies no one could be an expert in a domain they develop, even if no one else in the world knows anything about that domain except them, such as the first biologist or the person who created the game Go. Terry Pratchett makes this point ironically in his novel *Raising Steam*, when his character Dick Simnel, who creates the first working steam locomotive, says: "Since I've never done me indentures, I can never be a master because there's nobody who knows more about what I'm doing than, well, me. I've looked in all t'manuals and read all t'books and you can't be a master until all the other masters say you are a master" (2013: 105, italics his). Call this the *new domain problem* for expertise.

I think there are two replies available to the proponent of the cognitive systems model. First, few new types of expertise occur without any background information whatever. For example, most biology textbooks cite Aristotle as the first "biologist" because of his extensive documentation, classification, and accounts of the development of flora and fauna. But Aristotle was not the first to propound and apply hypotheses about animals. Animal husbandry in the Middle East can be traced to 7700 BCE, and Aristotle's own accounts suggest he spent ample time with people who worked directly with animals. Homer mentions domesticated sheep and cattle in *The Odyssey*, written sometime between the late eighth and late seventh centuries BCE.[9] Hesiod (in *Works and Days*) implicitly and Herodotus (in *The Histories*) explicitly demonstrate working knowledge of animal physiology. Thus, while Aristotle certainly gave substance and structure to the domain of biology, he was not working without a rich background knowledge that he spent years applying to develop this new domain of expertise.

A second reply is that, even in those cases where there is no background, such as someone who creates a new game, their knowledge of the game's dynamics upon creating it does not meet even the broadly intuitive criteria for expertise. Presumably, even the developer would admit that she has little competence in the game, and she would not have any more competence with the game than anyone to whom she had taught the rules.

One might object here that she is an expert in virtue of the fact that her knowledge of the game *constitutes* the state of the *domain-at-a-time*, and therefore, whatever minimal competence she has must be regarded as sufficient for expertise because there is no other standard in the domain at that time. But this does not follow.[10] Learning anything is a process during which one undergoes development from novice to some higher degree of competence. She certainly has a better understanding of the game than anyone, which gives her an epistemic advantage. But epistemic advantage is not expertise, and whether the game can be played better with additional practice is an open question.

The objector might persist: *But that is irrelevant; even if it could be played better, the standard cannot be how well the game could be played according to some idealized standard* (e.g., just because scientists *could* understand infinitely *more* about the universe than they currently do does not mean they are not experts now). In response, I would point out that the key here is not whether the game could be played better, but whether it admits of degrees of betterment in the first place. Processes that do not require rigorous training (voting, getting the mail, lowering the toilet seat[11]) are not candidate domains of expertise. The question is whether the game could be a domain of expertise. We can only learn whether the new game is a candidate for expertise—and therefore, whether its creator has become an expert—by playing the game, that is, through practice and feedback.

7.7 Conclusions

I opened this book with five big questions about expertise:

1 What is an expert?
2 How does someone become an expert?

3 What does it mean to say that an expert has "authority," and how much should we trust authorities?

4 How does anyone recognize an expert, and how do we choose which experts to listen to?

5 How do we decide what to believe or do when experts disagree?

Here, I have only addressed questions 1 and 2. But these are foundational. To explain what sort of authority experts have, we must know what sort of thing an expert is. In order to recognize an expert, we have to know what experts are supposed to be able to do. And to know whether and how much to trust experts, especially when they disagree, we have to have a sense of what makes them trustworthy.

In our technologically infused world that is increasingly structured to encourage us to avoid thinking too much, these questions about expertise will become ever more pressing. Recognizing the ways expertise can be confounded is a first line of defense against trusting the wrong set of folks. Understanding what makes an expert an expert is another. Each of these remaining questions could easily fill its own volume. But perhaps this book goes some way toward getting clear on what expertise is so that any discussion of expert authority, trustworthiness, or disagreement can start on a firm ground of what concept is at stake in each question. And even if disagreement remains, perhaps that disagreement can be articulated more effectively.

NOTES

Acknowledgments

1   Disjunctivism is the view that the fundamental constituents of a concept may be different and mutually exclusive under different circumstances, such that something is X if and only if it is Y or Z, where Y and Z are mutually exclusive. A classic example of disjunctivism of this sort comes from David Lewis ([1980]2010), where he argues that the causal processes we call "pain" in some circumstances may be fundamentally different from the causal processes that cause "pain" in another.
2   Oliver Scholz draws this distinction (2009: 188; 2018: 30).

Chapter 1

1   Cf. Audi (2006) for a defense of this definition.
2   See Tetlock (2005).
3   After reviewing dozens of studies of the effectiveness of therapy, psychological researchers J. T. Landman and R. M. Dawes (1982) and J. S. Berman and N. C. Norton (1985) conclude that minimally trained "parapsychologists" are roughly equal in effectiveness to professionally trained psychotherapists. Berman and Norton write: "We found that professional and paraprofessional therapists were generally equal in effectiveness. Our analyses also indicated that professionals may be better for brief treatments and older patients, but these differences were slight. Current research evidence does not indicate that paraprofessionals are more effective, but neither does it reveal any substantial superiority for the professionally trained therapist" (401, abstract).
4   Hodgson (2008).
5   See Bishop and Trout (2005: 24–53) for a review of how putative expertise in predicting employee success from interviews, criminal recidivism, loan defaults, and necessary length of psychiatric hospitalization has been obviated by Statistical Prediction Rules (SPRs).
6   This happens to be true in Pratchett's fictional universe.
7   Perhaps he thinks "peer affirmation" is a strictly necessary condition such that, if literally everyone stopped trusting experts, expertise would cease

to exist. If that were true, it would be an interesting question what follows, especially if people are still highly educated and specialized, and especially if people still trust one another locally (though not as experts).

8   There are a number of other caveats here. A small number of journals have the highest numbers of retractions, and retraction rates differ in different countries. Nichols doesn't point this out, but it is relevant to his claim.

9   Thanks to Markus Seidel for this point.

10 At one of our graduations for the medical school, a graduation speaker talked about "the power of the white coat" to calm patients as soon as they see it. He said they know it means they will be taken care of. That is not my experience with doctors, but I imagine some can relate to it.

11 See Rieder (2019).

12 For example, Hillsdale College in Michigan and Patrick Henry College in Virginia are dedicated to free-market economic principles. And Bioa University in California offers an advanced degree in Christian Apologetics, the domain of study committed to defending Christianity against critics, and often a specific set of Christian beliefs.

13 John Hardwig (1985) makes a similar case: "The list of things I believe, though I have no evidence for the truth of them, is, if not infinite, virtually endless. And I am finite. … I believe too much; there is too much relevant evidence (much of it available only after extensive, specialized training); intellect is too small and life too short" (328).

14 A caveat is worth mentioning here. The participants in this study were either in college or graduated, a majority were college graduates, and many had advanced degrees, so there are concerns about whether these findings generalize to Americans generally. While 60 percent of Americans over the age of twenty-five have had some college, only 34 percent have a bachelor's degree (US Census, 2014).

15 See David Coady (2012, chapter 5), "Conspiracy Theories and Conspiracy Theorists."

16 See Postman (1985) on how television changed the way expert information is disseminated.

17 I am speaking casually here about reasons. I don't mean to imply that traditional theories of justification are all "evidentialist" or "internalist" or "cognitivist" (see Watson n.d.). My point is that tribal epistemology is different in important ways from any of these.

18 See Flax (1983) and Hartsock (1987).

19 See Alison Wylie and Lynn Hankinson Nelson (2009). See also Miriam Solomon (2009).

20 Portions of this section are adapted from Watson (2016).

21 See also Cass Sunstein, *#Republic* (2017).

22 The idea here is that a company like Time Warner or Viacom would be making *their* opinions the rule of judgment, which is, arguably, no different from what a state official would do. For an example of how corporations might filter poorly, see the documentary *This Film Is Not Yet Rated* (IFC, 2006).

23 Following Pariser's example, I conducted an informal search, asking Facebook friends of various political and religious persuasions from around the world to search the phrases "net neutrality" and "media bias" on Google. The results are suggestive but not radical. Wikipedia came up first on almost every search, suggesting that popularity still drives the filters. The first two to three hits were the same on almost everyone's searches, from Bolivia to Korea to the United States. The results of those who used more ad blockers and security measures were much the same after the first two or three hits. But for those without such measures, the rest of the hits varied significantly.

24 "According to one *Wall Street Journal* study, the top fifty internet sites, from CNN to Yahoo to MSN, install an average of 64 data-laden cookies and personal tracking beacons each" (Pariser 2011: 6). The study Pariser references is Julia Angwin, "The Web's New Gold Mine: Your Secrets," *Wall Street Journal*, July 30, 2010, http://www.wsj.com/articles/SB10001424052748703940904575395073512989404.

25 Pariser attributes the phrase "persuasion profile" to Dean Eckles, from a phone interview (121).

26 The phrase "in the wrong hands" is important, since some argue that persuasion profiling can benefit consumers. As an example, Pariser cites DirectLife, "a wearable coaching device by Philips that figures out which arguments get people eating more healthily and exercising more regularly" (Pariser, 121). The popular *nudge* literature also advocates using persuasion profiling in ways that benefit individuals according to their own sense of what is beneficial (cf. Thaler and Sunstein 2009).

27 Adapted from Nguyen (2018a: 6–7).

28 See Fantl (2018) for an argument for the value of closed-mindedness in cases like these and others.

29 Consider physicist Frederick Seitz, former president of the US National Academy of Sciences, who was enlisted to defend the tobacco industry against the claim that cigarettes are harmful. "Seitz believed passionately in science and technology, both as the cause of modern health and wealth and the only means for future improvements, and it infuriated him that others didn't see it his way." Nevertheless, "Seitz saw irrationality everywhere, from the attack on tobacco to the 'attempt to lay much of the blame for cancer upon industrialization.' After all, the natural environment was hardly

carcinogen-free, he noted, and even 'the oxygen in the air we breathe … plays a role in radiation-induced cancer'" (Oreskes and Conway 2010: 28). Seitz would likely reject Lackey's echo chamber precisely because it seems to lack true content. (Thanks to Markus Seidel for pointing me to this reference.)

Chapter 2

1. To be sure, not all agents need be human. But until we discover (or create) other intelligent persons, I feel safe restricting my discussion to human experts.
2. Harold Fowler translates *gnostikein* as "intellectual."
3. This story is relayed in Diogenes Laertius's *Lives of Eminent Philosophers*, Book VI, chapter 2, section 40. Laertius notes that, in response to the jibe, someone added the qualification "having broad nails." Laertius doesn't say who added it.
4. Call this "definitional" reduction (Scholz 2018), where a concept can be explicated in terms of more basic concepts. Philosophers also debate the plausibility of "ontological" reduction, for example, whether the color red is reducible to its molecular composition or whether a particular university is reducible to any of its constituent parts, and "theoretical" reduction, where a scientific theory (e.g., Kepler's laws and Galileo's laws) can be explained by a more robust theory with fewer theoretical postulates (e.g., Newtonian laws).
5. For reference, Licon (2012) explicitly claims to offer a reductive account of expertise.
6. A person has a defeater for a disposition to act if they have good reasons for not keeping that disposition.
7. Assuming, of course, that knowledge is justified true belief. Most philosophers today add a fourth place-holder condition to the effect of "whatever would protect knowledge from Gettier cases."
8. An exception seems to be the Dreyfuses' view, as we will see in Chapter 4.
9. Plato draws a similar distinction in *Statesman*, but we will look more closely at that passage in 5.1.
10. Thanks to Dr. Scott Malm for this example.
11. See Dreyfus and Dreyfus (1986: chapter 4) and Buchanan et al. (2018) for more on the history of knowledge engineering and expert systems.
12. I took this example from David Epstein's book *Range* (2019).
13. Buchanan et al. (2018: 84).

14 See Howard and Dawes (1976), Edwards and Edwards (1977), and Thornton (1977). I am indebted to Bishop and Trout (2005) for this example.

15 Of course, this expert system might be a marvelous predictor without being able to offer much guidance. We can imagine a couple begging the researchers, "Yes, we understand *that* our marriage is on the rocks. But *how* do we fix it?"

16 For more on how technology enhances expertise, see journalist David Epstein's (2014b) TED Talk, "Are athletes really getting, faster, better, stronger?"

17 I am assuming without argument that we cannot meaningfully ascribe intentional states like belief, hope, knowledge, or justification to non-conscious technologies, and so any talk about the "authority" of a system simply reduces to talk about "reliability." But I am open to further discussion on this point, and see Freiman and Miller (2020) for an argument that artificial entities can express "quasi-testimony," which may imply that a richer set of mental terms may be appropriately ascribed to certain kinds of technology.

18 I can imagine reasonable disagreement on this point. There may be scholars who think there are intuitions in favor of treating expert systems as experts. For example, Goldman (2018) casually suggests that Google's search algorithm is an expert because, when prompted, it produces more true beliefs than false in a domain (lots of domains, in fact). But in order to make this case, one needs to defend an account of expertise (which Goldman does, as we will see in Chapter 3) and an account of authority that entail regarding an algorithm as an expert. For my money, an expert has to be an epistemic agent, and algorithms just don't fit the bill.

Chapter 3

1 Parts of this section are adapted and revised from Watson (2019).

2 Goldman ([2001] 2002): 144). Interestingly, cognitive psychologist Merim Bilalić (2017: 8) categorizes chess mastery as a type of cognitive expertise, whereas most philosophers and psychologists treat it as a species of performative expertise.

3 Specifically, he says "knowledge can be piecemeal, can grasp isolate truths one by one, whereas understanding always involves seeing connections and relations between the items known" and a claim like "'The only part of modern physics I understand is the formula '$E=mc^2$' is nonsense."

4 Goldman wrestles with several formulations of expertise, but this is the version he takes to be the least problematic. I set aside the parenthetical note about credences because Goldman doesn't elaborate.

5   The idea that experts should be able to solve "novel" problems has a rich history. John Dewey (1910) regards the ability to address novel problems as essential for expertise. And W. K. Clifford ([1872] 1886) says that competence with novelty distinguishes ordinary technical skill with scientific thinking: "Now it seems to me that the difference between scientific thought and merely technical thought ... is just this: Both of them make use of experience to direct human action; but while technical thought or skill enables a man to deal with the same circumstances that he has met with before, scientific thought enables him to deal with different circumstances that he has never met with before" (88).

6   Licon (2012: 450–1) also includes a condition like (C) in his account of expertise.

7   See, for example, Scholz (2009).

8   My wording here is intentional. I say "it shows how expertise could be objective" because simply defining expertise a certain way does not imply that there are instances of it in the world. There is a further question as to whether anyone actually meets the criteria set out by truth-based accounts.

9   Note that Quast (2018a) could not make this move because he argues that fulfilling a social function to make others better off epistemically is intrinsic to expertise.

10 "For Newton and some of his most illustrious contemporaries, including Robert Boyle (1627–1691) and John Locke (1632–1704), alchemy was a very serious part of chemistry that held great promise for understanding the nature of matter" (Davis 2009: 118–19). This view was not, however, held by all putative experts. Less than a generation prior, Descartes associated alchemy with astrology and magic, and regarded them all as "false sciences" (Descartes 1988: 24).

11 Note that claiming their beliefs were "approximately true" will not help here because that only means they were very close to what we believe today. But this presupposes that what we believe today is "actually true," despite the distinct possibility that we are in the same position as Copernicus or Newton.

12 This case is relayed by Hempel (1966, ch. 2).

13 Someone might object that this argument presupposes an instrumentalist or skeptical view of scientific progress. If one is a strong realist, it is argued, this pessimism is unwarranted, and therefore, the objection loses its force. Many of Newton's beliefs turn out to be true in practice and under certain restricted conditions. If one is a strong enough realist, I think this is right. But I think the advent of the historical perspective on science casts serious doubts on strong realism. This need not leave us with anti-realism or instrumentalism. One may continue to regard science as truth-oriented even if, given our cognitive and linguistic limitations, we are unable to obtain it reliably. It is important to note that even if many of Newton's conclusions were true, his arguments for them (assuming the Euclidean structure of space, and space's ontological distinctness from time) are not cogent. Thanks to Markus Seidel for this objection.

14 Perhaps the earliest presentation is in Book 2 of Sextus Empiricus's *Outlines of Pyrrhonism*, and it plays an important role in Michel de Montaigne's "Apology for Raimond Sebond" (see Kevin McCain 2014). But its most thorough explication was given by Roderick Chisholm (1973).

15 It is noteworthy that some epistemologists now deny that epistemic regress ad infinitum is an obstacle to justification. For example, Peter Klein and Scott Aikin (2009) defend what is known as "infinitism" about justification, according to which an infinite series of non-circular, successive reasons can plausibly justify a subject with respect to a belief. Nevertheless, infinitism remains an internalist view, and thereby cannot help test the reliability of a subject's access to truth.

16 Walton (2014: 142) says Mizrahi "argues that arguments from expert opinion are *inherently* weak," (italics mine). But this is not right. Mizrahi offers contingent, empirical evidence for believing that such arguments are weak. If experts got better at predictions, premise 2 would be false, and his conclusion would not follow. He gives no reason to think they are inherently weak or that experts couldn't, in principle, get better.

17 Mizrahi cites Freedman (2010) for evidence 2 and 3, but I could not find the sources Freedman cites for these. Retraction rates are difficult to track because they depend heavily on which disciplines are being measured. For example, Van Noorden (2011) cites retraction rates in "scientific" journals between about 280 and 340 for 2009, whereas Steen, Casadevall, and Fang (2013) cite well over a thousand retractions for 2009.

18 Mizrahi cites Freedman (2010) for this; Freedman attributes this to Dr. Jerome Groopman (p. 35) but gives no citation; see Groopman (2010) for doctor's perspective on medical error.

19 Three collections of articles in this domain are representative: Kahneman, Slovic, and Tversky (1982); Kahneman and Tversky (2000); Gilovich, Griffin, and Kahneman (2002).

20 This is an admittedly overly simplistic characterization. For more on how heuristics may have evolved, see Gigerenzer (2008).

21 They cite three other studies supporting this: Coughlin and Patel (1987); Patel and Ericsson (1990); and Patel et al. (1986).

22 See also Stichter (2015) for an argument against a strong distinction between cognitive and skilled expertise.

23 Elijah Chudnoff (2019) attempts to distinguish two kinds of cognitive expertise—intellectual and mental. There are two problems with Chudnoff's approach. First, he presupposes that the "traditional" taxonomy divides types of expertise into "perceptual," "cognitive," and "motor." This distinction is found only in the neurology of expertise

literature, as explained by Bilalić (2017). This leaves Chudnoff with a vague distinction between the perceptual and cognitive aspects of some types of expertise (such as chess expertise) that is not supported elsewhere in the literature. Second, as noted earlier, Bilalić defines "cognitive expertise" idiosyncratically, such that cognitive expertise is a subtype of what psychologists of expertise identify as superior performance. This leaves Chudnoff with a vague distinction between the cognitive and doxastic aspects of some types of expertise, such as art history and palliative care medicine. Since Chudnoff's starting assumptions are unmotivated in the mainstream literature, I take it his distinction is similarly unmotivated.

24 The domain-at-a-time standard also allows us to sidestep the question of whether the degree of expertise is due to genetic "giftedness." While Ericsson and colleagues argue that expertise has little or nothing to do with innate talent or gifts, even in the cases of savant syndrome (2016: 219–22), others argue that there are genetic bases at least for musical expertise (Mosing et al. 2018, and Tan et al. 2018) and drawing expertise (Drake and Winner 2018), and connections between autism and child prodigies (Ruthsatz et al. 2018). The domain-at-a-time standard allows that, no matter how a person arrives at that degree of competence, they could be considered an expert. There is, however, a concern about whether the rigor of training is necessary for expertise, which I will address later in this book. For now, what's notable in all of these research findings is that, even if genetic markers indicate that it will be *easier* for a child to master certain domains or gives them a proclivity for choosing those activities, that mastery still requires extensive practice or learning.

25 See also the Myles Burnyeat reference in footnote 4.

26 See Fantl (2008) for more on the philosophical debate over this distinction.

27 Note that "success" here should not be read in veritistic terms. What constitutes success will look different in different subject matters and social contexts, but it is still the case that no one has cognitive access to mind-independent truths.

28 It is also consistent with the following thought experiment from David Coady: "Suppose Jones has acquired significantly more accurate information about a subject than most people, but that, as a result of some cognitive impairment, Jones is no longer able to accurately answer new questions that arise about the subject. Is Jones an expert? It seems to me that Jones is an expert, at least until such a time that the subject in question has changed (or lay knowledge of it has expanded) to the point that Jones's store of accurate information on the subject is no longer significantly greater than most people's" (2012: 29–30).

Chapter 4

1. As mentioned in a previous note, experimental psychologist Merim Bilalić (2017) calls chess playing a type of "cognitive expertise," but he treats it as a type of performative expertise as discussed in this and the next chapters. This is an idiosyncratic use of cognitive expertise, which is primarily associated with the truth-tracking accounts discussed in Chapter 5.
2. The brackets indicate changes to reflect the introduction of gender-neutral pronouns.
3. Per Angela Duckworth (2016) (who, I take it, has an epistemic advantage because she has talked with him) his name is pronounced *chick-sent-mee-high*.
4. Dreyfus (2006) adds two more levels to this continuum: Mastery and Practical Wisdom. Unfortunately, this adds more confusion to the Dreyfus view than substance. Are masters no longer experts as advanced beginners are no longer novices? Thus, I leave evaluation of this more complex Dreyfusian view to others.
5. See Dreyfus (1979) for more on embodiment.
6. See George Bealer (1992) for a discussion of "physical intuition."
7. In fact, I think Leyva gets the standard accounts of knowledge-that and knowledge-how incorrect. He explicitly associates knowledge-that with *intellectualism* and knowledge-how with *anti-intellectualism*. Intellectualism treats all knowledge as reducible to propositions (knowledge-how always presupposes some knowledge-that). As Ryle explains the intellectualist tradition: "This point is commonly expressed in the vernacular by saying that an action exhibits intelligence, if, and only if, the agent is thinking what he is doing while he is doing it, and thinking what he is doing in such a manner that he would not do the action so well if he were not thinking what he is doing" ([1949] 2009: 18). Anti-intellectualists argue either that all knowledge reduces to abilities (knowledge-that always presupposes some knowledge-how) (Ryle's view) or that knowledge-how and knowledge-that are independent types of knowledge (see Fantl 2008). Leyva's view seems closest to what Dreyfus and Ryle describe as embodied knowledge, knowledge that is not rule-based. Here's an example from Ryle: "It should be noticed that the boy is not said to know how to play [a game], if all that he can do is to recite the rules accurately. He must be able to make the required moves. But he is said to know how to play if, although he cannot cite the rules, he normally does make the permitted moves, avoid the forbidden moves and protest if his opponent makes forbidden moves. His knowledge how is exercised

primarily in the moves that he makes, or concedes, and in the moves that he avoids or vetoes" ([1949] 2009: 29).

8   Sacks relays this story in *The Man Who Mistook His Wife for a Hat* (1985).
9   See Baumeister (1984); Beilock (2010); Yarrow et al. (2009).

Chapter 5

1   It is not clear to me that gardening, or at least horticulture, is not a plausible domain of expertise. Visit the gardens at the Biltmore Estate in Asheville, NC during spring to observe what is, ostensibly, the result of expertise. Further, Ericsson has worked with companies to apply deliberate practice-like principles in business management, so it is not clear that this list helps their case.

2   Ericsson and Pool define a mental representation as "a mental structure that corresponds to an object, an idea, a collection of information, or anything else, concrete or abstract, that the brain is thinking about" (2016: 58). This rather meagre description makes mental representations sound a lot like what John Locke (1975) called "ideas" when he says he means by that "whatever is meant by *phantasm, notion, species*, or whatever it is which the mind can be employed about in thinking" (Introduction, §8, italics his). But as they describe their role, it becomes clear that Ericsson and Pool mean something much richer by mental representation than "idea." It is much closer to what Scholz (2018) calls "understanding."

3   This example is taken from Ericsson (2018: 6).

4   Education researchers, for example, often express exasperation at the difficulties of identifying successful teaching techniques. Consider that, in a high school class, students are becoming adults biologically and emotionally, living in a variety of different home environments (some of which have disengaged or even dangerous families), struggling with varying degrees of health problems and disabilities, and have varying levels of interest in any particular subject. To say that it is the teacher's responsibility when a student fails a math test strains credulity.

5   Tetlock's actual statement: "When we pit experts against minimalist performance benchmarks—dilettantes, dart-throwing chimps, and assorted extrapolation algorithms—we find few signs that expertise translates into greater ability to make either 'well-calibrated' or 'discriminating' forecasts" (2005: 20).

Chapter 6

1. For further discussion of Campbell's work and a biological perspective on how ideas may be distributed via evolutionary mechanisms, see Blackmore (1999: 17, 29).

2. Harry Collins (2014) makes a similar point, saying the "relational theory" of expertise "provides no guidance on how to choose between competing experts; if all experts are there only because people call them experts, how can anyone choose one over another? The relational theory," Collins continues, "also fails to capture the day-to-day experience of life. Learn, or, more pertinently, fail to learn, to ride a bike, play the piano, read and write, or even speak a language, and the felt experience is of not having an expertise as opposed to having one" (50). Interestingly, Collins's conclusion is not that these critiques invalidate the relational view but simply show that it is inadequate. "The practical problems do not prove the relational theory wrong any more than bumping into a wall proves that life is not a dream, but the relational theory simply does not address the practical problems" (49–50).

3. Turner acknowledges that this taxonomy is not intended to be comprehensive (2014: 35).

4. See Kory Stamper (2017) for a wonderful discussion of the singular "they" from the perspective of a dictionary writer.

5. As Selinger (2011: 73) explains, "Collins believes that the (right kind) of talking computers and the (right kind) of talking lions would be examples of minimally embodied beings who are, in principle, capable of passing the Turing Test."

6. Note that this is not the same as "transmuted" expertise, since the localized expert has a degree of expertise in the domain they are judging. The same is true of the example Collins and Evans give of sheep farmers during the cleanup of radioactive material following Chernobyl. "The sheep farmers have a specialist contributory expertise ... highly relevant to the ecology of sheep on radioactive fells, but, unfortunately, it went unrecognized by Ministry scientists" (2007: 49). The fact that the sheep farmers' expertise overlaps with the domain of the Ministry scientists renders this an example of an expert coordination problem than a reason to introduce another type of expertise. In my view, Collins and Evans would be better served by dropping the transmuted/non-transmuted distinction and focusing instead on epistemic placement in a domain.

7. I don't think we need to distinguish this as a distinct type of meta-expertise. In this example, the localized expert can play this "meta-expert" role simply by being better placed with respect to copy machines than the electrical engineer. In Chapter 7, I argue that anyone with expertise that overlaps with other domains can serve in this meta-expert role, such that we don't need a distinct set of meta-expertises.

8. This critique was inspired by concerns raised by Selinger (2011: 76–7).

Chapter 7

1. According to Tetlock and Gardner (2015: 72–80), diversity of information, rather than amount, is the better predictor of accuracy in decision-making.
2. To act more like a fox than a hedgehog.
3. Let the reader understand that what I mean by "expansive practice" is distinct from what Yrjö Engeström (2018) means by "expansive learning." Engeström is working in what is called the Activity Theory of education and uses "expansive learning" to refer to a certain kind of learning process. Though expansive learning can contribute to expertise, it has different elements than my "expansive practice" and applies to a much broader set of learning conditions.
4. Portions of this section are adapted from Watson (2018). There, I called this the "Hollow Topics Problem."
5. Ron Numbers wrote a 600-page history of creationism called *The Creationists: From Scientific Creationism to Intelligent Design* (Cambridge, MA: Harvard University Press, 2006). Thomas Woodward wrote a history of the intelligent design movement called *Doubts about Darwin* (Grand Rapids, MI: Baker Books, 2004).
6. For an excellent discussion of the strengths and weaknesses of parapsychological research from a meta-expertise perspective, see Gilovich (1991), ch. 9. And for a discussion of how to reason through conflicting evidence claims, see Schick and Vaughn (2010).
7. I am naming her with permission.
8. In Watson (2019), I called this the "new expert problem." But after reflecting on the nature of the problem, it is centrally a problem about domains.
9. According to classicist Emily Wilson (2018: 14–15), the context for mentioning these animals is all the more interesting because the animals mentioned ("large, impressive domesticated animals like pigs, sheep, and cattle not chickens or geese") are not what people who lived around the Mediterranean at the time would have eaten ("fish, vegetables, cheese, and fruit"). Wilson concludes that "it seems most likely that Homeric elites do not eat meat as a reflection of reality, but because it is a way for the poem to demonstrate their distinguished and extraordinary status." This suggests that domestication was a very old practice that had, by the time of the Homeric writer, developed an association with social status.
10. One reason our intuitions may be pressed to think it does follow is a certain casual use of "expert," as when we say, "You're our resident expert on the copy machine" or "You're the expert on growing tomatoes." In these

instances, all we mean is that the person has an advantage—epistemic or technical—over us with respect to some domain. Being the best in the office or the best in the family does not entail that one is an expert in the objective sense.

11 I'm constantly told that someone can be better *about* lowering the toilet seat, that is, at doing it more consistently. But that is not the same thing as being better *at* doing it.

REFERENCES AND FURTHER READING

2U (2019). "To Future-Proof Your Career, Start by Embracing Cross-Disciplinary Thinking," *Quartz*, May 2. Available online: https://qz.com/1589490/to-future-proof-your-career-start-by-embracing-cross-disciplinary-thinking/.

AAP Task Force on Sudden Infant Death Syndrome (2016). "SIDS and Other Sleep-Related Infant Deaths: Updated Recommendations for a Safe Infant Sleeping Environment," *Pediatrics* 138 (5). Available online: https://pediatrics.aappublications.org/content/pediatrics/138/5/e20162938.full.pdf.

AARP (2018). "Online Pharmacy Scams," *AARP Fraud Resource Center*, December 3. Available online: https://www.aarp.org/money/scams-fraud/info-2019/online-pharmacy.html.

Abagnale, Frank and Stan Redding (1980). *Catch Me if You Can: The True Story of a Real Fake*, New York: Grosset & Dunlap.

Adams, Francis (1952). "Biographical Note: Hippocrates, fl. 400 B.C." in Robert Maynard Hutchins, ed., *Great Books of the Western World: Hippocrates, Galen*, Chicago, IL: William Benton, Encyclopedia Britannica.

Agnew, Neil M., Kenneth M. Ford, and Patrick J. Hayes ([1994] 1997). "Expertise in Context: Personally Constructed, Socially Selected, and Reality-Relevant?" in Paul J. Feltovich, Kenneth M. Ford, and Robert R. Hoffman, eds., *Expertise in Context*, 219–44, Cambridge, MA: AAAI /MIT Press.

Ahlstrom-Vij, Kristoffer (2013). *Epistemic Paternalism: A Defence*, Basingstoke: Palgrave Macmillan.

Aikin, Scott (2009). "Don't Fear the Regress: Cognitive Values and Epistemic Infinitism," *Think* 8 (23): 55–61.

Allen, James (1994). "Failure and Expertise in the Ancient Conception of Art," in Tami Horowitz and Allen Janis, eds., *Scientific Failure*, 83–110, Lanham, MD: Rowman & Littlefield.

"American Academy of Pediatrics" (n.d.). *American Academy of Pediatrics*. Available online: https://www.aap.org/en-us/Pages/Default.aspx.

"American College of Pediatricians" (n.d.). *American College of Pediatricians*. Available online: https://www.acpeds.org/.

The American Association for the Advancement of Science (AAAS) (n.d.). "Affiliates," *AAAS*. Available online: https://www.aaas.org/group/60/list-aaas-affiliates#p.

Anderson, Elizabeth (2011). "Democracy, Public Policy, and Lay Assessments of Scientific Testimony," *Episteme* 8 (2): 144–64.

Anderson, James G. and Kathleen Abrahamson (2017). "Your Health Care May Kill You: Medical Errors," *Studies in Health, Technology, and Informatics* 234: 13–17.
Anscombe, G. E. M. (1975). "What Is It to Believe Someone?" in Cornelius F. Delaney, ed., *Rationality and Religious Belief*, 1–10, Notre Dame: University of Notre Dame Press.
Arendt, Hannah ([1954] 1961). "What Is Authority?" in *Between Past and Future: Six Exercises in Political Thought*, 91–141, New York: Viking.
Ariely, Dan (2010). *Predictably Irrational: The Hidden Forces That Shape Our Decisions*. New York: Harper.
Aristotle (1955). *On Sophistical Refutations*, trans. Edward S. Forster. The Loeb Classics Library. Cambridge, MA: William Heinemann, Ltd.
Aristotle (2001). *Politics*, in Richard McKeon, ed., Benjamin Jowett, trans., *The Basic Works of Aristotle*, 1113–316, New York: Modern Library.
Arkes, Hal R., Robert L. Wortmann, Paul D. Saville, and Allan R. Harkness (1981). "Hindsight Bias among Physicians Weighing the Likelihood of Diagnoses," *Journal of Applied Psychology* 66: 252–5.
Armstrong, J. Scott (1997). "Peer Review for Journals: Evidence on Quality Control, Fairness, and Innovation," *Science and Engineering Ethics* 3 (1): 63–84.
The Associated Press (2019). "Japan's Supreme Court Uphold Transgender Sterilization Requirement," *NBC News*, January 25. Available online: https://www.nbcnews.com/feature/nbc-out/japan-s-supreme-court-upholds-transgender-sterilization-requirement-n962721.
Audi, Robert (2006). "Testimony, Credulity, Veracity," in Jennifer Lackey and Ernest Sosa, eds., *The Epistemology of Testimony*, 25–49, New York: Oxford University Press.
Austin, James L. (1946). "Other Minds, Part II," *Proceedings of the Aristotelian Society* 148: 148–87.
Bacon, Francis ([1612] 1980). "Of Studies," in *The Essays of Sir Francis Bacon*, 163–4, Norwalk, CT: The Easton Press.
Bacon, Francis ([1620] 2000). *New Organon*, Cambridge: Cambridge University Press.
Badcott, David (2005). "The Expert Patient: Valid Recognition or False Hope?" *Medicine, Health Care, and Philosophy* 8 (2): 173–8.
Baker, Peter and Julie Hirschfeld Davis (2015). "Obama Chooses Nike Headquarters to Make His Pitch on Trade," *New York Times*, May 7. Available online: http://www.nytimes.com/2015/05/08/business/obama-chooses-nike-headquarters-to-make-his-pitch-on-trade.html.
Ballantyne, Nathan (2019). "Epistemic Trespassing," *Mind* 128 (510): 367–95.
Barnes, Barry and David Bloor (1982). "Relativism, Rationalism and the Sociology of Knowledge," in Martin Hollis and Steven Lukes, eds., *Rationality and Relativism* 21–47, Basil Blackwell: Oxford.

Bartlett, James C., Amy L. Boggan, and Daniel C. Krawczyk (2013). "Expertise and Processing Distorted Structure in Chess," *Frontiers in Human Neuroscience* 7: 825 https://www.frontiersin.org/articles/10.3389/fnhum.2013.00825/full.

Bartz, Robert (2000). "Remembering the Hippocratics: Knowledge, Practice, and Ethos of Ancient Greek Physician-Healers," in Mark G. Kuczewski and Ronald Polansky, eds., *Bioethics: Ancient Themes in Contemporary Issues*, 3–29, Cambridge, MA: MIT Press.

Baumeister, Roy F. (1984). "Choking under Pressure: Self-Consciousness and Paradoxical Effects of Incentives on Skillful Performance," *Journal of Personality and Social Psychology* 46 (3): 610–20.

Bealer, George (1992). "The Incoherence of Empiricism." *Aristotelian Society Supplementary Volume* 66 (1): 99–138.

Beaman, Lori, Reghabendra Chattopadhyay, Esther Duflo, Rohini Pande, and Petia Topalova (2009). "Powerful Women: Does Exposure Reduce Bias?" *The Quarterly Journal of Economics* 124 (4): 1497–540.

Beckwith, Christopher I. (2012). *Warriors of the Cloisters: The Central Asian Origins of Science in the Medieval World*, Princeton, NJ: Princeton University Press.

Beebe, James R., Maria Baghramian, Luke Drury, and Finnur Dellsén (2019). "Divergent Perspectives on Expert Disagreement: Preliminary Evidence from Climate Science, Climate Policy, Astrophysics, and Public Opinion," *Environmental Communication* 13 (1): 35–50, DOI: 10.1080/17524032.2018.1504099.

Beilock, Sian (2010). *Choke: What the Secrets of the Brain Reveal about Getting It Right When You Have To*, New York: Free Press.

Berkman, Nancy, Stacey L. Sheridan, Katrina E. Donahue, David J. Halpern, and Karen Crotty (2011). "Low Health Literacy and Health Outcomes: An Updated Systematic Review," *Annals of Internal Medicine* 155 (2): 97–115.

Berlin, Isaiah (1953). "The Hedgehog and the Fox: An Essay on Tolstoy's View of History," London: Weidenfeld and Nicolson.

Berman, Jeffrey C. and Nicholas C. Norton (1985). "Does Professional Training Make a Therapist More Effective?" *Psychological Bulletin* 98: 401–7.

Bertamini, Marco, Alice Spooner, and Heiko Hecht (2004). "The Representation of Naïve Knowledge about Physics," in Grant Malcolm, ed., *Multidisciplinary Approaches to Visual Representations and Interpretations*, 27–36, Amsterdam: Elsevier.

Biederman, Irving and Margaret M. Shiffrar (1987). "Sexing Day-Old Chicks: A Case Study and Expert Systems Analysis of a Difficult Perceptual-Learning Task," *Journal of Experimental Psychology: Learning, Memory, and Cognition* 13 (4): 640–5.

Bilalić, Merim (2017). *The Neuroscience of Expertise*, Cambridge: Cambridge University Press.

Bishop, Michael A. and J. D. Trout (2005). *Epistemology and the Psychology of Human Judgment*, Oxford: Oxford University Press.

Biss, Eula (2014). *On Immunity: An Inoculation*, Minneapolis, MN: Graywolf Press.

Blackmore, Susan (1999). *The Meme Machine*, Oxford, UK: Oxford University Press.

Bloor, David (2011). *The Enigma of the Aerofoil: Rival Theories in Aerodynamics, 1909–1930*, Chicago, IL: University of Chicago Press.

Bochenski, Joseph (1965). "The Logic of Religion," *Journal of Symbolic Logic* 33 (2): 312–13.

BonJour, Laurence (1985). *The Structure of Empirical Knowledge*, Cambridge, MA: Harvard University Press.

Bornstein, Brian H., A. Christine Emler, and Gretchen B. Chapman (1999). "Rationality in Medical Treatment Decisions: Is There a Sunk-Cost Effect?" *Social Science & Medicine* 49 (2): 215–22.

Botting, David (2018). "Two Types of Argument from Position to Know," *Informal Logic* 38 (4): 502–30.

Bowell, Tracy (n.d.). "Feminist Standpoint Theory," *Internet Encyclopedia of Philosophy*. Available online: https://www.iep.utm.edu/fem-stan/#H2.

Brainard, Jeffrey and Jia You (2018). "What a Massive Database of Retracted Papers Reveals about Science Publishing's 'Death Penalty,'" *Science Magazine*, October 25. Available online: https://www.sciencemag.org/news/2018/10/what-massive-database-retracted-papers-reveals-about-science-publishing-s-death-penalty.

Breitenstein, Mirko (2014). "The Success of Discipline. The Reception of Hug of St. Victor's *De institutione novitorum* within the 13th and 14th Century," in Mirko Breitenstein, Julia Burkhardt, Stefan Burkhardt, and Jens Rohrkasten, eds., *Rules and Observance* 183–222, Berlin: Abhandlungen.

Brewer, Scott (1998). "Scientific Expert Testimony and Intellectual Due Process," *The Yale Law Journal* 107 (6): 1535–681.

Brewer, Scott (2006). "Scientific Expert Testimony and Intellectual Due Process," in Evan Selinger and Robert P. Crease, eds., *The Philosophy of Expertise*, 111–58, New York: Columbia University Press.

Brown, Mark B. (2014). "Expertise and Democracy," in Stephen Elstub and Peter McLaverty, eds., *Deliberative Democracy: Issues and Cases*, 50–68, Edinburgh: Edinburgh University Press.

Buchanan, Bruce, G., Randall Davis, Reid G. Smith, and Edward A. Feigenbaum (2018). "Expert Systems: A Perspective from Computer Science," in K. Anders Ericsson, Robert R. Hoffman, Aaron Kozbelt, and A. Mark Williams, eds., *The Cambridge Handbook of Expertise and Expert Performance*, 2nd ed. 84–104, Cambridge: Cambridge University Press.

Buckwalter (2014). "Intuition Fail: Philosophical Activity and the Limits of Expertise," *Philosophy and Phenomenological Research* 92 (2): 378–410.

Burge, Tyler (1993). "Content Preservation," *Philosophical Review* 102 (4): 457–88.

Burns-Piper, Annie (2016). "Advocates, Experts and Mothers Call for Action on the Mistreatment of Women during Childbirth," *CBC News*, November 19. Available online: https://www.cbc.ca/news/investigates/childbirth-mistreatment-reaction-1.3857635.

Burnyeat, Myles (1987). "Wittgenstein and Augustine De Magistro," *Proceedings of the Aristotelian Society Supplement* 61: 1–24.

Camerer, Colin F. and Eric J. Johnson (1991). "The Process-Performance Paradox in Expert Judgment: How Can Experts Know So Much and Predict So Badly?" in K. Anders Ericsson and Jacqui Smith, eds., *Toward a General Theory of Expertise*, 195–217, Cambridge: Cambridge University Press.

Campbell, Donald T. (1977). "Descriptive Epistemology: Psychological, Sociological, and Evolutionary," in *William James Lectures*, Cambridge, MA: Harvard University Press.

Castelvecchi, Davide (2016). "Fermat's Last Theorem Earns Andrew Wiles the Abel Prize," *Nature: International Weekly Journal of Science*, March 15. Available online: https://www.nature.com/news/fermat-s-last-theorem-earns-andrew-wiles-the-abel-prize-1.19552.

Cereda, Anna and John C. Carey (2012). "The Trisomy 18 Syndrome," *Orphanet Journal of Rare Diseases* 7: 81.

Chakravartty, Anjan (2017). "Scientific Realism," in Edward N. Zalta, ed., *The Stanford Encyclopedia of Philosophy*, Summer 2017 Edition. Available online: https://plato.stanford.edu/archives/sum2017/entries/scientific-realism/.

Chartonas, Dimitrios, Michalis Kyratsous, Sarah Dracass, Tennyson Lee, and Kamaldeep Bhui (2017). "Personality Disorder: Still the Patients Psychiatrists Dislike?" *BJ Psych Bulletin* 41: 12–17.

Chase, William G. and Herbert A. Simon (1973). "Perception in Chess," *Cognitive Psychology* 4: 55–81.

Chisholm, Roderick (1973). *The Problem of the Criterion*, Milwaukee, WI: Marquette University Press.

Chisholm, Roderick (1982). "A Version of Foundationalism," in Roderick Chisholm, ed., *The Foundations of Knowing*, 61–75, Minneapolis: University of Minnesota Press.

Chlebowski, Rowan T., Karen C. Johnson, Charles Kooperberg, Mary Pettinger, Jean Wactawski-Wende, Tom Rohan, Jacques Rossouw, Dorothy Lane, Mary J. O'Sullivan, Shagufta Yasmeen, Robert A. Hiatt, James M. Shikany, Mara Vitolins, Janu Khandekar, F. Allen Hubbell, and Women's Health Initiative Investigators (2008). "Calcium Plus Vitamin D Supplementation and the Risk of Breast Cancer," *Journal of the National Cancer Institute* 100 (22): 1581–91.

Cholbi, Michael (2007). "Moral Expertise and the Credentials Problem," *Ethical Theory and Moral Practice* 10 (4): 323–34.

Choudhry, Niteesh K., Robert H. Fletcher, and Stephen B. Soumerai (2005). "Systematic Review: The Relationship between Clinical Experience and Quality of Healthcare," *Annals of Internal Medicine* 142 (4): 260–73.

Chudnoff, Elijah (2019). "Two Kinds of Cognitive Expertise," *Nous*, Available online: https://doi.org/10.1111/nous.12305.

Cicero (1860). *De Oratore*, trans. John S. Watson, New York: Harper and Brothers Publishers.

Cicero (1988). *De Oratore*, trans. E. W. Sutton, Loeb Classical Library, Cambridge, MA: Harvard University Press.

Clifford, William K. (1877). "The Ethics of Belief," *Contemporary Review*, XXXIX January Edition.

Clifford, William K. ([1872] 1886). "On the Aims and Instruments of Scientific Thought," a lecture delivered to members of the British Association at Brighton, August 19, 1872, in Leslie Stephen and Frederick Pollock, eds., *Lectures and Essays*, 2nd ed., 85–109, London: Macmillan.

Coady, David (2012). *What to Believe Now: Applying Epistemology to Contemporary Issues*, Malden, MA: Wiley-Blackwell.

Cohen, I. Bernard (1985). *The Birth of a New Physics*, revised and updated ed., New York: W. W. Norton.

Cohen, Marvin S. (1993). "The Naturalistic Basis of Decision Biases," in Gary A. Klein, Judith Orasnu, Roberta Calderwood, and Caroline E. Zsambok, eds., *Decision Making In Action: Models and Methods*, 51–99, Norwood, NJ: Ablex Publishing Corporation.

Coleman, Clifford, Stanley Hudson, and Lucinda Maine (2013). "Health Literacy Practices and Educational Competencies for Health Professionals: A Consensus Study," *Journal of Health Communication* 18 (Supplement 1): 82–102.

Coleman, Clifford, Stanley Hudson, and Ben Pederson (2017). "Prioritized Health Literacy and Clear Communication Practices for Health Care Professionals," *Health Literacy Research and Practice* 1 (3): e91–e99.

Collins, Harry (2004). "Interactional Expertise as a Third Kind of Knowledge," *Phenomenology and the Cognitive Sciences* 3: 125–43.

Collins, Harry (2014). *Are We All Scientific Experts Now?* Cambridge: Polity Press.

Collins, Harry (2018). "Studies of Expertise and Experience," *Topoi* 37: 67–77, https://doi.org/10.1007/s11245-016-9412-1

Collins, Harry, and Robert Evans (2006). "The Third Wave of Science Studies: Studies of Expertise and Experience," in Evan Selinger and Robert P. Crease, eds., *The Philosophy of Expertise*, 39–110, New York: Columbia University Press.

Collins, Harry, and Robert Evans (2007). *Rethinking Expertise*, Chicago, IL: University of Chicago Press.

Collins, Harry, and Trevor Pinch (2005). *Dr. Golem: How to Think about Medicine*, Chicago, IL: University of Chicago Press.

Conly, Sarah (2012). *Against Autonomy*, Cambridge: Cambridge University Press.

Cotgrave, Randle (1611). *A Dictionarie of the French and English Tongues*, London: Adam Inslip. Available online: http://www.pbm.com/~lindahl/cotgrave/.

Coughlin, Lorence D. and Vimla L. Patel (1987). "Processing of Critical Information by Physicians and Medical Students," *Journal of Medical Education* 62: 818–28.

Crasnow, Sharon, Alison Wylie, Wenda K. Bauchspies, and Elizabeth Potter (2015). "Feminist Perspectives on Science," in Edward N. Zalta, ed., *The Stanford Encyclopedia of Philosophy*, Summer 2015 edition. Available online: http://plato.stanford.edu/archives/sum2015/entries/feminist-science/.

Croce, Michael (2019). "Objective Expertise and Functionalist Constraints," *Social Epistemology Review and Collective* 8 (5): 25–35.

Cross, Patricia K. (1977). "Not *Can*, but *Will* College Teaching Be Improved?," *New Directions for Higher Education*, 1–15.

Csikszentmihalyi, Mihaly (1975). *Beyond Boredom and Anxiety*, San Francisco, CA: Jossey-Bass Publishers.

Csikszentmihalyi, Mihaly (1988). "The Flow Experience and Its Significance for Human Psychology," in M. Csikszentmihalyi and I. S. Csikszentmihalyi, eds., *Optimal Experience: Psychological Studies of Flow in Consciousness*, 15–35, New York: Cambridge University Press.

Csikszentmihalyi, Mihaly (1990). *Flow: The Psychology of Optimal Experience*, New York: HarperCollins.

Dall'Alba, Gloria (2018). "Reframing Expertise and Its Development: A Lifeworld Perspective," in K. Anders Ericsson, Robert R. Hoffman, Aaron Kozbelt, and A. Mark Williams, eds., *The Cambridge Handbook of Expertise and Expert Performance*, 2nd ed., 33–9, Cambridge: Cambridge University Press.

Dancy, Jonathan, "Moral Particularism," in Edward N. Zalta, ed., *The Stanford Encyclopedia of Philosophy*, Winter 2017 Edition. Available online: https://plato.stanford.edu/archives/win2017/entries/moral-particularism/.

Dane, Erik, Kevin W. Rockmann, and Michael G. Pratt (2012). "When Should I Trust My Gut? Linking Domain Expertise to Intuitive Decision-Making Effectiveness," *Organizational Behavior and Human Decision Processes* 119: 187–94.

Davis, Dave, Mary Ann Thomson O'Brien, Nick Freemantle, Frederic M. Wolf, Paul Mazmanian, and Anne Taylor-Vaisey (1999). "Impact of Formal Continuing Medical Education: Do Conferences, Workshops, Rounds, and Other Traditional Continuing Education Activities Change Physician Behavior or Health Care Outcomes?" *Journal of the American Medical Association* 282 (9): 867–74.

Davis, Edward B. (2009). "That Isaac Newton's Mechanistic Cosmology Eliminated the Need for God," in Ron Numbers, ed., *Galileo Goes to Jail and Other Myths about Science and Religion*, 115–22, Cambridge, MA: Harvard University Press.

Dawes, Robyn (1994). *House of Cards: Psychology and Psychotherapy Built on Myth*, New York: Free Press.

Dawkins, Richard (1976). *The Selfish Gene*, Oxford: Oxford University Press.

De Groot, Adriaan ([1946] 1965). *Thought and Choice in Chess*, The Hague, Netherlands: Amsterdam Academic Archive.

Dellsén, Finnur (2018). "The Epistemic Value of Expert Autonomy," *Philosophy and Phenomenological Research*. doi: https://doi.org/10.1111/phpr.12550.

Derrida, Jacques (1977). "Signature, Event, Context," trans. Samuel Weber and Jeffrey Mehlman, *Glyph* 1: 172–97.

Descartes, René ([1637] 1988). "Discourse on the Method," in John Cottingham, Robert Stoothoff, and Dugald Murdoch, trans., *Descartes: Selected Philosophical Writings*, 20–56, Cambridge: Cambridge University Press.

Detienne, Marcel and Jean-Pierre Vernant ([1978] 1991). *Cunning Intelligence in Greek Culture and Society*, Chicago, IL: University of Chicago Press.

Dewey, John ([1910] 2009). *How We Think*, New York: BN Publishing.

Drake, Jennifer E. and Ellen Winner (2018). "Why Deliberate Practice Is Not Enough: Evidence of Talent in Drawing," in David Z. Hambrick, Guillermo Campitelli, and Brooke N. Macnamara, eds., *The Science of Expertise: Behavioral, Neural, and Genetic Approaches to Complex Skill*, 101–28, London: Routledge.

Dreyfus, Hubert (1979). *What Computers Can't Do: The Limits of Artificial Intelligence*, revised, New York: Harper Colophon Books.

Dreyfus, Hubert (1999a). "How Neuroscience Supports Merleau-Ponty's Account of Learning," Paper presented at the Network for Non-Scholastic Learning Conference, Sonderborg, Denmark.

Dreyfus, Hubert (1999b). "The Primacy of Phenomenology over Logical Analysis," *Philosophical Topics* 27 (2): 3–24.

Dreyfus, Hubert (2000). "Response to Carmen Taylor," in M. Wrathall and J. Malpas, eds., *Heidegger, Authencity, and Modernity: Essays in Honor of Hubert L. Dreyfus*, Vol. 1, pp. 306–12, Cambridge: MIT Press.

Dreyfus, Hubert (2006). "How Far Is Distance Learning from Education?," in Evan Selinger and Robert P. Crease, eds., *The Philosophy of Expertise* 196–212, New York: Columbia University Press.

Dreyfus, Hubert, Charles Spinosa, and Fernado Flores (1997). *Disclosing Worlds: Entrepreneurship, Democratic Action, and the Cultivation of Solidarity*, Cambridge, MA: MIT Press.

Dreyfus, Hubert L. (2001). *On the Internet*, New York: Routledge.

Dreyfus, Hubert L. and Stuart E. Dreyfus (1986). *Mind over Machine: The Power of Human Intuition and Expertise in the Era of the Computer*, New York: Free Press.

Dreyfus, Hubert L. and Stuart E. Dreyfus (2005). "Peripheral Vision: Expertise in Real World Contexts," *Organization Studies* 26: 779–92.

Driver, Julia (2006). "Autonomy and the Asymmetry Problem for Moral Expertise," *Philosophical Studies* 128 (3): 619–44.

Duckworth, Angela (2016). *Grit: The Power and Passion of Perseverance*, New York: Scribner.

Dunning, David (2011). "The Dunning-Kruger Effect: On Being Ignorant of One's Own Ignorance," in James M. Olson and Mark P. Zanna, eds., *Advances in Experimental Social Psychology*, 44, San Diego, CA: Academic Press.

Dunning, David (2016). "The Psychological Quirk That Explains Why You Love Donald Trump," *Politico*, May 25. Available online: https://www.politico.com/magazine/story/2016/05/donald-trump-supporters-dunning-kruger-effect-213904.

Dworkin, Gerald (1988). *The Theory and Practice of Autonomy*, Cambridge: Cambridge University Press.

Edwards, Dianne and Joseph Edwards (1977). "Marriage: Direct and Continuous Measurement," *Bulletin of the Psychonomic Society* 10: 187–8.

Elga, Adam (2011). "Reflection and Disagreement," in Alvin Goldman, ed., *Social Epistemology: Essential Readings*, 158–82, Oxford: Oxford University Press.

Elgin, Catherine Z. (2012). "Begging to Differ," *The Philosopher's Magazine*, 59: 77–82.

Elgin, Catherine Z. (2016). "Understanding," in *Routledge Encyclopedia of Philosophy*, New York: Routledge.

Elgin, Catherine Z. (2017). *True Enough*, Cambridge, MA: MIT Press.

Elgin, Catherine Z. (2018). "Epistemically Useful Falsehoods," in Brandon Fitelson, Rodrigo Borges, and Cherie Braden, eds., *Themes from Klein: Knowledge, Skepticism, and Justification*, 25–38, Cham, Switzerland: Springer Nature.

Elliot, Terri (1994). "Making Strange What Had Appeared Familiar," *The Monist* 77 (4): 424–33.

Elo, A. E. (1986). *The Rating of Chessplayers, Past and Present*, 2nd ed., New York: Arco.

Engeström, Yrjö (2018). *Expertise in Transition: Expansive Learning in Medical Work*, Cambridge: Cambridge University Press.

Epstein, David (2014a). *The Sports Gene: Inside the Science of Extraordinary Athletic Performance*, New York: Portfolio/Penguin.

Epstein, David (2014b). "Are Athletes Really Getting Faster, Better, Stronger?" TED Talk, https://www.ted.com/talks/david_epstein_are_athletes_really_getting_faster_better_stronger?language=en.

Epstein, David (2019). *Range: Why Generalists Triumph in a Specialized World*, New York: Riverhead Books.

Ericsson, K. Anders (1985). "Memory Skill," *Canadian Journal of Psychology* 39 (2): 188–231.

Ericsson, K. Anders (1990). "Peak Performance and Age: An Examination of Peak Performance in Sports," in Paul B. Baltes and Margeret M. Baltes, eds., *Successful Aging: Perspectives from the Behavioral Sciences*, 164–95, New York: Cambridge University Press.

Ericsson, K. Anders (2003). "Valid and Non-reactive Verbalization of Thoughts during Performance of Tasks: Toward a Solution to the Central Problems of Introspection as a Source of Scientific Data," *Journal of Consciousness Studies* 10: 1–18.

Ericsson, K. Anders (2009). "Deliberate Practice and Acquisition of Expert Performance: A General Overview," *Academic Emergency Medicine* 15 (11): 988–94.

Ericsson, K. Anders (2011). "The Surgeon's Expertise," in Heather Fry and Roger Kneebone, eds., *Surgical Education: Theorising an Emerging Domain* 107–21, Dordrecht: Springer.

Ericsson, K. Anders (2018). "An Introduction to the Second Edition of *The Cambridge Handbook of Expertise and Expert Performance: Its Development,*

Organization, and Content," in K. Anders Ericsson, Robert R. Hoffman, Aaron Kozbelt, and A. Mark Williams, eds., *The Cambridge Handbook of Expertise and Expert Performance*, 2nd ed., 3–20, Cambridge: Cambridge University Press.

Ericsson, K. Anders and Andreas C. Lehmann (1996). "Expert and Exceptional Performance: Evidence of Maximal Adaptation to Task Constraints," *Annual Review of Psychology* 47: 273–305.

Ericsson, K. Anders and Jacqui Smith, eds. (1991). *Toward a General Theory of Expertise*, Cambridge: Cambridge University Press.

Ericsson, K. Anders and Neil Charness (1994). "Expert Performance: Its Structure and Acquisition," *American Psychologist* 49 (8): 725–47.

Ericsson, K. Anders and Neil Charness (1997). "Cognitive and Developmental Factors in Expert Performance," in Paul J. Feltovich, Kenneth M. Ford, and Robert R. Hoffman, eds., *Expertise in Context*, 3–41, Cambridge, MA: AAAI/MIT Press.

Ericsson, K. Anders and Robert Pool (2016). *Peak: Secrets from the New Science of Expertise*, Boston, MA: Mariner.

Ericsson, K. Anders and William G. Chase (1982). "Exceptional Memory," *American Scientist* 70: 607–15.

Ericsson, K. Anders, William G. Chase, and Steven Faloon (1980). "Acquisition of a Memory Skill," *Science* 208: 1181–2.

Ericsson, K. Anders, Ralf Th. Krampe, and Clemens Tesch-Römer (1993). "The Role of Deliberate Practice in the Acquisition of Expert Performance," *Psychological Review* 100 (3): 363–406.

Ericsson, K. Anders, Robert R. Hoffman, Aaron Kozbelt, and Mark Williams, eds. (2018). *Expertise and Expert Performance*, 2nd ed., Cambridge: Cambridge University Press.

Euripides (1995). *Andromache*, trans. David Kovacs, Loeb Classical Library, Cambridge, MA: Harvard University Press.

Fantl, Jeremy (2008). "Knowing-How and Knowing-That," *Philosophy Compass* 3 (3): 451–70.

Fantl, Jeremy (2012). "Knowledge How," in Edward N. Zalta, ed., *The Stanford Encyclopedia of Philosophy*, Fall 2017 Edition. Available online: https://plato.stanford.edu/archives/fall2017/entries/knowledge-how/.

Fantl, Jeremy (2018). *The Limitations of the Open Mind*. New York: Oxford University Press.

Faulkner, Paul (2000). "The Social Character of Testimonial Knowledge," *Journal of Philosophy* 97: 581–601.

Feldman, Richard and Ted A. Warfield (2010). *Disagreement*, Oxford: Oxford University Press.

Feltovich, Paul J., Michael J. Prietula, and K. Anders Ericsson (2018). "Studies of Expertise from Psychological Perspectives: Historical Foundations and Recurrent Themes," in K. Anders Ericsson, Robert R. Hoffman, Aaron Kozbelt, and A. Mark Williams, eds., *The Cambridge Handbook of Expertise and Expert Performance*, 2nd ed., 59–83, Cambridge: Cambridge University Press.

Feyerabend, Paul ([1974] 2006). "How to Defend Society against Science," in Evan Selinger and Robert P. Crease, eds., *The Philosophy of Expertise*, 358–69, New York: Columbia University Press.

Finnis, John (1980). "Authority," in Joseph Raz, ed., *Authority*, 174–202, New York: New York University Press.

Fischer, Frank (2009). *Democracy and Expertise: Reorienting Policy Inquiry*, Oxford: Oxford University Press.

Flax, Jane (1983). "Political Philosophy and the Patriarchal Unconscious," in Sandra Harding and Merrill Hintikka, eds., *Discovering Reality*, 245–81, Dordrecht, Holland: Kluwer.

Foley, Richard (1994). "Egoism in Epistemology," in Frederick F. Schmitt, ed., *Socializing Epistemology: The Social Dimensions of Knowledge*, 53–73, London: Rowman & Littlefield.

Foley, Richard (2001). *Intellectual Trust in Oneself and Others*, Cambridge: Cambridge University Press.

Forsetlund, Louise, Arild Bjørndal, Arash Rashidian, Gro Jamtvedt, and Andrew D. Oxman (2009). "Continuing Education Meetings Workshops: Effects on Professional Practice and Health Care Outcomes," *Cochrane Database of Systematic Reviews* 2, CD003030.

Foucault, Michel ([1979] 2000). "What Is an Author?," repr. in Forrest E. Baird and Walter Arnold Kaufmann, eds., *Twentieth-Century Philosophy*, 2nd ed., Upper Saddle River, NJ: Prentice Hall.

Fowler, Harold N., ed. (1921). *Plato in Twelve* Volumes, *Vol. 12*, Cambridge, MA: Harvard University Press; London, William Heinemann Ltd.

Fricker, Elizabeth (2006). "Testimony and Epistemic Autonomy," in Jennifer Lackey and Ernest Sosa, eds., *The Epistemology of Testimony*, 225–50, Oxford: Oxford University Press.

Freedman, David H. (2010). *Wrong: Why Experts Keep Failing Us—And How to Know When Not to Trust Them*, New York: Little, Brown & Company.

Freiman, Ori and Boaz Miller (2020). "Can Artificial Entities Assert?," in Sanford C. Goldberg, ed., *The Oxford Handbook of Assertion*, Oxford: Oxford University Press.

Fuller, Steve (2006). "The Constitutively Social Character of Expertise," in Evan Selinger and Robert P. Crease, eds., *The Philosophy of Expertise*, 342–57, New York: Columbia University Press.

Funk, Cary and Brian Kennedy (2019). "Public Confidence in Scientists Has Remained Stable for Decades," *Pew Research Center*, March 22. Available online: https://www.pewresearch.org/fact-tank/2019/03/22/public-confidence-in-scientists-has-remained-stable-for-decades/?fbclid=IwAR2RsXV-9y1aUHEm5hebd5kWz7Pf85oEEAlCInpyeZi28ES5m-HiwR2kEj0.

Funk, Cary, Brian Kennedy, and Meg Hefferon (2018). "Public Perspectives on Food Risks," *Pew Research Center*, November 19. Available online: https://www.pewresearch.org/science/2018/11/19/public-perspectives-on-food-risks/.

Gagné, Francoys (1999). "Nature or Nurture? A Re-Examination of Sloboda and Howe's (1991) Interview Study on Talent Development in Music," *Psychology of Music* 27 (1): 38–51.

Garland, Cedric F., Frank C. Garland, Edward D. Gorham, Martin Lipkin, Harold Newmark, Sharif B. Mohr, and Michael F. Holick (2006). "The Role of Vitamin D in Cancer Prevention," *American Journal of Public Health* 96 (2): 252–61.

Gelfert, Axel (2011). "Expertise, Argumentation, and the End of Inquiry," *Argumentation* 25 (3): 297–312.

Gelfert, Axel (2014). *A Critical Introduction to Testimony*, London: Bloomsbury Academic.

Gibson, William and Bruce Sterling (1990). *The Difference Engine*, London: Victor Gollancz.

Gigerenzer, Gerd (2007). "Fast and Frugal Heuristics: The Tools of Bounded Rationality," in Derek J. Koehler and Nigel Harvey, eds., *Blackwell Handbook of Judgment & Decision Making*, 62–88, Malden, MA: Blackwell Publishing.

Gigerenzer, Gerd (2008). "Why Heuristics Work," *Perspectives on Psychological Science* 3 (1): 20–9.

Gilman, Benjamin Ives (1914). "The Day of the Expert," *Science* 39 (1013): 771–9.

Gilovich, Thomas (1991). *How We Know What Isn't So*, New York: Free Press.

Gilovich, Thomas, Dale Griffin, and Daniel Kahneman, eds. (2002). *Heuristics and Biases: The Psychology of Intuitive Judgment*, Cambridge: Cambridge University Press.

Gobet, F., and Charness, N. (2006). "Expertise in Chess," in K. Anders. Ericsson, Neil Charness, Paul J. Feltovich, and Robert R. Hoffman, eds., *The Cambridge Handbook of Expertise and Expert Performance*, 523–38, New York: Cambridge University Press.

Goldman, Alvin (1991). "Epistemic Paternalism: Communication Control in Law and Society," *The Journal of Philosophy* 88 (3): 113–31.

Goldman, Alvin (2001). "Experts: Which Ones Should You Trust?," *Philosophy and Phenomenological Research* 63 (1): 85–109.

Goldman, Alvin (2009). "Replies to Discussants," in Shurz, Gerhard and Markus Werning, eds., *Reliable Knowledge and Social Epistemology: Essays on the Philosophy of Alvin Goldman and Replies by Goldman*, 245–90, Amsterdam: *Grazer Philosophische Studien*.

Goldman, Alvin (2018). "Expertise," *Topoi* 37 (1): 3–10.

Goldman, Alvin I. ([2001] 2002). "Experts: Which Ones Should You Trust?," in Alvin I. Goldman, *Pathways to Knowledge: Private and Public*, 139–63, Oxford: Oxford University Press.

Goldman, Alvin I. and Dennis Whitcomb (2011). *Social Epistemology: Essential Readings*, Oxford: Oxford University Press.
Goodman, Nelson (1984). *Of Mind and Other Matters*, Cambridge, MA: Harvard University Press.
Gould, John (1955). *The Development of Plato's Ethics*, Cambridge: Cambridge University Press.
Graves, Robert ([1955] 1960). *The Greek Myths*, rev. ed., London: Penguin.
Grenz, Stanley J. (1996). *A Primer on Postmodernism*, Grand Rapids, MI: Wm. B. Eerdman's.
Grinsven, S. van, F. Hagenmaier, C.J. van Loon, M.J. van Gorp, J. van Kints, and A. van Kampen (2014) 'Does the Experience Level of the Radiologist, Assessment in Consensus, or the Addition of the Abduction and External Rotation View Improve the Diagnostic Reproducibility and Accuracy of MRA of the Shoulder?' *Clinical Radiology* 69 (11): 1157–1164.
Grob, Gerald N. (2011). "The Attack of Psychiatric Legitimacy in the 1960s: Rhetoric and Reality," *Journal of the History of the Behavioral Sciences* 47: 398–416.
Groopman, Jerome (2010). *How Doctors Think*, Boston, MA: Houghton, Mifflin, Harcourt.
Groopman, Jerome and Pamela Hartzband (2011). *Your Medical Mind: How to Decide What Is Right for You*, New York: Penguin.
Gross, Samuel R. (1991). "Expert Evidence," *Wisconsin Law Review* 1991: 1113–232.
Guerrero, Alex (2017). "Living with Ignorance in a World of Experts," in Rik Peels, ed., *Perspectives on Ignorance from Moral and Social Philosophy*, 156–85, New York: Routledge.
Guidry-Grimes, Laura K. (2017). *Mental Diversity and Meaningful Psychiatry Disabilities*, Ph.D. Dissertation, Georgetown University, http://hdl.handle.net/10822/1043860.
Guthrie, Chris, Jeffrey Rachlinski, and Andrew Wistrich (2001). "Inside the Judicial Mind," *Cornell Law Review* 86: 777–830.
Guthrie, Chris, Jeffrey Rachlinski, and Andrew Wistrich (2007). "Blinking on the Bench: How Judges Decide Cases," *Cornell Law Review* 93: 1–43.
Guthrie, Chris, Jeffrey Rachlinski, and Andrew Wistrich (2011). "Probable Cause, Probability, and Hindsight," *Journal of Empirical Legal Studies* 8: 72–98.
Hallett, Christine (2005). "The Attempt to Understand Puerperal Fever in the Eighteenth and Early Nineteenth Centuries: The Influence of Inflammation Theory," *Medical History* 49 (1): 1–28.
Hambrick, David Z., Guillermo Campitelli, and Brooke N. Macnamara, eds. (2018). *The Science of Expertise: Behavioral, Neural, and Genetics Approaches to Complex Skill*, London: Routledge.
Hampshire, Adam, Roger R. Highfield, Beth L. Parkin, and Adrian M. Owen (2012). "Fractionating Human Intelligence," *Neuron* 76 (6): 1225–37. DOI: 10.1016/j.neuron.2012.06.022.
Hand, Learned (1901). "Historical and Practical Considerations Regarding Expert Testimony," *Harvard Law Review* 15 (1): 40–58.

Hardwig, John (1985). "Epistemic Dependence," *Journal of Philosophy* 82 (7): 335–49.
Hart, Herbert L. A. (1982). *Essays on Bentham: Jurisprudence and Political Philosophy*, Oxford: Oxford University Press.
Hartsock, Nancy (1987). "The Feminist Standpoint: Developing the Ground for a Specifically Feminist Historical Materialism," in Sandra Harding, ed., *Feminism and Methodology: Social Science Issues*, 157–80, Bloomington: Indiana University Press.
Haskell, Thomas (1998). *Objectivity Is Not Neutrality: Explanatory Schemes in History*, Baltimore, MD: Johns Hopkins Press.
Hauser, Larry (n.d.). "Chinese Room Argument," *Internet Encyclopedia of Philosophy*. Available online: https://www.iep.utm.edu/chineser/.
Hawkins, Derek (2016). "Flight Attendant to Black Female Doctor: 'We're Looking for Actual Physicians,'" *Washington Post*, October 14. Available online: https://www.washingtonpost.com/news/morning-mix/wp/2016/10/14/blatant-discrimination-black-female-doctor-says-flight-crew-questioned-her-credentials-during-medical-emergency/?noredirect=on.
"Healthcare Ethics Consultant-Certified Program," *American Society for Bioethics and Humanities*, accessed July 11, 2019. Available online: http://asbh.org/certification/hcec-certification.
HEC-C Certification Commission (2019). *Healthcare Ethics Consultant-Certified (HEC-C) Examination Candidate Handbook*, Chicago, IL: American Society for Bioethics and Humanities.
Hecht, Jennifer Michael (2003). *Doubt: A History*, New York: HarperCollins.
Heldal, Frode and Aksel Tjora (2009). "Making Sense of Patient Expertise," *Social Theory and Health* 7: 1–19.
Hempel, Carl (1966). *Philosophy of Natural Science*, Englewood Cliffs, NJ: Prentice Hall.
Hester, D. Micah (2001). "Community as Healing: Pragmatist Ethics in Medical Encounters," Lanham, MD: Rowman and Littlefield.
Hinton, Martin David (2015). "Mizrahi and Seidel: Experts in Confusion," *Informal Logic* 35 (4): 539–54.
Hochschild, Arlie Russell (2016). *Strangers in Their Own Land: Anger and Mourning on the American Right*, New York: The New Press.
Hodgson, Robert T. (2008). "An Examination of Judge Reliability at a Major U.S. Wine Competition," *Journal of Wine Economics* 3(2) 105–13.
Hoffman, Diane E. and Anita J. Tarzian (2001). "The Girl Who Cried Pain: A Bias against Women in the Treatment of Pain," *Journal of Law, Medicine and Ethics* 29: 13–27.
Hoffman, Kelly M., Sophie Trawalter, Jordan R. Axt, and M. Norman Oliver (2016). "Racial Bias in Pain Assessment and Treatment Recommendations, and False Beliefs about Biological Differences between Blacks and Whites," *PNAS* 113 (16): 4296–301.

Hogarth, Robin M. (2001). *Educating Intuition*, Chicago, IL: University of Chicago Press.
Hogarth, Robin M. (2010). "Intuition: A Challenge for Psychological Research on Decision Making," *Psychological Inquiry* 21: 338–53.
Hogarth, Robin M., Tomás Lejarraga, and Emre Soyer (2015). "The Two Settings of Kind and Wicked Learning Environments," *Current Directions in Psychological Science* 24 (5): 379–85.
Homer (1900). *The Odyssey*, trans. Samuel Butler, London: A.C. Fifield. https://en.wikisource.org/wiki/The_Odyssey_(Butler).
Homer (2018). *The Odyssey*, trans. Emily Wilson, New York: W. W. Norton.
"How to Taste Whisky" (n.d.). *Master of Malt*. Available online: https://www.masterofmalt.com/c/guides/how-to-taste-whisky/.
Howard, John W. and Robin M. Dawes (1976). "Linear Prediction of Marital Happiness," *Personality and Social Psychology Bulletin* 2 (4): 478–80.
Huemer, Michael (2013). *The Problem of Political Authority*, New York: Palgrave Macmillan.
"Human Health Risk Assessment," US EPA, accessed July 15, 2019. Available online: https://www.epa.gov/risk/human-health-risk-assessment.
Huxley, Aldous (1963). *Literature and Science*, New Haven, CT: Leete's Island Books, Inc.
Ingelfinger, Franz J. (1980). "Arrogance," *New England Journal of Medicine* 303 (26): 1507–11.
International Association of Memory, http://iam-stats.org/.
Irwin, Alan (1995). *Citizen Science: A Study of People, Expertise and Sustainable Development*, New York: Routledge.
Jackson, Mark (1994). "Suspicious Infant Deaths: The Statute of 1624 and Medical Evidence at Coroners' Inquests," in Michael Clark and Catherine Crawford, eds., *Legal Medicine in History*, 64–86, Cambridge: Cambridge University Press.
James, William ([1890] 1950). *Principles of Psychology*, New York: Dover.
Jamieson, Kathleen Hall and Joseph N. Cappella (2010). *Echo Chamber: Rush Limbaugh and the Conservative Media Establishment*, Oxford: Oxford University Press.
Jobs, Steve (2011). "Technology and Liberal Arts," *YouTube*, October 6. Available online: https://www.youtube.com/watch?v=KlI1MR-qNt8.
John, Esther M., G. G. Schwarz, D. M. Dreon, and J. Koo (1999). "Vitamin D and Breast Cancer Risk: The NHANES I Epidemiologic Follow-up Study, 1971-1975 to 1992," *Cancer Epidemiology, Biomarkers & Prevention* 8 (5): 399.
John, Stephen (2018). "Epistemic Trust and the Ethics of Science Communication: Against Transparency, Openness, Sincerity and Honesty," *Social Epistemology* 32 (2): 75–87.
Johnson, Dave (2015). "Obama to Visit Nike to Promote TPP. Wait, Nike? Really?," *Huffington Post*, May 7. Available online: http://www.huffingtonpost.com/dave-johnson/obama-to-visit-nike-to-pr_b_7233118.html.

Jones, James ([1981] 1993). *Bad Blood: The Tuskegee Syphilis Experiment*, rev. ed., New York: The Free Press.

"Journal of Parapsychology" (n.d.). *Parapsychological Association*. Available online: https://www.parapsych.org/section/17/journal_of_parapsychology.aspx.

Kahneman, Daniel (2011). *Thinking Fast and Slow*, New York: Farrar, Straus, & Giroux.

Kahneman, Daniel and Amos Tversky, eds. (2000). *Choices, Values and Frames*, Cambridge: Cambridge University Press.

Kahneman, Daniel and Dan Lovallo (1993). "Timid Choices and Bold Forecasts: A Cognitive Perspective on Risk Taking," *Management Science* 39 (1): 17–31.

Kahneman, Daniel, Paul Slovic, and Amos Tversky (1982). *Judgment under Uncertainty: Heuristics and Biases*, Cambridge: Cambridge University Press.

Kaiser, Mary Kister, John Jonides, and Joanne Alexander (1986). "Intuitive Reasoning about Abstract and Familiar Physics Problems," *Memory and Cognition* 14 (4): 308–12.

Kant, Immanuel (1784). "What Is Enlightenment?" trans. Mary C. Smith, http://www.columbia.edu/acis/ets/CCREAD/etscc/kant.html.

Kant, Immanuel ([1785] 2006). *Anthropology from a Pragmatic Point of View*, trans. Robert B. Louden, Cambridge: Cambridge University Press.

Kellogg, Ronald T. (2018). "Professional Writing Expertise," in K. Anders Ericsson, Robert R. Hoffman, Aaron Kozbelt, and Mark Williams, eds., *Expertise and Expert Performance*, 2nd ed., 413–30, Cambridge: Cambridge University Press.

Kelly, Thomas (2005). "The Epistemic Significance of Disagreement," in Tamar Gendler and John Hawthorne, eds., *Oxford Studies in Epistemology*, Vol. 1, 167–96, Oxford: Oxford University Press.

Keren, Gideon (1987). "Facing Uncertainty in the Game of Bridge: A Calibration Study," *Organizational Behavior and Human Decision Processes* 39: 98–114.

Khan, Carrie-Ann Biondi (2005). "Aristotle's Moral Expert: The Phronimos," in Lisa Rasmussen, ed., *Ethics Expertise: History, Contemporary Perspectives, and Applications*, 39–53, Dordrecht: Springer.

Klein, Gary (1998). *Sources of Power: How People Make Decisions*, Cambridge, MA: MIT Press.

Klein, Gary (2003). *The Power of Intuition: How to Use Your Gut Feelings to Make Better Decisions at Work*, New York: Currency.

Klein, Gary (2013). *Seeing What Others Don't: The Remarkable Ways We Gain Insight*, New York: Public Affairs.

Klein, Gary (2015). "A Naturalistic Decision Making Perspective on Studying Intuitive Decision Making," *Journal of Applied Research in Memory and Cognition* 4: 164–8.

Klein, Gary A. (2016). "The Naturalistic Decision Making Approach: What We Have Learned by Studying Cognition in the Wild," *Psychology Today*, https://www.psychologytoday.com/nz/blog/seeing-what-others-dont/201602/the-naturalistic-decision-making-approach?amp.

Klein, Gary, Roberta Calderwood, and Anne Clinton-Cirocco (2010). "Rapid Decision Making on the Fireground: The Original Study Plus a Postscript," *Journal of Cognitive Engineering and Decision Making* 4: 186–209.

Klein, Gary, Steve Wolf, Laura Militello, and Caroline Zsambok (1995). "Characteristics of Skilled Option Generation in Chess," *Organizational Behavior and Human Decision Processes* 62 (1): 63–9.

Klein, Gary A., Judith Orasnu, Roberta Calderwood, and Caroline E. Zsambok, eds. (1992). *Decision Making In Action: Models and Methods*, 51–99, Norwood, NJ: Ablex Publishing Corporation.

Klein, Peter (2005). "Infinitism Is the Solution to the Regress Problem," in Matthius Steup and Ernest Sosa, eds., *Contemporary Debates in Epistemology*, 131–9, Malden, MA: Blackwell.

Koehler, Daniel J., Lyle Brenner, and Dale Griffin (2002). "The Calibration of Expert Judgment: Heuristics and Biases beyond the Laboratory," in Thomas Gilovich, Dale Griffin, and Daniel Kahneman, eds., *Heuristics and Biases: The Psychology of Intuitive Judgment*, 686–715, Cambridge: Cambridge University Press.

Koppl, Roger (2018). *Expert Failure*. Cambridge, UK: Cambridge University Press.

Koppl, Roger (2019). "Roger Koppl: Expert Failure," on *This Is Not a Pipe Podcast*, interviewed by Chris Richardson, September 5. Available online: https://www.tinapp.org/episodes/expertfailure

Kornbith, Hilary (2002). *Knowledge and Its Place in Nature*, Oxford: Oxford University Press.

Kornblith, Hilary (2010). "Belief in the Face of Controversy," in Richard Feldman and Ted A. Warfield, eds., *Disagreement*, 40–1, Oxford: Oxford University Press.

Kuhn, Thomas (1962). *The Structure of Scientific Revolutions*, Chicago, IL: University of Chicago Press.

Kutrovátz, Gábor. (2011). "Expert Authority and Ad Verecundiam Arguments," in France H. van Eemeren, Bart J. Garssen, David Godden, and Gorden Mitchell, eds., *Proceedings of the Seventh Conference of the International Society of the Study of Argumentation*, 1050–61, Amsterdam: Rozenberg.

LaBarge, Scott (1997). "Socrates and the Recognition of Experts," *Apeiron* 30 (4): 51–62.

Lackey, Jennifer (2006). "Introduction," in Jennifer Lackey and Ernest Sosa, eds., *The Epistemology of Testimony*, 1–21, Oxford: Oxford University Press.

Lackey, Jennifer (2018a). "Experts and Peer Disagreement," in Matthew A. Benton, John Hawthorne and Dani Rabinowitz, eds., *Knowledge, Belief, and God: New Insights in Religious Epistemology*, 228–45. Oxford: Oxford University Press.

Lackey, Jennifer (2018b). "True Story: Echo Chambers Are Not the Problem," *Morning Consult Blog*, https://morningconsult.com/opinions/true-story-echo-chambers-not-problem/.

Landman, J. T. and R. M. Dawes (1982). "Psychotherapy Outcome: Smith and Glass' Conclusions Stand Up to Scrutiny," *American Psychologist* 37: 504–16.

Landwehr, Achim (2004). "The Expert in a Historical Context: The Case of Venetian Politics," in Elke Kurz-Milcke and Gerd Gigerenzer, eds., *Experts in Science and Society*, 215–28, New York: Kluwer Academic / Plenum Publishers.

Lappe, Joan M., Dianne Travers-Gustafson, K. Michael Davies, Robert R. Recker, and Robert P. Heaney (2007). "Vitamin D and Calcium Supplementation Reduces Cancer Risk: Results of a Randomized Trial," *American Journal of Clinical Nutrition* 85 (6): 1586–91.

Lee, Carole J., Cassidy R. Sugimoto, Guo Zhang, and Blaise Cronin (2012). "Bias in Peer Review," *Journal of the American Society for Information Science and Technology* 64 (1): 2–17.

Lagay, Faith (2002). "The Legacy of Humoral Medicine," *AMA Journal of Ethics Virtual Mentor* 4 (7): DOI 10.1001/virtualmentor.2002.4.7.mhst1-0207.

Leventhal, Laura., Barbee Teasley, and Diane Rohlman (1994). "Analyses of Factors Related to Positive Test Bias in Software Testing," *International Journal of Human-Computer Studies* 41: 717–49.

Lewis, Clive S. (1954). *The Horse and His Boy*, London: Geoffrey Bles.

Lewis, Clive S. (1960). *The Four Loves*, New York: Harcourt Brace.

Lewis, David ([1980] 2010). "Mad Pain and Martian Pain," in Nils Ch. Rauhut and Robert H. Bass, eds., *Readings on the Ultimate Questions*, 3rd ed. 241–9, Boston, MA: Prentice Hall.

Leyva, Arturo (2018). "Embodied Rilkean Sport-Specific Knowledge," *Journal of the Philosophy of Sport* 45 (2): 1–16.

Licon, Jimmy Alfonso (2012). "Skeptical Thoughts on Philosophical Expertise," *Logos and Episteme* 3 (4): 449–58.

Lindberg, David C. (2002a). "Early Christian Attitudes toward Nature," in Gary B. Ferngren, ed., *Science and Religion: A Historical Introduction*, 47–56, Baltimore, MD: Johns Hopkins University Press.

Lindberg, David C. (2002b). "Medieval Science and Religion," in Gary B. Ferngren, ed., *Science and Religion: A Historical Introduction*, 57–72, Baltimore, MD: Johns Hopkins University Press.

Linshi, Jack (2015). "10 CEOs Who Prove Your Liberal Arts Degree Isn't Worthless," *Time Magazine*, July 23. Available online: https://time.com/3964415/ceo-degree-liberal-arts/.

Lippmann, Walter (1922). *Public Opinion*, New York: Harcourt.

Lippmann, Walter (1927). *The Phantom Public*, Transaction Publishers.

Lloyd, Geoffrey. E. R. (1987). *Revolutions of Wisdom: Studies in the Claims and Practice of Ancient Greek Science*, Berkeley: University of California Press.

Locke, John (1975). *An Essay Concerning Human Understanding*, Peter H. Nidditch, ed., Oxford: Oxford University Press.

London, Alex John (2000). "Thrasymachus and Managed Care: How Not to Think about the Craft of Medicine," in Mark G. Kuczewski and Roland

Polansky, eds., *Bioethics: Ancient Themes in Contemporary Issues*, 131–54, Cambridge, MA: MIT Press.

Lopez, German (2019). "For the First Time, the Feds Criminally Charged a Pharma Distributor for the Opioid Epidemic," *Vox*, April 23. Available online: https://www.vox.com/policy-and-politics/2019/4/23/18512781/rochester-drug-cooperative-opioid-epidemic-drug-trafficking.

Luscombe, Belinda (2011). "10 Questions for Daniel Kahneman," *Time Magazine*, November 28. Available online: http://content.time.com/time/magazine/article/0,9171,2099712,00.html.

Lyotard, Jean-François ([1979] 1984). *The Postmodern Condition: A Report on Knowledge*, trans. Geoff Bennington and Brian Massumi (Manchester: Manchester University Press, 1984). Trans. of *La Condition postmoderne: rapport sur le savoir* (Paris: Minuit, 1979).

Machuca, Diego E., ed. (2013). *Disagreement and Skepticism*, London: Routledge.

Majdik, Zoltan P. and William M. Keith (2011). "The Problem of Pluralistic Expertise: A Wittgensteinian Approach to the Rhetorical Basis of Expertise," *Social Epistemology* 25 (3): 275–90.

Makary, Martin A. and Michael Daniel (2016). "Medical Error: The Third Leading Cause of Death in the US," *BMJ* 353, doi: https://doi.org/10.1136/bmj.i2139.

Marr, Bernard (2017). "Machine Learning, Artificial Intelligence—And the Future of Accounting," *Forbes Magazine*, https://www.forbes.com/sites/bernardmarr/2017/07/07/machine-learning-artificial-intelligence-and-the-future-of-accounting/#2fc34b1c2dd1.

Martin, Ben L. (1973). "Experts in Policy Processes: A Contemporary Perspective," *Polity* 6 (2): 149–73.

Martini, Carlo (2015). "The Paradox of Proof and Scientific Expertise," *Journal of Philosophical Studies* 28: 1–16.

Martinson, Brian C., Melissa S. Anderson, and Raymond de Vries (2005). "Scientists Behaving Badly," *Nature* 435: 737–8.

Maruthappu, Mahiben, Antoine Duclos, Stuart R. Lipsitz, Dennis Orgill, Matthew J. Carty (2015). "Surgical Learning Curves and Operative Efficiency: A Cross-Specialty Observational Study," *BMJ Open* 5 (3). doi: 10.1136/bmjopen-2014-006679.

Mascaro, Jennifer S. Patrick D. Hackett, and James K. Rilling (2013). "Testicular Volume Is Inversely Correlated with Nurturing-Related Brain Activity in Human Fathers," *PNAS* 110 (39): 15746–51.

Matheson, Jonathan (2015). *The Epistemic Significance of Disagreement*, New York: Palgrave Macmillan.

Matheson, Jonathan and Brandon Carey (2013). "How Skeptical Is the Equal Weight View?," in Diego E. Machuca, ed., *Disagreement and Skepticism*, 131–49, New York: Routledge.

Matheson, Jonathan, Scott McElreath, and Nathan Nobis (2018). "Moral Experts, Deference & Disagreement," in Jamie Carlin Watson and Laura Guidry-Grimes, eds., *Moral Expertise*, 87–105, Cham, Switzerland: Springer.

Mazza, Ed (2016). "Florida 18-Year-Old Arrested for Allegedly Operating Fake Medical Practice," *Huffington Post*, February 2. Available online: https://www.huffpost.com/entry/malachi-love-robinson-teen-fake-doctor_n_56c40019e4b0c3c5505328df?guccounter=1.

McCain, Kevin (2014). "The Problem of the Criterion," *Internet Encyclopedia of Philosophy*. Available online: https://www.iep.utm.edu/criterio/.

McCloskey, Michael, Alfonso Caramazza, and Bert Green (1980). "Curvilinear Motion in the Absence of External Forces: Naïve Beliefs about the Motion of Objects," *Science* 210: 1139–41.

McGrath, Alister (2007). *Christianity's Dangerous Idea*, New York: HarperCollins.

McGrath, Sarah (2008). "Moral Disagreement and Moral Expertise," in Russ Shafer-Landau (ed.), *Oxford Studies in Metaethics: Volume 3*, pp. 87–108, Oxford: Oxford University Press.

McLean vs. Arkansas Documentation Project (2005). "Statement of Purpose," *AntiEvolution.org*. Available online: http://www.antievolution.org/projects/mclean/new_site/index.htm.

McMyler, Benjamin (2011). *Testimony, Trust, & Authority*, Oxford: Oxford University Press.

McNeil, Barbara J., Stephen G. Pauker, Harold C. Sox, Jr., and Amos Tversky (1982). "On the Elicitation of Preferences for Alternative Therapies," *New England Journal of Medicine* 306: 1259–62.

Merleau-Ponty, Maurice (1945). *Phenomenology of Perception*, Paris: Éditions Gallimard.

Mie, Axel, Christina Rudén, and Philippe Grandjean (2018). "Safety of Safety Evaluation of Pesticides: Developmental Neurotoxicity of Chlorpyrifos and Chlorpyrifos-methyl," *Environmental Health* 17 (77): 1–5.

Mieg, Harald and Julia Evetts (2018). "Professionalism, Science, and Expert Roles: A Social Perspective," in K. Anders Ericsson, Robert R. Hoffman, Aaron Kozbelt, and A. Mark Williams, eds., *The Cambridge Handbook of Expertise and Expert Performance*, 2nd ed., 127–48, Cambridge: Cambridge University Press.

Millgram, Elijah (2015). *The Great Endarkenment*, Oxford: Oxford University Press.

Mitchell, Georgina (2017). "Man Charged after 'Impersonating Doctor' at NSW Hospitals for 11 Years," *Sydney Morning Herald*, March 7. Available online: https://www.smh.com.au/national/nsw/man-charged-after-impersonating-a-doctor-at-nsw-hospitals-for-11-years-20170307-guswh5.html.

Mizrahi, Moti (2013). "Why Arguments from Expert Opinion Are Weak Arguments," *Informal Logic* 33 (1): 57–79.

Mizrahi, Moti (2016). "Why Arguments from Expert Opinion Are Still Weak: A Reply to Seidel," *Informal Logic* 36 (2): 238–52.

Mizrahi, Moti (2018). "Arguments from Expert Opinion and Persistent Bias," *Argumentation* 32 (2): 175–95.

Mlodinow, Leonard (2008). *The Drunkard's Walk: How Randomness Rules Our Lives*, New York: Pantheon Books.

Montague, Jules (2017). "Trust Me, I'm a Fake Doctor: How Medical Imposters Thrive in the Real World," *The Guardian*, August 14. Available online: https://www.theguardian.com/global/2017/aug/14/trust-me-im-a-fake-doctor-how-medical-imposters-thrive-in-the-real-world.

Montero, Barbara (2016). *Thought in Action: Expertise and the Conscious Mind*, Oxford: Oxford University Press.

Mosing, Miriam A., Isabelle Peretz, and Frederick Ullén (2018). "Genetic Influences on Music Expertise," in David Z. Hambrick, Guillermo Campitelli, and Brooke N. Macnamara, eds., *The Science of Expertise: Behavioral, Neural, and Genetic Approaches to Complex Skill*, pp. 272–282, London: Routledge.

Murray, Charles and Richard Hernstein (1994). *The Bell Curve: Intelligence and Class Structure in American Life*, New York: Free Press.

Murray-Close, Marta and Misty L. Heggeness (2018). "Manning Up and Womaning Down: How Husbands and Wives Report Their Earnings When She Earns More," *United States Census Bureau* Working Paper Number: SEHSD-WP2018-20. Available online: https://www.census.gov/content/dam/Census/library/working-papers/2018/demo/SEHSD-WP2018-20.pdf.

Nelson, Katherine E., Laura C. Rosella, Sanjay Mahant, and Astrid Guttman (2016). "Survival and Surgical Interventions for Children with Trisomy 13 and 18," *JAMA* 316 (4): 420–28.

Newell, Allen and Herbert Simon (1972). *Human Problem Solving*, Upper Saddle River, NJ: Prentice Hall.

Newton, Isaac (1952). *Mathematical Principles of Natural Philosophy*, trans. Andrew Motte, rev. Florian Cajori, Chicago, IL: Encyclopedia Britannica Inc.

Nguyen, C. Thi (2018a). "Echo Chambers and Epistemic Bubbles," *Episteme* 1–21, https://doi.org/10.1017/epi.2018.32.

Nguyen, C. Thi (2018b). "Cognitive Islands and Runaway Echo Chambers: Problems for Epistemic Dependence on Experts," *Synthese*, 1–19, DOI: https://doi.org/10.1007/s11229-018-1692-0.

Nichols, Tom (2017). *The Death of Expertise: The Campaign against Established Knowledge and Why It Matters*, New York: Oxford University Press

Nietzsche, Friedrich ([1878] 1986). *Human, All Too Human: A Book for Free Spirits*, trans. R. J. Hollingdale, Cambridge: Cambridge University Press.

Nietzsche, Friedrich ([1886] 2009). *Beyond Good and Evil*, trans. Helen Zimmern, Urbana, IL: Project Gutenberg.

Norman, Geoffrey R., Lawrence E. M. Grierson, Jonathan Sherbino, Stanley J. Hamstra, Henk G. Schmidt, and Silvia Mamede (2018). "Expertise in Medicine and Surgery," in K. Anders Ericsson, Robert R. Hoffman, Aaron Kozbelt, and Mark Williams, eds., *Expertise and Expert Performance*, 2nd ed., 331–55, Cambridge: Cambridge University Press.

Norton, Kevin and Tim Olds (2001). "Morphological Evolution of Athletes over the 20th Century," *Sports Medicine* 31 (11): 763–83.

Noveck, Beth Simone (2015). *Smart Citizens, Smarter State: The Technologies of Expertise and the Future of Governing*, Cambridge, MA: Harvard University Press.

Numbers, Ron (2006). *The Creationists: From Scientific Creationism to Intelligent Design*, Cambridge, MA: Harvard University Press.

Oreskes, Naomi and Erik M. Conway (2010). *Merchants of Doubt: How a Handful of Scientists Obscured the Truth on Issues from Tobacco Smoke to Global Warming*, New York: Bloomsbury.

Origgi, Gloria (2015). "What Is an Expert That a Person May Trust Her? Towards a Political Epistemology of Expertise," *Journal of Philosophical Studies* 28: 159–68.

Pariser, Eli (2011). *The Filter Bubble: What the Internet Is Hiding from You*, New York: Penguin Press.

Parry, Richard (2014). "Episteme and Techne," in Edward N. Zalta, ed., *The Stanford Encyclopedia of Philosophy*, Fall 2014 Edition. Available online: https://plato.stanford.edu/archives/fall2014/entries/episteme-techne/.

Paskin, Janet (2008) "10 Things Your Tax Preparer Won't Tell You," SmartMoney.

Patel, Vimla L. and Guy J. Groen (1986). "Knowledge-Based Solution Strategies in Medical Reasoning," *Cognitive Science* 10: 91–116.

Patel, Vimla L. and Guy J. Groen (1991). "The Nature of Medical Expertise: A Critical Look," in K. Anders Ericsson and Jacqui Smith, eds. *Toward a General Theory of Expertise*, 93–125, Cambridge: Cambridge University Press.

Patel, Vimla L. and K. Anders Ericsson (1990). "Expert-Novice Differences in Clinical Text Understanding," (Technical Report CME90-CS13). Montreal: Centre for Medical Education, McGill, University.

Perceptions of Science in America (2018). Cambridge, MA: American Academy of Arts and Sciences. Available online: https://www.amacad.org/sites/default/files/publication/downloads/PFoS-Perceptions-Science-America.pdf.

Peters, Richard S., Peter G. Winch, and Austin E. Duncan-Jones (1958). "Authority," *Proceedings of the Aristotelian Society* 32: 207–60.

Philips, Jennifer K., Gary Klein, and Winston R. Sieck (2007). "Expertise in Judgment and Decision Making: A Case for Training Intuitive Decision Skills," in Derek J. Koehler and Nigel Harvey, eds., *Blackwell Handbook of Judgment and Decision Making*, 297–315, Malden, MA: Blackwell Publishing.

Pico Della Mirandola, Giovanni (1956). *Oration on the Dignity of Man*, trans. A. R. Caponigri, Chicago, IL: H. Regnery.

Plato (1903). *Statesman*, trans. John Burnet, Oxford: Oxford University Press.

Plato (1967). *Protagoras*, trans. W. R. M. Lamb. Plato in Twelve Volumes, Vol. 3, Cambridge, MA, Harvard University Press; London, William Heinemann Ltd. 1967.

Plato (1968). *The Republic of Plato*, trans. Allan Bloom, 2nd ed., New York: Basic Books.

Plato (1992). *Republic*, trans. G. M. A. Grube, revised by C. D. C. Reeve, New York: Hackett.

Plato (1997a). "Ion," in John M. Cooper, ed., Paul Woodruff, trans., *Plato: Complete Works*, 937–49, Indianapolis, IN: Hackett Publishing Company.

Plato (1997b). *Laches*, trans. Rosamond Kent Sprague, in John M. Cooper, ed. *Plato: Complete Works*, 664–86, Indianapolis, IN: Hackett Publishing Company.

Plato (1997c). "Protagoras," in John M. Cooper, ed., Stanley Lombardo and Karen Bell, trans., *Plato: Complete Works*, 746–90, Indianapolis, IN: Hackett Publishing Company.

Plato (1997d). "Statesman," in John M. Cooper, ed., C. J. Rowe, trans., *Plato: Complete Works*, 294–358, Indianapolis, IN: Hackett Publishing Company.

Plutarch (1874). *Plutarch's Morals*, translated from the Greek by several hands, rev. William W. Goodwin, Boston, MA: Little, Brown, and Co; Cambridge: Press of John Wilson and Son.

Polanyi, Michael ([1958] 1962). *Personal Knowledge: Towards a Post-Critical Philosophy*, New York: Harper Torchbooks.

Porter, Roy (2003). *Cambridge History of Science, Vol. 4: Eighteenth-Century Science*, Cambridge: Cambridge University Press.

Porter, Theodore M. (1995). *Trust in Numbers: The Pursuit of Objectivity in Science and Public Life*, Princeton, NJ: Princeton University Press.

Postman, Neil (1985). *Amusing Ourselves to Death: Public Discourse in the Age of Show Business*, New York: Penguin.

Pottash, Michael (2019). "Comfort Care, Whatever Does That Mean?" *Pallimed: A Hospice and Palliative Care Blog*, https://www.pallimed.org/2019/05/comfort-care-whatever-does-that-mean_4.html.

Prasad, Vinayak K., and Adam S. Cifu (2015). *Ending Medical Reversal: Improving Outcomes, Saving Lives*, Baltimore, MD: Johns Hopkins University Press.

Pratchett, Terry (2013). *Raising Steam*, London: Doubleday.

Putnam, Hilary (1975). *Mind, Language, and Reality: Philosophical Papers Volume Two*, Cambridge: Cambridge University Press.

Qian, M. K., P. C. Quinn, G. D. Heyman, O. Pescalis, G. Fu, and K. Lee (2017). "Perceptual Individuation Training (but Not Mere Exposure) Reduces Implicit Bias in Preschool Children," *Developmental Psychology* 53(5): 845–59.

Quast, Christian (2018a). "Expertise: A Practical Explication," *Topoi* 37 (1): 11–27.

Quast, Christian (2018b). "Towards a Balanced Account of Expertise," *Social Epistemology* 32 (6): 397–418.

Rachels, James, and Stuart Rachels (2015). *The Elements of Moral Philosophy*, 8th ed., New York: McGraw-Hill Education.

Rakel, Horst (2004). "Scientists as Expert Advisors: Science Cultures Versus National Cultures?," in Elke Kurz-Milcke and Gerd Gigerenzer, eds., *Experts in Science and Society*, 3–25, New York: Klewer Academic.

Rao, T. S. Sathyanarayana and Chittaranjan Andrade (2011). "The MMR Vaccine and Autism: Sensation, Refutation, Retraction, and Fraud," *Indian Journal of Psychiatry* 53 (2): 95–6.

Rapport Du Comité D'Orientation (2016). "Ensemble: Améliorons Le Dépistage du Cancer du Sein," http://www.concertation-depistage.fr/wp-content/uploads/2016/10/depistage-cancer-sein-rapport-concertation-sept-2016.pdf.

Ray, C. Claiborne (2019). "A Barnyard Mystery: Are the Chicks Male or Female?," *New York Times*, June 24. Available online: https://www.nytimes.com/2019/06/24/science/chicken-

Raz, Joseph ([1975]1999). *Practical Reasons and Norms*, Oxford: Oxford University Press.

Raz, Joseph ([1985] 1990). "Authority and Justification," in Joseph Raz, ed., *Authority*, 116–41, New York: New York University Press.

Raz, Joseph (1988). *The Morality of Freedom*, Oxford: Oxford University Press.

Reade, Charles ([1868] 1896). *Foul Play*, London: Chatto & Windus, Piccadilly.

Reeves, Josh (2018). "Should Christians Trust Scientific Experts?," *BioLogos Blog*, https://biologos.org/articles/should-christians-trust-scientific-experts.

Reichenbach, Hans (1958). *The Philosophy of Space & Time*, New York: Dover.

Reiheld, Alison (2017). "What You Don't Know CAN Hurt You: Epistemic Injustice and Conceptually Impoverished Health Promotion," *IJFAB Blog*, November 3. Available online: https://www.ijfab.org/blog/2017/11/what-you-dont-know-can-hurt-you-epistemic-injustice-and-conceptually-impoverished-health-promotion/.

Rieder, Gernot and Judith Simon (2016). "Datatrust: Or, the Political Quest for Numerical Evidence and the Epistemologies of Big Data," *Big Data and Society* 3 (1): 1–6.

Rieder, Travis (2019). *In Pain: A Bioethicist's Personal Struggle with Opioids*, New York: HarperCollins.

Rilke, Rainer Maria ([1910] 1985). *The Notebooks of Malte Laurids Brigge*, trans. S. Mitchell, New York: Vintage.

Ritchie, Earl J. (2016). "Fact Checking the Claim of 97% Consensus on Anthropogenic Climate Change," *Forbes Magazine*, December 14. Available online: https://www.forbes.com/sites/uhenergy/2016/12/14/fact-checking-the-97-consensus-on-anthropogenic-climate-change/#7ad367271157.

Roberts, David (2017). "Donald Trump and the Rise of Tribal Epistemology," *Vox*, May 19. Available online: https://www.vox.com/policy-and-politics/2017/3/22/14762030/donald-trump-tribal-epistemology.

Robertson, Josefina (2014). "Waiting Time at the Emergency Department from a Gender Equality Perspective," MA diss., Institute of Medicine at the Sahlgrenska Academy, University of Gothenburg.

Rogers, John C., David E. Swee, and John A. Ullian (1991). "Teaching Medical Decision Making and Students' Clinical Problem Solving Skills," *Medical Teacher* 13 (2): 157–64.

Rorty, Richard (1979). *Philosophy and the Mirror of Nature*, Princeton, NJ: Princeton University Press.

Rorty, Richard (1990). "Introduction," in John P. Murphy, ed., *Pragmatism: From Peirce to Davidson*, Boulder, CO: Westview Press.

Rowlands, Mark (2015). "Rilkean Memory," *Southern Journal of Philosophy* 53 (S1): 141–54.
Russell, Bertrand (1912). *Problems of Philosophy*, Home University Library, http://www.ditext.com/russell/russell.html
Russell, Bertrand (1968). *The Art of Philosophizing and Other Essays*, New York: Philosophical Library.
Ruthsatz, Joanne, Kimberley Stephens, and Mark Matthews (2018). "The Link between Child Prodigies and Autism," in David Z. Hambrick, Guillermo Campitelli, and Brooke N. Macnamara, eds., *The Science of Expertise: Behavioral, Neural, and Genetic Approaches to Complex Skill*, 87–100, London: Routledge.
Ryle, Gilbert (1945). "Knowing How and Knowing That: The Presidential Address," *Proceedings of the Aristotelian Society* 46: 1–16.
Ryle, Gilbert ([1949] 2009). *The Concept of Mind: The 60th Anniversary Edition*, New York: Routledge.
Sacks, Oliver (1985). *The Man Who Mistook His Wife for a Hat*, New York: Touchstone.
Sahni, V. Anik, Patricia C. Silveira, Nisha I. Sainani, and Ramin Khorasani (2016). "Impact of a Structured Report Template on the Quality of MRI Reports for Rectal Cancer Staging," *American Journal of Roentgenology* 205 (3): 584–8, doi: 10.2214/AJR.14.14053.
Samuel, Arthur L. (1959). "Some Studies in Machine Learning Using the Game of Checkers," *IBM Journal* 3 (3): 210–29.
Schick, Theodore and Lewis Vaughn (2010). *How to Think about Weird Things: Critical Thinking for a New Age*, 6th ed., New York: McGraw-Hill.
Schmitt, Frederick F. 2006. "Testimonial Justification and Transindividual Reasons," in Jennifer Lackey and Ernest Sosa, eds., *The Epistemology of Testimony*, 193–224, Oxford: Oxford University Press.
Scholz, Oliver (2009). "Experts: What They Are and How We Recognize Them—A Discussion of Alvin Goldman's Views," in Shurz, Gerhard and Markus Werning, eds., *Reliable Knowledge and Social Epistemology: Essays on the Philosophy of Alvin Goldman and Replies by Goldman*, 187–208, Amsterdam: Grazer Philosophische Studien.
Scholz, Oliver (2018). "Symptoms of Expertise: Knowledge, Understanding, and Other Cognitive Goods," *Topoi* 37 (1): 11–27.
Schwitzgebel, Eric and Fiery Cushman (2012). "Expertise in Moral Reasoning? Order Effects on Moral Judgment in Professional Philosophers and Non-philosophers," *Mind and Language* 27 (2): 135–53.
Scott, Robert and Henry G. Lidell (1843). *A Greek-English Lexicon*. Oxford: Oxford University Press.
Scott, Robert and Henry G. Lidell (1945). *An Intermediate Greek-English Lexicon*. Oxford: Oxford University Press.
Searle, John (1980). "Minds, Brains, and Programs," *Behavioral and Brain Sciences* 3: 417–24.

Searle, John (1984). *Minds, Brains, and Science*, Cambridge, MA: Harvard University Press.
Searle, John (1989). "Reply to Jacquette," *Philosophy and Phenomenological Research* 49: 701–8.
Searle, John (2002). *Consciousness and Language*, Cambridge: Cambridge University Press.
Seidel, Markus (2014). "Throwing the Baby out with the Water: From Reasonably Scrutinizing Authorities to Rampant Scepticism about Expertise," *Informal Logic* 34 (2): 192–218.
Selinger, Evan (2011). *Expertise: Philosophical Reflections*, US: Automatic Press.
Selinger, Evan and John Mix (2006). "On Interactional Expertise: Pragmatic and Ontological Considerations," in Evan Selinger and Robert Crease, eds., *The Philosophy of Expertise*, 302–21, New York: University of Columbia Press.
Selinger, Evan, and Robert P. Crease (2006). "Dreyfus on Expertise: The Limits of Phenomenological Analysis," in Evan Selinger and Robert Crease, eds., *The Philosophy of Expertise*, 213–45, New York: Columbia University Press.
Sevin, Cory, Gorden Moore, John Shepherd, Tracy Jacobs, and Cindy Hupke (2009). "Transforming Care Teams to Provide the Best Possible Patient-Centered, Collaborative Care," *J Ambulatory Care Manage* 32 (1): 24–31.
Shackelford, Jole (2009). "That Giordano Bruno Was the First Martyr of Modern Science," in Ronald L. Numbers, ed., *Galileo Goes to Jail: And Other Myths about Science and Religion*, 59–67, Cambridge, MA: Harvard University Press.
Shaffer, Michael J. (2013). "Doxastic Voluntarism, Epistemic Deontology, and Belief-Contravening Commitments," *American Philosophical Quarterly* 50 (1): 73–81.
Shalowitz, David I., Elizabeth Garrett-Myer, and David Wendler (2006). "The Accuracy of Surrogate Decision Makers: A Systematic Review," *Arch Intern Med* 166 (5): 493–7.
Shanteau, James (1989). "Psychological Characteristics and Strategies of Expert Decision Makers," in Bernd Rohrmann, Lee R. Beach, Charles Vlek, and Stephen R. Watson, eds., *Advances in Decision Research*, 203–15, Amsterdam: North Holland.
Shapen, Steven and Simon Schaffer (1985). *Leviathan and the Air-Pump: Hobbes, Boyle, and the Experimental Life*. Princeton, NJ: Princeton University Press.
Shapin, Steven (1994). *A Social History of Truth: Civility and Science in Seventeenth-Century England*, Chicago, IL: University of Chicago Press.
Shema, Hadas (2014). "The Birth of Modern Peer Review," *Scientific American*, April. Available online: https://blogs.scientificamerican.com/information-culture/the-birth-of-modern-peer-review/.
Shorto, Russell (2008). *Descartes' Bones: A Skeletal History of the Conflict between Faith and Reason*, New York: Vintage.
Simon, Herbert (1957a). *Administrative Behavior: A Study of Decision-Making Processes in Administrative Organization*, 2nd ed., New York: Macmillan.
Simon, Herbert (1957b). *Models of Man*, New York: John Wiley.

Simon Herbert, A. and William G. Chase (1973). "Skill in Chess," *American Scientist* 61 (4): 394–403.

Simonton, Dean Keith (1999). "Talent and Its Development: An Emergenic and Epigenetic Model," *Psychological Review* 106 (3): 435–57.

Sinkivec, Maja (2016). *How Good Is Google Translate Really? Evaluation of Google Translate for the Language Direction Slovenian-German*, Masters Thesis at Karl-Franzens-University Graz, Austria.

Skotko, Brian G., Susan P. Levine, and Richard Goldstein (2011). "Self-Perceptions from People with Down Syndrome," *American Journal of Medical Genetics* Part A 155: 2360–9.

Slowik, Edward (2017). "Descartes' Physics," in Edward N. Zalta, ed., *The Stanford Encyclopedia of Philosophy*, Fall 2017 edition. Available online: https://plato.stanford.edu/entries/descartes-physics/#ForcCartPhys.

Smith, Barry and Roberto Casati (1994). "Naïve Physics: An Essay in Ontology," *Philosophical Psychology* 7 (2): 225–44.

Smith, James F. and Thomas Kida (1991). "Heuristics and Biases: Expertise and Task Realism in Auditing," *Psychological Bulletin* 109 (3): 472–89.

Smith, Tom W. and Jaesok Son (2013). "Trends in Public Attitudes about Confidence in Institutions," NORC at the University of Chicago. Available online: http://www.norc.org/PDFs/GSS%20Reports/Trends%20in%20 Confidence%20Institutions_Final.pdf.

Solomon, Miriam (2009). "Standpoint and Creativity," *Hypatia* 24 (4): 226–37.

Sosa, Ernest (2006). "Knowledge: Instrumental and Testimonial," in Jennifer Lackey and Ernest Sosa, eds. *The Epistemology of Testimony* 116–23, Oxford: Oxford University Press.

Specter, Michael (2007). "The Denialists: The Dangerous Attacks on the Consensus about H.I.V. and AIDS," *The New Yorker*, March 12. Available online: https://www.newyorker.com/magazine/2007/03/12/the-denialists.

Spier, Raymond (2002a). "The History of the Peer Review Process," *Trends in Biotechnology* 20 (8): 357–8.

Spier, Raymond (2002b). "Peer Review and Innovation," *Science and Engineering Ethics* 8 (1): 99–108.

Stamper, Kory (2017). *Word by Word: The Secret Life of Dictionaries*, New York: Penguin Random House.

Starks, J. L. and J. Deakin (1984). "Perception in Sport: A Cognitive Approach to Skilled Performance," in William F. Straub and Jean M. Williams, eds., *Cognitive Sport Psychology*, 115–28, Lansing, NY: Sport Science Intl.

Steen, R. Grant, Arturo Casadevall, and Ferric C. Fang (2013). "Why Has the Number of Scientific Retractions Increased?," *PLOS ONE* 8 (7): e68397.

Stevenson, Matthew (2017). "Killing Bill O'Reilly: The Disgraced Broadcaster's Distortions of History," *Harper's Magazine*, July.

Stich, Stephen (1990). *The Fragmentation of Reason*. Cambridge, MA: MIT Press.

Stichter, Matt (2015). "Philosophical and Psychological Accounts of Expertise," *Journal of Philosophical Studies* 28: 105–28.

Sunday, Mackenzie and Isabel Gauthier (2018). "The Neural Underpinnings of Perceptual Expertise," in David Z. Hambrick, Guillermo Campitelli, and Brooke N. Macnamara, eds., *The Science of Expertise: Behavioral, Neural, and Genetic Approaches to Complex Skill*, 200–17, London: Routledge.

Sunstein, Cass (2017). *#Republic*, Princeton, NJ: Princeton University Press.

The Talk Origins Archive (1996). "McLean vs. Arkansas Board of Education," *Talk Origins Archive*. Available online: http://www.talkorigins.org/faqs/mclean-v-arkansas.html.

Tan, Yi Ting, Gary E. MacPherson, and Sarah J. Wilson (2018). "The Molecular Genetic Basis of Music Ability and Music-Related Phenotypes," in David Z. Hambrick, Guillermo Campitelli, and Brooke N. Macnamara, eds., *The Science of Expertise: Behavioral, Neural, and Genetic Approaches to Complex Skill*, 283–304, London: Routledge.

Tanesini, Alessandra (2020). "Standpoint Then and Now," in Miranda Fricker, Peter J. Graham, David Henderson, and Nikolaj J. L. L. Pedersen, eds., *The Routledge Handbook of Social Epistemology*, 335–43, New York: Routledge.

Tetlock, Philip E. (2005). *Expert Political Judgment: How Good Is It? How Can We Know?* Princeton, NJ: Princeton University Press.

Tetlock, Philip E. and Dan Gardner (2015). *Superforecasting: The Art and Science of Prediction*, New York: Crown Publishers.

Thaler, Richard H. and Cass R. Sunstein (2003a). "Libertarian Paternalism," *American Economic Review* (Papers and Proceedings) 93 (2) Fall: 175–9.

Thaler, Richard H. and Cass R. Sunstein (2003b). "Libertarian Paternalism Is Not an Oxymoron," *The University of Chicago Law Review* 70 (4): 1159–202.

Thaler, Richard and Cass Sunstein (2009). *Nudge: Improving Decisions about Health, Wealth, and Happiness*, New York: Penguin.

Thornton, Billy (1977). "Linear Prediction of Marital Happiness: A Replication," *Personality and Social Psychology Bulletin* 3: 674–6.

Turner, Stephen P. (2014). *The Politics of Expertise*, London: Routledge.

Tversky, Amos and Daniel Kahneman (1974). "Judgment under Uncertainty: Heuristics and Biases," *Science* 185: 1124–31.

Tversky, Amos and Daniel Kahneman (1981). "The Framing of Decisions and the Psychology of Choice," *Science* 211: 453–8.

Tversky, Amos and Daniel Kahneman (1986). "Rational Choice and the Framing of Decisions," *The Journal of Business* 59 (4) Part 2: The Behavioral Foundations of Economic Theory: S251–S278.

United States, Congress, Subcommittee on Health and Long-Term Care (1985). *Fraudulent Medical Degrees: Hearing before the Subcommittee of Health and Long-Term Care of the Select Committee on Aging, House of Representatives, Ninety-Eighth Congress, Second Session, December 7, 1984*, Washington: US GPO. Available online: https://babel.hathitrust.org/cgi/pt?id=mdp.39015031766556&view=1up&seq=7.

US Census (2014). United States Census Bureau, https://www.census.gov/programs-surveys/acs/news/data-releases/2014.html.

Van Cleve, James (2006). "Reid on the Credit of Human Testimony," in Jennifer Lackey and Ernest Sosa, eds., *The Epistemology of Testimony*, 50–74, Oxford: Oxford University Press.

Van Noorden, Richard (2011). "Science Publishing: The Trouble with Retractions," *Nature* 478: 26–8.

Veatch, Robert M. (2000). "Doctor Does Not Know Best: Why in the New Century Physicians Must Stop Trying to Benefit Patients," *Journal of Medicine and Philosophy: A Forum for Bioethics and Philosophy of Medicine* 25 (6): 701–21.

Veatch, Robert M. and Laura Guidry-Grimes (2020). *The Basics of Bioethics*, 4th ed., New York: Routledge.

Vickers, Andrew J., Fernando J. Bianco, Angel M. Serio, James A. Eastham, Deborah Schrag, Eric A. Klein, Alwyn M. Reuther, Michal W. Kattan, J. Edson Pontes, and Peter T. Scardino (2007). "The Surgical Learning Curve for Prostate Cancer Control after Radical Prostatectomy," *Journal of the National Cancer Institute* 99 (15): 1171–7.

Vickers, Andrew J., Fernando J. Bianco, Mithat Gonen, Angel M. Cronin, James A. Eastham, Deborah Schrag, Eric A. Klein, Alwyn M. Reuther, Michael W. Kattan, J. Edson Pontes, and Peter T. Scardino (2008). "Effects of Pathologic Stage on the Learning Curve for Radical Prostatectomy: Evidence That Recurrence in Organ-Confined Cancer Is Largely Related to Inadequate Surgical Technique," *European Urology* 53 (5): 960–6.

Vlastos, Gregory (1957). "Socratic Knowledge and Platonic 'Pessimism,'" *The Philosophical Review* 66 (2): 226–38.

Voyer, Benjamin G. (2015). "Nudging Behaviors in Healthcare: Insights from Behavioural Economics," *British Journal of Healthcare Management* 21 (3): 130–5.

Wada, Kyoko, Louis C. Charland, and Geoff Bellingham (2019). "Can Women in Labor Give Informed Consent to Epidural Analgesia?," *Bioethics* 33 (4): 475–86.

Wagemans, Jean H. M. (2011). "The Assessment of Argumentation from Expert Opinion," *Argumentation* 25: 329–39.

Wai, Jonathan and Harrison Kell (2017). "What Innovations Have We Already Lost? The Importance of Identifying and Developing Spatial Talent," in Myint S. Khine, ed., *Visual-Spatial Ability in STEM Education* 109–24, Cham, Switzerland: Springer.

Walton, Douglas (1992). *The Place of Emotion in Argument*, University Park: Pennsylvania State University Press.

Walton, Douglas (1997). *Appeal to Expert Opinion*. University Park: Penn State Press.

Walton, Douglas (2014). "On a Razor's Edge: Evaluating Arguments from Expert Opinion," *Argument and Computation* 5 (2–3): 139–59.

Ware, Mark and Michael Mabe (2015). *The STM Report: An Overview of Scientific and Scholarly Journal Publishing*, 4th ed., The Hague: International Association of Scientific, Technical and Medical Publishers.

Watson, James (1913). "Psychology as the Behaviorist Views It," *Psychological Review* 20: 158–77.

Watson, Jamie Carlin (2014). "Prolegomena to an Epistemic Case for Classical Liberalism," *Libertarian Papers* 6 (1): 21–55.
Watson, Jamie Carlin (2016). "Filter Bubbles and the Public Use of Reason: Applying Epistemology to the Newsfeed," in Frank Scalambrino, ed., *Social Epistemology and Technology: Toward Public Self-Awareness Regarding Technological Mediation*, 47–58, London: Rowman & Littlefield.
Watson, Jamie Carlin (2017). *Winning Votes by Abusing Reason: Responsible Belief and Political Rhetoric*, Lanham, MD: Lexington Books.
Watson, Jamie Carlin (2018). "The Shoulders of Giants: A Case for Non-Veritism about Expert Authority," *Topoi* 37 (1): 39–53.
Watson, Jamie Carlin (2019). "What Experts Could Not Be," *Social Epistemology* 33: 74–87.
Watson, Jamie Carlin (n.d.). "Epistemic Justification," *Internet Encyclopedia of Philosophy*. Available online: https://www.iep.utm.edu/epi-just/.
Watson, Jamie Carlin and Laura Guidry-Grimes, eds. (2018). *Moral Expertise*, New York: Springer.
Watson, John B. (1913). "Psychology as the Behaviorist Views It," *Psychological Review* 20: 158–77.
Watson, Katherine D. (2006). "Medical and Chemical Expertise in English Trials for Criminal Poisoning, 1750–1914," *Medical History* 50 (3): 373–90.
Waylen, A. E., M. S. Horswill, J. L. Alexander, and F. P. McKenna (2004). Do Expert Drivers Have a Reduced Illusion of Superiority? *Transportation Research Part F—Traffic Psychology and Behavior* 7: 323–31.
Wegwarth, Odette and Gerd Gigerenzer (2011). "Statistical Illiteracy in Doctors," in Gerd Gigerenzer and J. A. Muir Gray, eds., *Better Doctors, Better Patients, Better Decisions: Envisioning Health Care 2020*, 137–52, Cambridge, MA: MIT Press.
Weinberg, Jonathan, Shaun Nichols, and Stephen Stich (2001). "Normativity and Epistemic Intuitions," *Philosophical Topics* 29: 429–60.
Wheeler, Gregory (2018). "Bounded Rationality," *The Stanford Encyclopedia of Philosophy* (Spring 2020 Edition), Edward N. Zalta (ed.), Available online: https://plato.stanford.edu/archives/spr2020/entries/bounded-rationality/.
Wiland, Eric (2018). "Moral Advice and Joint Agency," in Mark C. Timmons, ed., *Oxford Studies in Normative Ethics*, 102–23, Vol. 8, Oxford: Oxford University Press.
Williams, Bernard (1972). *Morality: An Introduction to Ethics*, New York: Harper Torchbooks.
Williams, Bernard (2002). *Truth and Truthfulness*, Princeton, NJ: Princeton University Press.
Williams, James (2018). *Stand Out of Our Light: Freedom and Resistance in the Attention Economy*, Cambridge, UK: Cambridge University Press.
Wilson, Emily (2018). "Introduction," in Emily Wilson, trans., *The Odyssey*, pp. 1–91, New York: W. W. Norton.

Wilson, I. B., M. L. Green, L. Goldman, J. Tsevat, E. F. Cook, and R. S. Phillips (1997). Is Experience a Good Teacher? How Interns and Attending Physicians Understand Patients' Choices for End-of-Life Care. *Medical Decision Making* 17: 217–27.

Winter, Tom and Elisha Fieldstadt (2019). "First Major Drug Distribution Company, Former Executives, Charged in Opioid Crisis," *NBC News*, April 23. Available online: https://www.nbcnews.com/news/us-news/former-ceo-major-drug-distribution-company-first-face-criminal-charges-n997571.

Wittgenstein, Ludwig ([1958] 2000). "Philosophical Investigations," in Forrest E. Baird and Walter Kauffman, eds., *Twentieth Century Philosophy*, 2nd ed., 168–85, Upper Saddle River, NJ: Prentice Hall.

Wolff, Robert Paul ([1970] 1990). *In Defense of Anarchism*, New York: Harper Books.

Woodward, Thomas (2004). *Doubts about Darwin*, Grand Rapids, MI: Baker Books.

Wouk, Herman (1951). *The Cain Mutiny*. New York: Doubleday.

Wylie, Alison and Lynn Hankinson Nelson (2009). "Coming to Terms with the Value(s) of Science: Insights from Feminist Science Scholarship," in Harold Kincaid, John Dupré, and Alison Wylie, eds., *Value-Free Science? Ideals and Illusions*, pp. 58–86, Oxford: Oxford University Press.

Yarrow, Kielan, Peter Brown, and John W. Krakauer (2009). "Inside the Brain of an Elite Athlete: The Neural Processes That Support High Achievement in Sports," *Nature Reviews Neuroscience* 10: 585–96.

Yates, J. Frank, Laith Alattar, David W. Eby, Lisa J. Molnar, David LeBlanc, Mark Gilbert, Michelle Rasulis, and Renáe St. Louis (2011). "An Analysis of Seatbelt Use Decision Making among Part-Time Users," *The University of Michigan Transportation Research Institute* (April 2011). Available online: https://deepblue.lib.umich.edu/bitstream/handle/2027.42/85177/102755.pdf?sequence=1&isAllowed=y.

Zagzebski, Linda (2012). *Epistemic Authority: A Theory of Trust, Authority, and Autonomy in Belief*, New York: Oxford University Press.

Zenger, Todd R. (1992). "Why Do Employers Only Reward Extreme Performance? Examining the Relationships among Performance, Pay, and Turnover," *Administrative Science Quarterly* 37 (2): 198–219.

INDEX

(Transliterated words and titles appear in italics.)

abilities ix, 17, 19, 25, 34, 44, 48, 60–1, 73, 96, 98, 105–6, 132, 154, 156, 160, 167, 187, 204 (n. 7)
Activity Theory 207 (n. 3)
anti-vaxxers 41
Aristotle xx, 43, 77, 134, 139, 193
art/arts xx, 14, 29, 43–4, 50, 162, 186, 187
artificial intelligence (AI) 45, 77, 88–91
authoritative x, 47, 58, 85, 141, 147, 150, 178, 182
authority
  administrative 71, 141, 148, 150–1
  cognitive (*see* authority, epistemic)
  epistemic xi, xiii, xv, xviii, 2–4, 6–8, 51, 57–8, 63, 65, 76–8, 80–1, 83, 85, 99, 107, 134, 143, 145–53, 156, 160–1, 163, 177, 180, 182–3, 195, 200 (n. 17, n. 18)
  expert (*see* authority, epistemic)
  pragmatic 141
  scientific (*see* authority, epistemic)
automaticity 103, 183
autonomy 177
autotelic experience (*see* flow)

Bacon, Roger 125
Brewer, Scott 51

Cicero 29
climate science 5, 13–15, 20, 26, 91, 139, 141
Coady, David 51, 56–7, 60–1, 97, 151, 177, 197 (n. 15), 203 (ch 3. N. 28)
cognitive bias (*see* heuristics and biases)
cognitive systems account of expertise 172–8
Collins, Harry xiii, xviii, xxii, 37, 84, 98–103, 128, 137–8, 140, 153–63, 170, 180–1, 192, 206 (n. 2, n. 5, n. 6)
competence xi–xiii, xv, xviii, xx, 5–7, 12, 19–20, 35–7, 41–2, 44, 47, 51, 54–5, 57, 65, 73–5, 77, 80–4, 87, 89–92, 94, 96, 99–100, 102–3, 105, 112, 116, 118, 120–2, 126, 128–9, 134, 139–40, 143, 151, 153–4, 156–60, 163–70, 173, 175–8, 180, 183, 188–90, 194, 201 (n. 5), 203 (n. 24)
skill (non-specialized) ix, xii–xiii, 19, 38–9, 45, 50, 57, 73, 75, 81, 91, 98–100, 106, 121, 123, 155, 167, 178, 184, 201 (n. 5)
specialized competence (training, skill) 5, 7, 11, 31–2, 43, 47, 57, 73, 76, 98, 104, 118, 121, 144, 167, 170–2, 197 (n. 7), 197 (n. 13), 201 (n. 5)

competent xiii, xix–xx, 6–7, 19,
  44–5, 54, 57, 62, 84, 89–90,
  93, 99, 103, 106, 134, 138, 141,
  151, 155–6, 167–8, 182
confounding of expertise 1, 14–26
creationism (creationists) 178–83,
  207 (n. 5)
Csikszentmihalyi, Mihaly 90, 96,
  119–21

death of expertise 7–11, 26
definitional accounts of expertise xvi,
  33–5, 40, 199 (n. 4)
Deliberate Practice (Ericsson) xvii–
  xviii, 37, 74, 103–6, 109–35,
  159, 163–4, 170–6, 183, 192
Descartes, René 167, 201 (n. 10)
Dewey, John 201 (n. 5)
disagreement 13, 23, 39, 110, 122,
  179, 182, 195, 200 (n. 18)
doctor (see physician)
domain (field of study; subject
  matter; specialization)
  (definition) xix
  specialized domains xx, 85,
    151–2, 154, 159, 192
domain-at-a-time condition 81, 167,
  169, 173, 175, 194,
  203 (n. 24)
Dreyfus, Hubert xvii, 33, 37, 87–107,
  116–17, 119, 121, 132, 154–5,
  161–3, 199 (n. 8, n. 11), 204
  (n. 4, n. 5, n. 7)
Dreyfus, Stuart xvii, 32, 37, 87–107,
  116–17, 119, 121, 132, 154–5,
  161–3, 199 (n. 8, n. 11), 204
  (n. 4, n. 5, n. 7)
Duckworth, Angela 109, 120–4, 132,
  204 (n. 3)
Dunning-Kruger Effect, the xvi,
  19–20

echo chambers xvi, 24–6, 199
Elgin, Catherine 82–3, 179

engineers (engineering) 8, 10, 15, 19,
  41, 45, 71, 79–80, 114, 146,
  160, 180, 199 (n. 11), 206 (n. 7)
embodied knowledge xiii, 91, 96, 106,
  154, 204 (n. 7), 206 (n. 5)
epistemic advantage 156, 194,
  204 (n. 3)
epistemic authority (see authority,
  epistemic)
epistemic facility account of expertise
  49, 83–5, 182, 187–188
epistemic placement 52, 55, 61, 76,
  83, 146, 177, 179–80, 192, 206
  (n. 6)
Ericsson, K. Anders xiii, xvii, 37, 73–
  4, 76, 88, 98, 103–106, 109–35,
  143, 158, 162, 170–2, 174, 183,
  186, 192, 202 (n. 21), 203 (n.
  24), 205 (n. 1, n. 2. n. 3)
Evans, Robert xiii, 37, 84, 98–102,
  140, 153–8, 160–1, 163, 180,
  206 (n. 6)
expansive practice 170–6, 183, 186–7,
  207 (n. 3)
experience (relevant for expertise)
  xiv, xvii, xx, 2, 5, 7, 12, 15,
  20, 55–6, 60, 80, 92, 99–100,
  103–6, 111, 127, 133, 157,
  161, 163, 172, 178, 186, 201
  (n. 5)
expert (cognitive systems) 176
expert (opening definition) xii
expertise (accounts of)
  cognitive systems 172–8
  definitional xvi, 33–5, 40, 199 (n. 4)
  epistemic facility 49, 83–5, 182,
    187–8
  methodological xvi, 33–5
  non-reductive xvi, 33, 35–6, 41
  operational xi, xvi, 37
  performance-based xvii, 49
  philosophical (embodied)
    87–107, 153, 154
  psychological 109–35, 153

INDEX   241

process xvi, 33, 36–7, 153
reductive xvi, 33, 35–6, 52, 199 (n. 5)
social role xvii–xviii, xxi, 49, 59, 137–64
truth-based xvi–xvii, 34, 48, 49–85, 88, 92, 169, 179, 201 (n. 8)
expertise (opening definition) xii
expertise (types)
  cognitive 29–33, 50–3, 61, 76–9, 173, 200 (n. 2), 204 (n. 1)
  contributory 153, 157–9, 161, 163, 181, 206 (n. 6)
  default x, 153, 156
  embodied xvii, 91–7, 106, 154
  expertise* (definition) 175
  interactional 84–5, 102, 153, 157–9, 161–3, 180–1, 192
  localized 44, 99, 104, 160, 206 (n. 6), 206 (n. 7), 207 (n. 6)
  meta-expertise(s) 159–61, 180, 206 (n. 7)
  interactional meta-expertise 181–2
  performative 76–9, 93, 159, 162, 173, 188, 200 (n. 2), 204 (n. 1)
  practical 30–2, 76
  specialized (specialized art) 41, 44, 47–8, 51, 73, 84, 99, 138, 140, 153, 160
  ubiquitous 98, 153, 156–60, 163
expert coordination 139–40, 159, 169, 206 (n. 6)
expert systems xii, xv–xvi, 41–8, 68, 72, 75, 125, 134, 199 (n. 11), 200 (n. 18)
expertise producers 41–8
expertise users (expert and novice) 41–8, 176
expertise vs experts xii, 175–6
expertises (Collins) 98, 153, 156–9, 161–2, 181, 206 (n. 7)
explicit knowledge xiii, 66

family resemblance xvi, 29, 39
filter bubbles xvi, 20–3
fixed criteria accounts of expertise xvi, 33, 36–7
flow (autotelic experience, optimal experience) 90–1, 96, 105–6, 109, 119–21
Fricker, Elizabeth 51, 53

Goldman, Alvin 52–5, 59, 61, 63, 79–81, 95, 140, 191, 200 (n. 18, n. 2, n. 4)
Gorgias xiii–xiv

Hardwig, John 65, 139, 197 (n. 13)
heuristics and biases xv, xix, 46, 58, 69–71, 75, 110–11, 131, 142, 150, 174, 187, 202 (n. 20)
  anchoring bias 131
  confirmation bias 71, 75, 127
  framing bias 70
  hindsight bias 70
  race- and sex-based bias 48
  self-selection bias 24
  standpoint bias xvi
  survivorship bias 127

indicators of expertise (see symptoms of expertise) 10, 66, 83, 128–9, 131
insight (Klein) 172
insight (self-awareness, self-insight) 19, 75
intelligence (IQ) 44, 51, 123, 130, 137, 162, 204 (n. 7)
intuition 92, 133, 170–1, 173–4, 186, 204 (n. 6)
intuition-primed decision-making 171
IQ (see intelligence)

just do it principle (Montero) 96, 98, 104
justification, epistemic 15, 36, 40, 53, 59, 63–5, 82–4, 134, 197 (n. 17), 200 (n. 17), 202 (n. 15)

Keith, William M. 33, 37–41
kind learning environment (Hogarth)
  126–9, 131–2, 170, 173
Klein, Gary 73–4, 110, 132–4, 171–2,
  202 (n. 15)
Koppl, Roger 4–7

Laches ix
Lackey, Jennifer 26
layperson (*see* novice)
liberal arts 187
linguistic immersion 100, 102
Locke, John 201 (n. 10), 205 (n. 2)

Majdik, Zoltan P. 33, 37–41
mechanic 12, 41–4, 47
methodological accounts of expertise
  xvi, 33–5
Mizrahi, Moti 58, 66–76, 129, 202
  (n. 16, n. 17, n. 18)
Montero, Barbara 36–7, 73, 78, 96–7,
  105–6

Nguyen, C. Thi 23–6, 198 (n. 27)
Nichols, Tom 7–11, 13–14, 20–1, 26,
  197 (n. 8)
non-expert (*see* novice)
nonminded 96, 100, 104–6, 116, 119,
  132, 170, 174
non-reductive accounts of expertise
  xvi, 33, 35–6, 41
normative xi, 5, 17, 58, 78, 80, 144,
  146, 153, 160, 164,
novice (layperson, non-expert)
  (definition) xix–xx

Odyssey, The 193
operational accounts of expertise xi,
  xvi, 37
operational definition (account) xi,
  111, 163–4
optimal experience (*see* flow)

parapsychology (parapsychologists)
  178–83, 196 (n. 3), 207(n. 6)

performance-based accounts of
  expertise xvii, 49
philosophical (embodied) 87–107,
  153, 154
psychological 109–35, 153
periodic table of expertises (Collins)
  153, 157
physician (doctor) x, xiii–xv, xx, 1, 2,
  6, 8, 10–12, 15, 41, 48, 54, 62,
  67–9, 70–4, 77, 84, 91, 99–100,
  109, 133, 141, 143, 168, 172,
  177–9, 197
physicist 63, 81, 101–2, 138–9, 147–8,
  158, 192
physics xx, 61, 63, 77, 101–2, 138,
  143, 158–60, 162, 167, 188,
  191–2, 200 (n. 3)
  Gravitational Wave 102, 138,
    158–9, 162, 192
  Naïve Physics 77
Plato ix, xiii, 29–33, 41, 50, 76, 139,
  199 (n. 9)
process accounts of expertise xvi, 33,
  36–7, 153
profession 138, 148
professional (adjective) 42, 44, 75,
  80, 97, 100, 106, 123, 148, 150,
  178
professional(s)(noun) ix, 4–7, 12, 67,
  130, 138, 145, 196 (n. 3)
professionalism xv, 7
purposeful practice (Ericsson)
  113–15

recognition problem for expertise 6,
  95, 144, 161
Recognition-Primed Decision
  Making (Klein) 133, 172
reductive accounts of expertise xvi,
  33, 35–6, 52, 199 (n. 5)
relativism, epistemic xviii, 29, 37, 40–1,
  53, 57–8, 65–6, 79–81, 85, 141–2,
  144–6, 149, 152–3, 166–8, 179
  descriptive reputational relativism
    79–81

normative reputational relativism 80–1, 153
reputational accounts of expertise 79–82, 137, 140–1, 166–7
reliable access condition (RA) xvi, 40, 49, 53–76, 79–82, 167
Russell, Bertrand 35

Scholz, Oliver 33–4, 55–6, 61, 82, 196 (n. 2), 199 (n. 4), 201 (n. 7), 205 (n. 2)
skepticism (skeptical) 2, 7, 11, 13, 65, 73, 80, 154, 164, 201 (n. 13)
skill (*see* competence)
social role accounts of expertise xvii–xviii, xxi, 49, 59, 137–64
sociology 33
Socrates ix, xiii–xiv
sophia xx
Stamper, Kory 206 (n. 4)
standpoint epistemology 16–19, 27
subject matter (*see* also domain) xix, 51, 68
symptom(s) of expertise 34–6
indicator(s) of expertise 10, 66, 83, 128–9, 131
System 1 Cognitive Processing (Kahneman) xviii, 117, 132, 171–6, 185
System 1 Expertise xviii, 171–87
System 2 Cognitive Processing (Kahneman) xviii, 132–3, 171
System 2 Expertise xviii, 171–87

tacit knowledge xiii, 60, 66, 98, 103, 127, 132–3, 137, 139, 153–7, 157 (Fig. 6.1), 159, 161–3, 190
technai 30
techne xx
testimony (simple testimony) 2, 3, 65, 72, 94, 181, 192
expert testimony xi, 53–4, 68, 71, 85, 181
legal testimony 181–3

Tetlock, Philip 67, 73, 110, 123, 129–33, 162, 170–3, 177, 186, 196 (n. 2), 205 (n. 5), 207 (n. 1)
tribal epistemology 15–18, 25, 197 (n. 17)
trust x, xiii–xv, xviii, 1–4, 5, 9, 11–26, 64, 72, 78–9, 81–2, 139, 141, 144–53, 160, 166, 177, 195, 197 (n. 7)
public trust (social trust) 10–11, 13–14, 147–53
quasi-testimony 200 (n. 17)
social trust (*see* trust, public trust)
trustworthy xiv, xv, 1, 5, 9, 11, 20, 23, 24–6, 60, 72, 140, 195
truth-based accounts of expertise xvi–xvii, 34, 48, 49–85, 88, 92, 169, 179, 201 (n. 8)
Turing Test 206 (n. 5)
Turner, Stephen 43, 66, 137, 139, 146–51, 206 (n. 3)

ubiquitous discrimination 157 (Fig. 6.1), 160

veritism (*see also* truth-based accounts of expertise) 40, 52–3, 59, 61, 63–6, 71, 76–7, 81–2, 85, 144, 177, 190, 211
vertisitic accounts 40, 51, 61, 65, 81, 85

Watson, Jamie Carlin 15, 36, 81, 84–85, 197 (n. 17), 207 (n. 8)
Whitehead, Alfred North 35
wicked learning environment (Hogarth) 126–30, 132–3, 170–3, 186
Williams, James 23
Wilson, Emily 207 (n. 9)
Wittgenstein 37–9, 155
Wittgensteinian approaches xvi, 29, 38–41

Xenophon 87

www.ingramcontent.com/pod-product-compliance
Lightning Source LLC
Chambersburg PA
CBHW060947230426
43665CB00015B/2093